**The Global Association for
Marketing at-Retail**

The Power of
Marketing
at-Retail

**The Global Association for
Marketing at-Retail**

The Power of
Marketing
at-Retail

Edited by Robert Liljenwall

The Definitive Guide for Practitioners and Students

REVISED THIRD EDITION

Point-Of-Purchase Advertising International,
The Global Association for Marketing at-Retail
1600 Duke Street
Suite 400
Alexandria, VA 22314
p: 703.373.8800
f: 703.373.8801
www.popai.com

Graphic Design:
Mercury Publishing Services
Rockville, Maryland

Printed in USA
ISBN 0-9707099-2-7

Cover photo: Fashion Show/General Growth Properties

CONTENTS

CONTENTS

FOREWORD

Dick Blatt,
President and CEO, POPAI

It remains true that the constant of our world is change. Marketing continues to undergo significant changes as the old models of effectively reaching shoppers and consumers no longer apply as they once did. When we all wanted to be "normal" two generations ago, mass media proved a wondrous tool to convey the advertising message. But, today's "individual" shopper wants to receive a message not only targeted to that person, but delivered in a way that person is comfortable receiving it.

Why Marketing at-Retail? The medium takes three forms today: the traditional consumer products goods companies branding and selling their products at retail, the retailers branding and selling their own generic and premium private label brands at their stores, and the retailers differentiating, branding and customizing the store and its location from its channel competitors.

The changes and evolution provide great opportunity for better understanding and more effective utilization of the Marketing at-Retail medium. POPAI is proud to publish the third edition of its industry text: The Power of Marketing at-Retail. It remains the only book published to cover all aspects of the medium in practice and in theory. It is an outstanding volume for students to learn about the medium and its role in marketing and for practitioners to refresh and update their knowledge and to ensure that knowledge is comprehensive.

The third edition has been further expanded to reflect this ongoing evolution of practice, research, technology, and globalization. It is a must read for all who have a desire to know the medium and who desire to broaden their perspective of it.

POPAI has a vision of education for the industry of which this book is a foundation. We believe a better educated industry observes a higher standard of practice. It is our further thinking that the industry needs information which it can actually use and apply. The text serves as the foundation for understanding the medium. We offer 20 stand-alone educational events in North America annually and about three times that number among our 20 international country chapters. POPAI has introduced an industry certification program at the most advanced end of this educational continuum. The vision for industry certification is to expand people's knowledge of the medium beyond their immediate practice and information base so longer term all those who are certified may practice our profession more effectively by knowing colleagues' exposure to industry knowledge.

Soon we will move to distance learning to better accommodate the nearly insatiable desire for information about the medium. That, too, will utilize this text as a basis for learning. By its next edition we will see other texts from other country chapters of POPAI to share information from around the world and to work toward consistent knowledge in our ever shrinking world.

I hope you find it an easy and informative read thanks to our editor Bob Liljenwall and all of the authors of the individual chapters. My thanks extended to Lucy Bolden, POPAI's Manager of Education who was instrumental in delivering this book and all POPAI staff through their continued dedication to elevating our industry.

As of printing, significant developments in industry research continue. Breakthroughs in the establishment of syndicated measure of gross ratings points by Nielsen are expected. POPAI continues its complimentary research on the measure of shopper engagement and expects to progress to a larger scale version of that research for these reasons. We will be making available some form of white paper for the industry as these developments occur.

PREFACE

Robert Liljenwall,
Editor

This is the third edition of Marketing at-retail: The Power of Point of Purchase Advertising. First published in 2001 by POPAI, the response to the first two editions has been outstanding with both editions selling out.

As the global organization responsible for promoting and monitoring the point-of-purchase advertising industry, POPAI brought together industry leaders to create a definitive guide and textbook for Marketing at-Retail professionals – brand marketers, retailers, vendors and suppliers, advertising and promotional agencies, and especially newcomers to the industry.

One of the most important functions of this publication is for it to serve as the primary teaching guide and benchmark for the MaRC exam (Marketing at-Retail Certification). This examination process greatly assists POPAI in creating long-term professional standards and executives who are thoroughly trained and educated about all facets of the Marketing at-Retail industry.

Each of the contributors for this updated version again provide their insight, opinion, and industry knowledge to serve the reader in understanding the evolving and fast-changing world of what is happening in the world of Marketing at-Retail.

"Marketing at-retail" is a term that is growing in awareness and acceptance among all three stakeholders – retailers, brand marketers, and at-retail vendors and suppliers. Not only is the industry providing innovative and effective point-of-purchase displays through all retail segments, but the broadening influence of new technologies and methods of reaching the consumer at retail – both inside and outside the retail environment – are responsible for retailers and brand marketers enjoying the strongest growth in history.

We have several new contributors this time around: Martin Block Ph.D., Professor of Marketing Research at Northwestern University, covers post-promotion evaluation; Jim Eby, Senior Vice President and Creative Director for Wunderman provides the chapter on Advertising Design and Creativity; Paul Reidl, Associate General Counsel at E. & J. Gallo Winery, covers Trade Practices & Intellectual Property; and Kurt Witzel, Sr. Manager,

Marketing Communications, Anheuser Busch presents a unique and valuable case study on AB's point-of-purchase programs.

Kat Chociej, Marketing Director for Weyerhaeuser Retail Experience Network, provides an in-depth review of POP advertising displays; and Laura Davis-Taylor, a media consultant, reviews digital signage, which is one of POPAI's major new industry initiatives.

In addition, we have returning Editorial authors from the last publication – John Anderson, U.S. Manager of Marketing/Merchandising BP Oil Corporation; and Merrill Howard of Artisan Complete. Two new editorial authors have added their industry knowledge – Brian McCormick, Vice President, Rapid Displays; and Robert Plante, Manager, Kiosk Programs for BMW, North America.

Our coveted CD (enclosed) includes the popular POPAI desktop reference guide and we have doubled the size of our industry Glossary of Terms – from 2,000 to 4,000 definitions, thanks to Brian McCormick.

As Editor, it is clear that since the first publication, we have been successful in addressing the core issues facing industry education: creating a comprehensive document that would further the understanding of the Marketing at-Retail industry especially for mid-level managers and new entrants into the industry who needed a one-stop publication that contained "all they needed to know".

It is also important to note that this publication would not have succeeded without the diligent and positive contribution of POPAI Manager of Education, Lucy Bolden, who devoted countless hours of coordination and proof reading with our printer Mercury Publications. We also recognize Sharon L. Dukes for her tireless editing efforts.

In conclusion, all involved in this project believe that this effort continues to strengthen the professionalism of the point-of-purchase advertising industry. And we also continue to believe that Marketing at-Retail is changing the world as never before.

Robert Liljenwall, MBA, Editor

ABOUT THE EDITOR

Robert Liljenwall, MBA

Mr. Liljenwall is head of The Liljenwall Group a marketing and branding consultancy in Newport Beach, CA. He has more than 40 years of top-level marketing experience, and travels widely as a consultant. He was head of advertising and promotion for Disneyland and, venue press chief for the 1984 Olympics. He was the founder and chief executive for Real Time Sports Network, the largest interactive retail television and kiosk network in the US. Liljenwall teaches strategic marketing, IMC, and brand management at University California-Los Angeles Extension, where he was named Distinguished Instructor for 2007. He received a BA degree in journalism from San Jose State University and his MBA from Pepperdine University. He served as Editor and co-author of the first and second editions of The Power of Point of-Purchase Advertising: Marketing at-Retail.

From Marketing Management to Marketing at-Retail

Francis J. Mulhern, Ph.D.
Department of Integrated Marketing Communications
Medill School, Northwestern University

INTRODUCTION

Marketing is unique among business fields because it represents companies to consumers, and consumers to companies. As such, marketers want to manage the touchpoints where brands and consumers meet. All touchpoints fall into one of three categories – media, people, and places.

For many decades, marketers have put most of their emphasis, and their money, on media. From just after World War II until the present decade, mass media has represented a broad, efficient way to reach hordes of consumers with messages and incentives. Until recently, media has been relatively easy to manage, and marketers have had a host of agencies and vendors facilitate ways to spend enormous amounts of money on advertising and promotion through the major media vehicles.

Reaching consumers through people has never been a real strength of marketing. The primary people connections between companies and consumers are field sales people and customer service, neither of which is under the control of Marketing Departments. The third type of touchpoint, places, has had an odd history in marketing. When marketing began, it was all about place – getting products to the market. That's what the fourth *P* was all about. Over the years marketing has ceded much of physical distribution to business logistics. What remained of place were channels of distribution – a mix of retailing and direct marketing through which customers could make purchases.

Today, marketing is in the midst of a dramatic transformation characterized by the digitization of media and the resurgence of place. Digitization of media, featuring e-commerce, online and mobile advertising, and interactivity of communications, garners a great deal of attention. The resurgence of place is occurring more quietly. Places are becoming more central to marketing practice because of:

- The rise of major retail stores as places where consumers go, not just to make purchases, but to have experiences;
- The role of stores as place media – providing marketers with enormous reach for disseminating messages and interacting with consumers;
- The evolution of stores into social communities where people interact with other people; and
- The linking of GPS technologies with mobile marketing to tie media into very specific locations.

Since the mid 1980s, marketing has put an enormous amount of emphasis on brands. Brands represent a psychological point of differentiation that, when used properly, can lead to long-term profitability. Brands are, and will always be, central to marketing practice. But what matters most is the relevance of a brand, communication, promotion or offer to the consumer at any given point in time and place. In this context, retail stores emerge as the most important place where consumers and brands interact. Mass media is fragmenting and audiences are shrinking. Filtering technologies and regulation are constraining direct and interactive marketing. What remains, and even grows, is the relevance of physical places where consumers interact with brands, and increasingly, do so in ways that involve meaningful experiences and social interaction. What we call *Marketing at-retail* represents the realization that marketers need to understand how stores have emerged as a dominant part of consumer brand experiences.

Marketing at-retail realizes that:

- Retail places have more immediate and comprehensive effects on people than media;
- Retail is blending with media as place-based media, such as digital signage becomes networked and measured;
- Retail takes on a stronger role for brand strategy – long the domain of big media; branding through retail is now central to marketing practice; and
- The most important brand-related interactions consumers have with people take place in retail stores.

In this chapter, we explore some of these themes and develop a framework for thinking of marketing from the consumers' perspective – which features retail stores as a central element.

CHALLENGES FOR MARKETING TODAY

In many respects, marketing is experiencing an identity crisis. Top managers at many organizations consider marketing a huge cost center that may not deserve the monies allocated to it. Critics view marketing as little more than selling, advertising, and a host of other rudimentary tactics assembled to support sales. Whereas part of the blame for this perception lies with executives who fail to understand all of the ways marketing contributes to corporate performance, some of the blame also must be shared by marketing itself — and by its failure to assume financial accountability and demonstrate its true contribution to profitability. Companies that do marketing well realize they represent customers to the organization, and all of the functions they perform serve the dual purposes of satisfying customer wants and generating revenue for the company.

Marketing is the only part of an organization that understands and measures consumers and competitors. As the external side of a business, it gathers information on customers and competitors, identifies profit-making opportunities, and develops business practices that match corporate offerings with marketplace demands. From this vantage point, marketing makes a contribution to corporate performance that is unmistakable and irreplaceable.

Many of the difficulties taking place in marketing stem from a dramatically shifting landscape both in the marketplace and within organizations themselves. Key among these changes are environmental factors, such as the shifting demographic and ethnic composi-tions of consumers, rapidly developing technologies for market research and marketing communications, and a shifting value system within corporations whereby marketing can no longer exist as a loosely managed cost center but must justify itself for the financial contributions it generates. The changes taking place for the marketing function are occur-ring at the same time dramatic changes are taking place in the retail environment. These changes, as depicted below, require a rethinking about how marketers regard retailing.

Consolidation of Retailing

As is the case in many industries, retailing is in the midst of a major consolidation whereby a fewer number of larger retail establishments are supplanting a greater number of smaller, independently owned retailers. Wal-Mart, the world's largest company in revenues, con-tinues its global expansion with a retailing model featuring efficient distribution, precise inventory management, and aggressive retail pricing. Major grocery chains continue to merge with large operators such as Kroger, Albertson's, and Safeway, gaining an increas-ingly national presence. The top 50 grocery chains account for three-fourths of grocery sales. Similar patterns of major chain growth and consolidation are taking place in phar-macies, gas stations, restaurants, and nearly all areas of retailing and service marketing. The implications of retail consolidation are far-reaching and dramatic. For manufacturers, this means that access to consumer markets is dominated by fewer, larger retailers that, in addition to controlling increasing portions of the distribution channel, are controlling both the means through which consumers experience a significant portion of their brand interactions and detailed information on how they buy.

Retailer as Media

In part due to the increasing size of major retailers, stores are becoming a primary form of media. While traditional broadcast and print media struggle with fragmentation of media markets and an overabundance of media choices for consumers, retailers have emerged as a key source of information and service for the consumer marketplace. Traditional media will always be important because manufacturers must make their brands famous through advertising. But any information that consumers need to make brand choices and learn about product and service performance is better suited for retailer-based communications. An excellent example of this is the in-store demonstration of televisions and audio-visual equipment. Because of the complexity introduced by flat-screen, plasma, LCD, and HD technologies, major electronic retailers now provide extensive in-store display, sampling and performance areas. These areas simulate living rooms, complete with couches and recliners. By having shoppers experience the audio-visual performance in the store, retail-ers not only provide a more complete purchase experience, they reduce product returns. This is one of many instances in which the retail establishment serves as a primary com-munication medium that can achieve things unattainable through media communications.

Experiential Retailing

Many retailers are transforming traditional stores from places where a shopper goes to obtain a product to places where a shopper goes to enjoy an experience. Examples include bookstores featuring a coffee shop and lounge chairs, shopping malls featuring community events and entertainment, and sporting goods and outdoor stores that feature product demonstration and instructional programs. Purchasing takes place in a broader context that includes interpersonal interaction, entertainment, and on-site consumption experiences. What this means is that Marketing at-retail is no longer just about finding ways to increase the likelihood of purchase; it is also about finding ways to enhance the shopper's experience. As a result, Marketing at-retail is broadening to include many nontraditional practices, such as entertainment or education, which enhance the shopper's experience, not just promote the sale of a product.

Data and Technology

During the 1980s, retailing experienced dramatic changes brought on by point-of-sale data from store checkout scanner technology. Although the original uses of that data were for inventory management and centralized pricing, scanner data generated a boom in the level of understanding of consumer brand choice, the impact of price and promotions, and in-store merchandising. This information was one of the contributing factors in the migration of marketing expenditures to marketing at-retail. Today, retailing is on the cusp of another revolution in knowledge. This time it is the individual-level purchase data generated by retailer frequent-shopper programs. Purchase transaction data on the individual customer is the finest level of data possible on shopping behavior. Accordingly, great strides are being made in understanding not just the impact of pricing, promotions, and all aspects of marketing at-retail, but also the impact of market baskets, cross-time purchasing, consumer expenditures, and store patronage. Dunnhumby, a British retail consultancy, provides major retailers such as Tesco and Kroger grocery chains with extensive analytic systems that mine frequent-shopper data to help retailers and manufacturers do more precise target marketing and measure the impact of their efforts, particularly at the point of purchase.

Over the next few years, retailers will experience continued improvements in their ability to manage customers by selectively offering merchandise and promotions to shoppers based on customer buying patterns. The fact that retailers control the collection and ownership of customer-level purchase data will contribute to the power of retailers and the importance of Marketing at-retail relative to media-based marketing. Presently, most Marketing at-retail is targeted either to all shoppers or to broad segments of shoppers in a store. Because of the availability of customer databases, Marketing at-retail is increasingly gravitating toward customer-specific communications and merchandising. This is a dramatic and sustainable shift in retailing practice, one that puts the retailer further to the forefront of all marketing.

Measurement

No topic is of greater interest to marketing today than measurement. Relative to other business areas, marketing has performed poorly with respect to measurement. However, data collection systems now in place are bringing about a control revolution in marketing whereby measurement and financial quantification will be the norm. In scientific and professional fields, advances take place in conjunction with the quality of measures. The improvements now occurring in marketing measurement will generate more precise targeting, more relevant communications, and more profitable allocation of marketing dollars. The key areas of measurement include (1) *customer profitability*—the computation of the dollar contribution individual customers make to manufacturer and retailer revenues and profits; (2) *brand equity*—the evaluation of the financial values of brands and the role of marketing communications in generating brand value; and (3) *customer response analysis*—the assessment of the financial contribution of individual marketing tactics—such as coupons, in-store displays, and feature advertising—to revenues, both as independent marketing elements as well as an integrated whole.

Marketing at-retail AND CUSTOMER MANAGEMENT

At the core of marketing today is a mindset that marketing is, above all else, about managing customers. This transcends the traditional view that marketing is about managing the functional areas of products, pricing, distribution, and communications.

Managing customers entails market research and consumer insight analysis, strategically oriented customer segmentation, brand positing, targeted distribution, and marketing communications. Within this framework companies can shift their thinking to the performance of customer segments as opposed to product groups. However, the transformation taking place in digital media and the emerging retail environment is less about managing customers and more about engagement, participation, conversations, and communities. In this context, retailing is much different from the channel caption of traditional marketing, and much more about understanding consumers and interacting with them in relevant ways. Within this context, Marketing at-retail establishes itself as the apparatus for facilitating relevant experiences for consumers – experiences built around social interaction and relevant communications.

Several challenges exist that make it difficult for manufacturers and retailers to adapt this more experiential and community perspective. First, organizational structures largely reflect from a production point of view to facilitate product development and manufacture, physical distribution efficiency, service delivery, media buying, and additional facets of business, from the perspective of the businessperson. Shifting corporate values toward consumer experiences often conflicts with the inherent structure and capabilities of many organizations. For example, many manufacturers make decisions on in-store promotions and advertising based on scanner data on sales by SKU. Such information tells the manufacturer nothing about the shopper experiences or social interactions. Yet, those factors increasingly determine the quality of a store visit.

The second difficulty in making business focus on consumer experiences relates the measures that businesses use to make decisions. Most companies, by and large, run their businesses based on measures that have very little to do with consumers. The prevailing measures represent the performance of brands, product groups, market areas, regional sales districts, media markets, and so forth. Accordingly, most marketing managers spend their time attempting to maximize the revenue or profit performance of these areas, not the profitability of customers or the quality of consumer experiences. Customer measurement is the only thing that will make businesses shift toward managing customers. Hence, we are seeing the gradual incorporation of financial measures of customers, largely through retailer and service marketing data and point-of-purchase measurement.

IMPLICATIONS FOR Marketing at-retail

Marketing at-retail is most powerful when it connects directly to the strategic objectives of manufacturers, service providers, and retailers. The most effective Marketing at-retail practices are those based on the following six strategic foundations.

Know Your Customers

Marketing at-retail should be based on market research and consumer insight. The abundance of information available on shopping behavior, brand choice, and customer response to marketing tactics provides extensive information for marketing at-retail. Brand marketers need to understand the underlying motivations that drive shopping behavior. These motivations go well beyond the acquisition of merchandise and often have more to do with consumer aspirations and self-actualization – things that are very much the part of shopper experiences.

Connect Marketing at-retail to Marketing Strategy

Too often, Marketing at-retail is treated as an add-on tactical element to a more broadly established marketing effort. This reflects an outdated advertising-centric perspective. Marketing at-retail should be conducted with the same strategic focus of marketing communication and channels of distribution, but with an eye to shopper experiences at the point of purchase.

Integrate Marketing at-retail with Media Communications

A fundamental aspect of integrated marketing communications is that all marketing efforts, through the media and through retailers, should be driven by the same marketing objectives and strategy. In particular, advertising and promotions at the point of purchase should complement communications through the media.

Understand the Contribution Made by Each Tactic and Their Synergies

Every Marketing at-Retail tactic makes a contribution to the overall marketing effort. For proper planning to take place, each element of Marketing at-retail must be managed with an understanding of what that specific element can contribute. For example, point-of-purchase advertisements reinforce brand messages, checkout coupons allow for precise targeting based on brand purchasing, and packaging and product displays provide tactile communications not possible through the media.

Practice Targetability

Retailers are increasingly customizing product assortment, store atmosphere, prices and promotions to match the customers in narrowly defined geographic markets, particularly with respect to socioeconomic factors and ethnicity. This customization, enabled by detailed information on geodemographics, allows retailers to offer a merchandising mix that suits the needs of local residents and provides some differentiation from nearby competitors. Relative to print and broadcast media, Marketing at-retail has a particular advantage in this respect because of the countless opportunities to do highly targeted communications and promotions at the point of purchase.

Measure Everything

Marketing expenditures are increasingly being allocated to practices that provide quantified metrics of impact. Precise and timely measures of the impact of Marketing at-retail ensure continued spending in this area. Retailers control more data than anyone else. By leveraging the information collected at point of purchase, retailers can strengthen their influence on how brands reach consumers.

SUMMARY

This chapter began by identifying the three main touchpoints for brands – media, people, and places. Retailing has long been viewed solely as the place component among these three. Today, we now know that retail stores feature many elements of media, communication channels for brands to reach consumers, and people, sales clerks who represent brands and stores to shoppers. The advantage of Marketing at-retail over many other areas of the field is that it serves as the primary connecting point between companies and their customers. The challenge to Marketing at-retail is to rise above the view that it is merely a set of merchandising tactics to be appended to a brand or distribution strategy. The chapters that follow depict the many areas of Marketing at-retail where specific practices can be implemented to truly contribute to core marketing and business objectives. This is achieved by leveraging consumer insight to bring forth merchandising practices that connect with shoppers, by representing brand positioning and message strategies at the point of purchase, and, ultimately, by providing the measures that capture the effectiveness of marketing and integrating those measures into marketing planning. A concerted effort to view stores as the places where consumers have many of their most important brand experiences helps marketers focus on the real relevance of retailing in modern marketing.

2

Consumer Behavior at the Point-of-Purchase

Hugh Phillips, Ph.D.
McGill University

AN OVERVIEW OF THE SHOPPING EXPERIENCE

In the last few years, immense changes have occurred in our understanding of how customers shop. Traditionally the approach was dominated by classical economics. The shopper was regarded as a rationalist – in the sense of applying ratio-deductive logic to purchasing decisions. Decision making could be neatly wrapped up in the value equation: Value = quality/cost. Thus shopping could be reduced to nothing more than a rational trade off between the best values at the lowest price. When this theory was developed in the eighteenth century, it had a great deal going for it. Shops were small, carried a limited range and housewives had plenty of leisure time in which to shop. In addition, the number of products they bought were limited and not that technically complex. Shoppers had the time and ability to, as we would say nowadays, 'comparison shop'.

However now even the most hard-bitten, ultra-conservative, economics professors doubt the literal truth of this approach; the modern world has become too complex. Time is short, products multifaceted, the range enormous, and the number of product choices immense. In other words, we don't have the time, the ability, or usually even the inclination to shop as the classical economists supposed. A gentleman by the name of Herbert Simon administered the coup de grace to the notion that classical economics theory was the truth, the whole truth, and nothing but the truth. As far back as the 1970s he proposed that we only sum up the benefits against the cost, if we have the capability and the time. In fact, most of the time, we actually make sub-optimal decisions. We expend just as much effort to make us satisfied with our decision. The amount of time and effort we allocate to a decision, is roughly proportionate to the perceived risk of getting it wrong.

Experimentalism

So if rationalistic, classical, economics theory, has been badly mauled what can we put in its place? Towards the end of the last century, researchers developed the concept of experimentalism:[1, 2] that the 'shopping experience' was an integral part of the shopping process and of the satisfaction we gained from shopping. For example, research showed that the perceived value placed on goods customers purchased varied according the place where they were purchased.[3] The higher the satisfaction with the retailer, the higher value we placed on the products we had purchased there. In addition, it was also found that consumers would deliberately search out retailers where there had a good shopping experience – that is for their target market. An interesting manifestation of this realization is that Wal-Mart, the world's number one discount retailer, has recently been enhancing the shopping experience in their stores. This demonstrates that the master of 'value' retailing has realized that nowadays just low prices are not enough.

Even after having grasped the concept of the shopping experience, some retailers and store designers saw it as an end in itself, and we entered the era of 'In-store

As it was.

As it is now.

Theatre'. Shoppers were bombarded with visual stimuli and diversions, without any concept of what they actually wanted or needed. The solution was, of course, – segmentation. Different segments have different needs, the luxury shopper in Galleries Layfette in Paris has different needs than the homemaker providing for a family for a week in Costco. Not only did the range, the price-point, and the service levels have to adapt to the segment but the whole 'shopping experience' had to be orientated to the specific target market. This is easier said than done as we have entered the age of market fragmentation, the trend to more and smaller market sectors. While the causes of this fragmentation are complex, for retailers the key factor is the major shifts in demographics that have been occurring.

KEY DEMOGRAPHIC CHANGES

The major demographic challenge to retailers has been the decline of the once all pervasive nuclear family. In the 2000 US Census only 36% of households could be considered "traditional" families, that is, consisting of a married couple with children. We now have significant segments of single people; couples without children – either before having children or after the children have flown the nest; single parents and just about every other permutation you can think of. This is then overlaid with major variations in income. Despite both being 'singles', an affluent foreign exchange dealer in New York will have totally different needs than an elderly single widow in Mississippi. Add to this the fact that most mature women now work, which not only changes their income but also reduces their time for shopping.

Any normal human being has probably now passed the information overload stage. There are just too many sectors to cope with, certainly too many to form the basis of a coherent marketing strategy. So let me cut through this morass and draw out the key underlying factors, which are simply time and discretionary income.

Time

It is well known that we are working longer hours and that this varies by demographics4. Plus, of course, different demographic groups have different priorities in terms of how they wish to spend their time.[5] Both the products we buy and our satisfaction with the shopping experience is governed by time pressure.[6] Thus, a key criterion of shopping satisfaction is how much time your customers have available. Masses of 'in-store theatre' may be appropriate in say an up-market department store or a specialist sport or hobby outlet, where customers have allocated time for that shopping adventure. However, it is totally counter productive to impose this distraction on time constrained shopping situations, especially those for the harassed working mom.

As a result, we find that the leader in 'clean store' policy – Target – stating:

*"We design our stores to be easy and intuitive to shop, with related depart-
ments conveniently placed next to each other (décor next to home improvement, toys next to sporting goods) and a "racetrack" central aisle to speed
you on your way... We also work hard to make sure your experience is
consistently enjoyable, with a clean environment, friendly team members
and feel-good details on all sides."*[7]

In contrast, the philosophy of the award-winning Apple stores is:

*"We wanted to create very distinct experiences for customers, in what they
perceive as a public place. More like a great library, which has natural
light, and it feels like a gift to the community. In a perfect world, that's what
we want our stores to be. And we don't want the store to be about the product, but about a series of experiences that make it more than a store"*[8]

The question as to which is right is obviously both; it depends on the target market – what
they are shopping for and how much time they have.

Income

Even leaving aside the immense and fraught topic of the discrepancies in incomes, income
trends have had a marked effect on how we shop. The key factor is that we have 'never
had it so good' and certainly never for so long.

The chart below shows that since the end of the last real recession in the 1980's, the
average consumer in the US has experienced a period of consistent personal income growth.

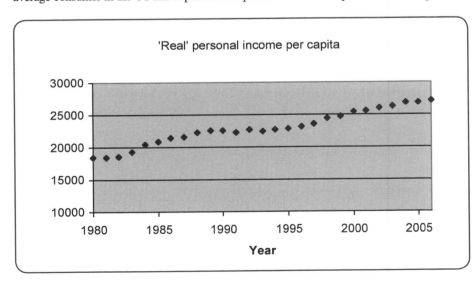

*Source: Derived from:
Aggregate Income and
Productivity Trends:
Canada vs. United States:
Centre for the Study of
Living Standards, Ottawa
Canada (2007)*

For retailers the obvious and compelling question is what are consumers doing with all this extra income? Let us breakdown where this largess goes. First, we pay our taxes, which may leave many of us with 'disposable income'. Then we must pay for the necessities of life; – we have to eat, put some sort of roof over our head, buy clothing, etc. If we deduct the cost of surviving from our disposable income, some of us may have something left over – which is our 'discretionary income'. We now have a choice how we can spend this money.

Perhaps a broader view of the definition will better illustrate just how discretionary income affects retailing. After we have bought a dishwasher or a flat screen TV, we won't be in the market for these outlays again for a number of years. This releases real discretionary income that we can spend on popcorn, beer, concert tickets, DVD's, or whatever takes our fancy. However, there is a limit to the amount of popcorn and beer we can consumer or the number of concerts or DVD's we want to see. When our obvious needs and inclinations are satisfied, most of us switch to investing this discretionary income in quality. We don't so much consume more, but we consume the same sorts of products, only of higher quality.

Obviously one manifestation is the trend to 'trading up'. Increased discretionary income gives the consumer the opportunity, the means and perhaps even the inclination to trade-up the perceived quality of the products they purchase. To illustrate this, the premium or luxury market is apparently growing at a robust rate of roughly 10% versus other categories at 2% to 3%[9].

The previous section provided an equally compelling criterion of 'quality', which was where we chose to shop – the 'quality' of the shopping experience. As discussed at length, the right shopping experience depends on the target market and the task that they have on hand at the time. While this may seem self evident by now, it has taken a new twist, at least in North America. The European retail sector has traditionally been segmented into 'service' (quality) and discount. The most striking manifestation of this is that it applies even to the supposedly mundane area of grocery shopping. British-based Tesco, the leader of the service retailing pack, has declined to enter into a head-to-head price war with Wal-Mart,[10] but is still gaining market share! Is this just a European phenomenon? Not anymore. The same trend is developing in the U.S., with the likes of Kroger, Safeway, and Super Valu Inc. sidestepping a price war with the traditional discounters[11] – which they can never win – by offering 'service' or 'quality' as an alternative to everything retail starts and finishes with the ticket price.

Thus, the new and compelling factor in the North American consumer behaviour equation is the polarization of consumer choice into the 'service' or 'discount' sectors. This is of course facilitated, or even caused, by the high discretionary income that is available to the 'haves' in our society to buy into this service concept. The implications of this trend are both immense and straightforward – the middle ground is disappearing rapidly.

This is not only for the retailers but also their suppliers – who will have to choose on which side of the great divide they are going to position themselves or at the very minimum devise alternative strategies for the different and diverging camps.

TACTICAL TO STRATEGIC

Those who study marketing will realize that we have now entered the realm of formal marketing strategies. We have established the fundaments of segmentation, addressing the needs of those segments and created market positioning. In line with this, a sea change occurred recently when the in-store marketing sector en masse reoriented itself from tactical to strategic. The cause was a classic – supply and demand had gotten out of kilter.

Marketers had been transferring budget to in-store communications as a reaction to a shift in consumer behaviour[12]. The effectiveness of classical media has been reducing, at a time when consumers were postponing their product decision making until they were in-store. To address the former and to capitalize on the latter, there has been a massive growth in in-store communications, which in turn lead to saturation. For example, POPAI UK found that in an average sized supermarket, there were 4,624 display items[13].

There have been two clear, straightforward and overwhelming reactions to this saturation. The first is from the retailers and the second from the customers. As was discussed earlier, retailers in certain sectors are moving to a more 'clean store' policy. Naturally this has lead to a culling of in-store displays and communications in general. Retailers were reacting to the needs of the consumer for efficiency and effectiveness in their shopping experience. A key factor has been the frustration of customers with their inability to find products in the communications plethora of 'junked up' stores. This is, of course, particularly irksome at a time when the consumer is more time constrained and also more demanding in terms of the level of service they expect in-store. The ability to easily find products has been found to be the fourth most important element in creating store loyalty[14] (Selection and Price are the first equal components and Quality the third). Thus, the current challenge of the in-store communications expert is how to cut through this plethora, simply to get noticed and be given the opportunity to communicate.

The solution to this problem lies right back in the first section of this chapter, which is the experts no longer accept that we shop rationalistically. Rather, they now accept that the majority of shopping isn't even conscious. The reason is that it would be impossible. Even in a comparatively small store customers are faced with 20,000 SKU's in a typical store. If they spent just one second inspecting each product, it would take five and a half hours to shop. But in reality they complete the task in around 15 minutes. Thus they cannot be shopping predominantly rationalistically or consciously.

There are two principal means that customers cope with in store shopping with these modern over-complex stores:

- Selective perception
- The use of schemata

Selective perception

Human perception is essentially selective. It has to be, as the capacity of the attention span is surprising limited. Psychologists measure the capacity of the attention span, 'Short Term Memory,'[15] in terms of chunks – a chunk being a well-known word or phrase. Under laboratory conditions, it has been found to be around seven 'chunks'. However in the real world situation it is less – how much less – I am afraid no-one really knows. It is probably only three to four of these chunks.[16] However this discussion is academic, since the key factor is that our attention span is at any one time very limited indeed. It is also tiring to use conscious attention, so we avoid using it whenever possible. Instead, selective perception is one of the primary means we use to cope with the complexity of life, despite having only a limited attention span.

What impinges on the eye and what is processed by the brain is different; we mentally process only a small fraction of what we 'see'. The classical illustrations of the selective perception of information are optical illusions. In the famous illusion below, we can see either a young or an older woman, depending on which elements we chose in the selective process.

The same applies to in-store communications.

- We selectively perceive only some of the displays in-store.
- Even if we do perceive a display, we will selectively process only some of the information it contains. This will determine the meaning to us of the communication. In turn this determines if it is relevant to us and thereby whether it will affect our behaviour

The six easy steps to lose customers

We have now reached a key factor – potentially *the* key factor – in in-store marketing. If you produce a display, what chance does it have of communicating to the customer base? To help assess that potential, perhaps it is helpful to consider six potentially harmful factors which strongly aid in losing customers.

1. The individual store may not even put up the display. The level of this 'non-compliance' can be as bad as 50%[17].

2. The customer may not pass the point in-store where the display is located. (Measuring the number of customers passing a display location in-store is the objective of the POPAI MARI project)

3. Even passing customers may not look at your display. The average for passing customers who physically look at a display is around a fifth[18]. (Again, quantifying this is a key objective of the MARI project.)

4. Customers may look at the display – the image enters the eye – but it may not be selectively perceived and so does not enter the conscious mind.

5. The display appears to have no relevance to the customer and consequently they ignore it.

6. Finally the customer may selectively misinterpret it; what they actually perceive is not what was intended.

It is impossible to accurately quantify the losses at each of these levels. However, if you were able to restrict the losses across all the levels to 90%, you would be doing very well indeed. As a result of this major, multi-level, loss in communications, many leading practitioners are now re-orientating their conceptual approach. They now see the key principal underlying shopper behaviour as a process of deselection – what gets deselected, and what I lose at each step. Thus, the key challenge for effective in-store communication is how to combat being visually deselected.

SUBCONSCIOUS PROCESSING

A second way we cope with our complex world, is that the great majority of our cognitive processing is at the subconscious / unconscious level[19]. This not only allows us to screen masses of data – parallel process – but is relatively effort free, unlike conscious processing[20]. Let us return to the example of shopping a small store with 20,000 SKU's.

It appears customers are using some form of short cut or heuristic. In order to cope with the size and complexity of modern stores, customers are using what psychologists call schemata. These are subconscious reactions to regularly encountered or stereotypical situations, which we have stored in our memories. The classical example of the use of schemata is driving. When we first learn to drive we follow the instructions of our teacher consciously – "Mirror, indicate, maneuver," "Stop at the red light," etc. We practice these a few times and they become stored subconscious reactions – that is they have become schemata. Now we drive mostly, 'on autopilot". We subconsciously react to road signs, other drivers, etc. 'without thinking'. Unless the unexpected happens – the non-typical, non-stereotypical situation – we quite adequately process information and react subconsciously – via these schemata.

The same happens when we shop. On our first shopping trips we shop consciously. During this phase, we find routines that work in terms of how to effectively shop modern stores. If they work, we repeat them on subsequent trips, and just as in the case of driving they rapidly become 'schemata'.

In shopping, we use mainly two types of these subconscious schemata:

- *Visual schemata:* Visual 'cues' that evoke a whole host of associations – brand, positioning, product field, etc.
- *Scanning schemata:* Used for product search, browsing, etc.

These are used in conjunction with each other and simultaneously.

Visual schemata

Visual schemata are the basic building blocks of shopping behaviour. Their origins lie in the fundaments of how we identify objects. Initially, we selectively perceive elements from the scene in front of us. At the lowest level, this would be a series of lines, colors, visual textures, etc. These act as 'pointers' to schemata in the memory, which provide the identification of that object. This organizes the elements into a coherent whole and then binds them together to form a meaningful entity.

STEP 1 – SELECTION OF ELEMENTS

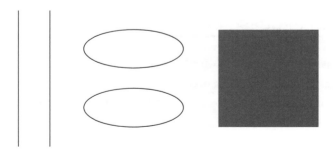

STEP 2 – ORGANIZATION INTO AN ENTITY

STEP 3 – BINDING THEM TOGETHER INTO A RECOGNIZABLE ENTITY

There are infinite categories of these visual schemata – sometimes called visual cues – that we use for recognition of objects. Some are specific to that object, such as the pack illustration above. Others apply to types or classes of objects: flowers, Christmas, romantic occasions or product fields. For designers or communicators, these schemata act as a sort of pallet, from which we can draw on a common culture of imagery to create and define our communications with customers.

Within this multitude of categories of visual schemata three are particularly relevant to in-store communications:

- Brand
- Product Field
- Positioning

Branding

A not uncommon experience often occurs when a pack is re-launched and sales plummet. The cause is at first sight inexplicable, as the redesign had 'passed' the conventional research checks. However critical branding visual cues had been removed. These had hitherto been thought to be visual trivia and their crucial role is not normally revealed by conventional research. From the authors' experience these can be a simple as the line above the name of the company, a box around the edge of the pack and two curved lines on each side of the label. Trivia yes, but essential trivia, as they were primary visual cues used by consumers to identify the brand.

Below is a selection of packs that were deconstructed by a research associate Dr. Deuksoo Kim. Brand recognition varied from 10% to 95%.[21] The recognition level depended totally on which cues were removed, some had virtually no effect, but others (virtually) destroyed recognition.

What his research also showed was that brand name and logo, the most protected brand properties, usually had little or no effect. The most effective brand recognition cues were outside shape and colour, though as mentioned earlier there can also be unexpected and hitherto unrecognized surprises!

Positioning cues

Alongside the branding cues exists a further set of brand positioning cues. These are an analogous set of colors, shapes, design features, etc. The pack design illustrated below simply had two of these cues altered; the result was a significant shift in the quality perception.

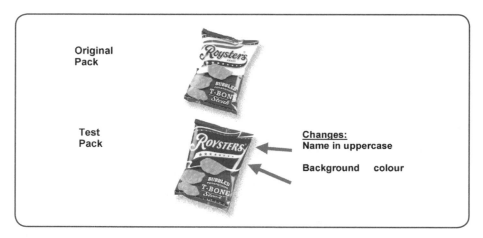

Product field

It is sufficient to say that a third category of visual cues exists that is used for product field recognition.

GETTING SELECTED

Our objective as in-store marketers is to get selected (or at least not get deselected). What initially strikes the customers eye in-store is a mass of lines colors, visual textures, etc., sort of vaguely reminiscent of the following:

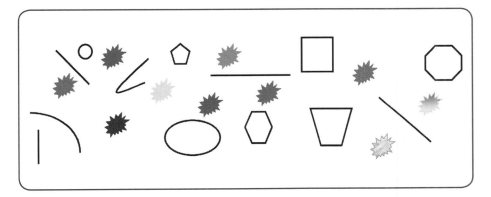

In reality it is nothing like this, as in reality it is a series of electronic pulses through the neurological system but this is about as close as I can get. However, it does make the point that we expect the customer in-store to sort out from this 'mess' – the lines, colors, etc. – that belong to our product and our promotion and then assemble them into the message that we wish to communicate. There are two blatantly obvious questions raised at this point.

1. How can they?
2. Why should they?

In fact, as demonstrated earlier, in most cases it is easier and therefore in their interest to ignore it. The key to unlocking this problem is the 'pain – pleasure' principle. We reduce the pain – the effort of decoding the visual imagery we are using – while giving customers, if not necessarily pleasure, then at least an incentive for doing so.

The sure-fire route for reducing the pain or effort is clarity: creating visual imagery that is clear, uncluttered and easily decoded by the passing customers. This means that your communication will be elevated from the eyes seeing it, to the brain processing it. We have now passed a key hurdle in not getting de-selected. (Points four and six in "The six easy steps to lose customers.")

We then need to communicate something relevant: addressing point five. This can be basic – a monetary discount or whatever – but increasingly marketers use the experiential approach, discussed at length earlier, partly because of the consumer trend toward the service approach to retailing.

The maxim is simple: create clarity and then overlay it with the shopping experience. However, there is a necessary order in these events; clarity must precede the shopping experience, which is also the reason so many retailers are moving to 'clean store' and throwing out displays.

Scanning schemata

However, we still have to get noticed at-retail, which leads us onto the scanning schemata that are used for product search, and browsing.

We have already established that customers do not inspect every product and display at-retail, nor do they shop at random, or meekly follow the predetermined walkways at-retail. All experienced shoppers follow a search pattern for circulating, browsing and scanning a store for products, services or offers that might interest them on that shopping trip.

The existence of these scanning schemata has been known since the birth of modern retailing. They were developed over a centenary or so by trial and error, into an accepted body of recognized merchandising principles. Recently it has been discovered that these 'rules of thumb' have a sound scientific basis in cognitive psychology. That is, they are grounded in schematas. These display principles include:

- Block merchandising
- Visual segmentation
- Book ending
- Sign post branding
- Sight lines
- Adjacencies, etc.

The first principle of marketing is to satisfy customer needs. The customers have invested in developing these schematas to scan, browse, etc., because of their *need* to cope with modern, complex, stores. Therefore the real marketer satisfies this need and develops their strategies around this need. As they are conforming to the customer's preferred mode of shopping, they make it easier for the shopper to identify their display/product/communications. In other words it is less effort, less likely to be misinterpreted and therefore less likely to be ignored or 'deselected.'

The illustrations below show the effect of re-merchandising a display according to these principals. There was no change in pricing or lines stocked, in-store location, category, space allocation, or P.O.P. In other words, apart from the display technique, the in-store offering was identical. However, category sales, for the 'after' design, increased by 37%. The reason was the customer base rewarded the retailer for fitting in with their needs in-store, which was to be able to shop in the way they wanted via use of the schemata they had invested time and effort in developing.

Before    After

Bringing visual and scanning schemata together

We have emphasized the need to create clarity, to aid the customer in identifying and processing communications in-store; in other words, to help the customer assemble the visual building blocks into a comprehensible image. The application of scanning schemata is a major step forward in this direction. If we design the macro image – store, gondola run, display, or whatever – to be easily scanned and processed, we help the customer identify the design elements we want them to process.

Again, let us use visual examples. In the pictures below, which is easier to identify visual elements – the black square and the white triangle?

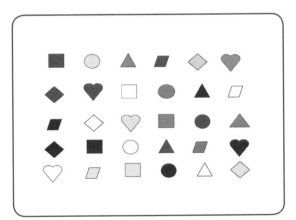 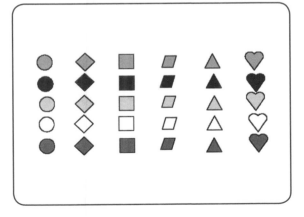

In the right-hand picture it is easier to identify these elements, as the macro image has been organized according to one of the recognized schemas we use to scan for objects.

The same applies to displays at-retail. In the two at-retail environments below, which would be easier to identify products, displays, or promotions?

FITTING THIS INTO CONSUMER DECISION MAKING

The current vogue is to divide purchase decisions into 'impulse' and 'destinational' purchases. Research shows that this black and white, categorical division is totally over simplified.

What is an impulse purchase?

We tend to associate an 'impulse' with spur of the moment, non-rational, activities based on some sort of emotive motivation. In fact pure impulse purchasing is low[22] – certainly less then 10% of all transactions and possibly around 8% in routine purchasing environments. Researchers prefer not to use the term 'impulse,' but rather 'unplanned' purchasing of which pure impulse is a small sub-set[23]. They have identified many different categories of this activity. For example, one leading researcher divided purchasing into:

- **Specifically Planned:** the need was anticipated and the person bought the exact item planned.
- **Generally Planned Purchase:** the need was anticipated, but the person decided in the store upon the item to satisfy the need.
- **Reminder Purchase:** the person was reminded of the need by some influence in the store.
- **Entirely Unplanned Purchase:** the need had been anticipated on entering the store, not prior to that.[24]

Other researchers have produced different typologies, all illustrating that there is no such thing as a simple or categorical split between an impulse purchase on one hand and a destinational purchase on the other. Planned and unplanned purchasing lie on a continuum, a question of degree; while some purchases are very planned, some marginally so, some appear to be completely unplanned and so on.

The theory behind this is that we have pre-dispositions to buy certain products or brands before we enter the store. These are created 'by the normal channels' – marketing, prior experience, the influence of friends, etc. What appears to happen is that this predisposition is either activated or not – either we don't buy or may buy a competitor – because of in-store influences.[25] (i.e., the famous 'shopping experience' which we discussed earlier). Thus identifying products in-store, which may activate this predisposition to buy, is crucial.

Therefore, which visual images are perceived and thereby enter the decision making process is now a critical factor. What we perceive and mentally process is driven by that image's relevance to us or our interests on that shopping trip. It may be something that is high up on our search priorities – a potentially much-planned purchase – or low down – a (semi) unplanned purchase. The key issue now to be addressed is how we select these images that have the potential to alter our buying.

Broad and narrow scan

It is generally accepted in cognitive psychology that our attention – 'short-term memory' – resembles a search light. It can be set on broad scan, absorbing information at the macro level over a wide area or on narrow scan, when it absorbs more detail but over a restricted area.

Referring to the previous section on visual cues – on the macro scan we adsorb little more than the fundamental cues – lines, shapes, colors, etc. However, as we narrow down, we begin to process more information, until the point where we are processing the object in reasonable detail.

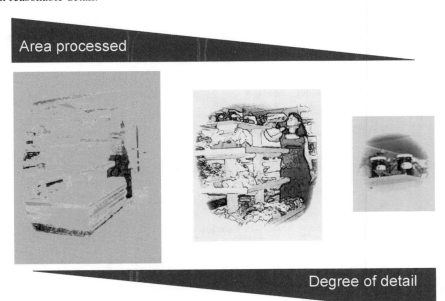

In addition, on macro scan customers are parallel processing, absorbing cues from a large number of objects, products, displays, etc. and over a wide area. This is the process in which we say customers are browsing or scanning for the objects they might want to buy. At this stage customers are working predominantly subconsciously.

If customers assemble the visual cues presented to them into the representation of a product or offer that might interest them, customers then narrow their scan and start seeking 'more information'. At this stage, customers will be starting the decision making process and working more at the conscious level

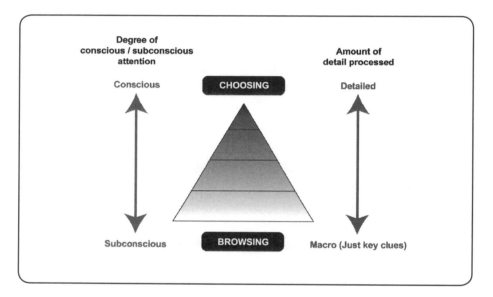

The take out for at-retail marketing is that any marketing communications must be able to operate at multiple levels (at varying degrees of detail, at different levels of conscious/unconscious processing, and as part of an array of images or focused as a single image. However there is a definite hierarchy of communication:

1. Attract attention subconsciously by correctly manipulating the 'visual' and 'scanning' schemata.

2. This elevates customers' degree of conscious attention, because it is relevant to the target market.

3. They then focus down and engage – now hit them with the message.

But it is 1 ◆ 2 ◆ 3

The fault of many in-store materials is that the sole criterion is how it looked in the manager's office. The decision-maker jumps straight to the third stage, ignoring that to get to that third stage they equally have to work at the initial levels. Customers have to have an incentive to elevate through the first two before you can start communicating the brand strategy![26]

SUMMARY

This chapter has covered a great deal of territory in an effort to encourage re-orientating in-store marketing away from the antiquated and now over-simplistic approach of '...he who shouts loudest and most often gets heard.'

The modern approach is based on a sound understanding of shopper behaviour. It emphasizes the need to apply the basic principles of marketing to the in-store situation – target marketing and satisfying the target market's needs. Modern research has identified that critical elements in this include the fact that customers shop predominantly subconsciously, that deselection is the underlying factor, and that they rely on subconscious stored routines, called schemata, to cope with the size and complexity of modern stores. These elements build up to the crucial element in modern retailing – the customer experience. Value is still the key criterion that drives customer choice, but in this day and age, value is more than just the product and price. The elusive customer experience is integral to the way our increasingly affluent and discriminating society shops and thereby the decisive factor in the success or failure at retail.

ENDNOTES

[1] Holdbrook M.B. and Hirschman E.C. (1982) "The experiential aspects of consumption: consumer fantasies, feelings and fun" *Journal of Consumer Research* 9 p132-140.

[2] Tauber E.M. (1972) Why people shop *Journal of Marketing* 36 October p46-59.

[3] Groppel A. and Bloch B. (1990) "An investigation of experience-orientated consumers in retailing" *The International Review of Retail, Distribution and Consumer Research* 1 (1) p101-118.

[4] Heisz A. and LaRochelle-Côté S. (2003) Analytical Studies Branch research paper series "Working hours in Canada and the United States". Stats Canada:

[5] *The American Time Use Survey* 2006 The Bureau of Labor Statistics

[6] Iyer, E.S. (1989) "Unplanned purchasing: knowledge of shopping environment and time pressure." *Journal of Retailing*, 65 (1): 63-80.

[7] Target's corporate web site http://sites.target.com/site/en/corporate/page.jsp?contentId=PRD03-001088

[8] Sr. vice-president for Retail Ron Johnson Apple, speaking at a design conference in Providence (RI). http://www.ifoapplestore.com/stores/risd_johnson.html

[9] Daniels C. (2006) "Almost Rich" *Marketing* April 26.

[10] Hill A. (2007) "Going up: the new Tesco price strategy" The Observer September 2.

[11] McWilliams G. (2007) "Not Copying Wal-Mart Pays Off for Grocers". Wall Street Journal June 6 2007

[12] Deloitte & GMA (2007) "Shopper Marketing".

[13] Marketing at-retail Initiative (MARI) POPAI UK & Ireland 2007.

[14] Hutton R. (2007) Customers Tell Us What They Expect from the "Experience" Conference paper "Store" conference: Retail Council of Canada: http://www.storeconference.ca/presentations/2007/pollara.pdf

[15] The scientific term for attention is 'short-term memory'. The vernacular terms Attention or Conscious Attention will be used here to avoid confusion.

[16] Hoyer W.D and Macinnis D.J (2007) *Consumer Behaviour* 4th Edition. (Houghton-Mifflin Company Boston). p 177

[17] POPAI research found that only 50 percent of non-digital, in-store advertising is displayed in the manner, location, and period intended "Effectiveness of Point of Purchase Displays as a Measured Medium with Selected SPAR UK Stores," 2004.

[18] POPAI UK, MARI project 2007

[19] There has been a perpetual debate in psychology as to the degree of conscious versus unconscious / subconscious processing. John F. Kihlstrom has written an interesting review of this debate "The Rediscovery of the Unconscious" which can be found at http://ist-socrates.berkeley.edu/~kihlstrm/rediscovery.htm

[20] The seminal work in this area is Schneider W. and Schiffrin R.M. (1977). "Controlled and automatic human information processing: 1. detection, search and attention" Psychological Review 84. p1-66. It has been subjected to much debate and refinement but is broad direction is still substantially accepted.

[21] Kim D (2004) "How do we recognise a brand in point-of-purchase communications? - Analyses of Visual Structure of fast-moving-consumer-goods Packages" PhD thesis but a summary is available on http://www.dmi21.co.kr/zeroboard/view.php?id=CognitivePsychology&no=28

[22] Rook D. W. (1987) "The buying impulse" *Journal of Consumer Research* 14 Sept p189 - 199.

[23] Prasad V.K. (1975) "Unplanned buying in two retail settings" *Journal of Retailing* 51 (3) p3-12.: Kollat D.T and Willet R.P. (1969) "Is impulse purchasing really a useful concept for marketing decisions" Journal of Marketing 33 (January) p79-83.

[24] McGoldrick P. (1982) "How planned are unplanned purchases?" *Retail and Distribution Management* January/February p27-30.

[25] Bradshaw R.P. and Phillips H.C. (1993) "the point of sale: the customers point of view" *Maximising retail sales in a recession* ESOMAR p125-154.

[26] For infomration on research techniques for assessing communications of communications in-store go to www.instore-research.com

3

Introduction to P-O-P Project Management

Rick De Herder
CEO
Array

OVERVIEW

"What is needed to make every P-O-P project successful is complete and thorough participation from all stakeholders. Every stakeholder must be committed to clear and open communication of the project objectives, and all must understand the challenges that may be encountered along the way."

Barbara Daugherty, Frito-Lay, Inc.

Every project is initiated to meet a goal. The role of project management is to oversee the process of delivering a program that meets its goals while minimizing the effort it takes to deliver the project and maximizing the return. At its heart, project management is rooted in the effective use of communication to share necessary information between all participants in a timely manner in a clearly understandable format and language so that each participant can fulfill his or her role to achieve mutual goals.

Because Marketing at-Retail programs necessarily involve multiple participants with interests that at times converge and diverge, the role of project management assumes increased complexity and plays a vital role in the timely, cost-effective, and successful program. A failure by any participant can easily cascade into a series of negative actions that doom a program. A clear understanding of the role of project management in delivering successful Marketing at-Retail programs, along with clear delineation of intersecting responsibilities and the use of simple tools to define and manage projects, can dramatically increase the success ratio of projects.

This chapter discusses the scope of responsibility associated with project management, the key players involved, the interrelationships between players, the process involved in moving a project from ideation to placement in store, and tools that can be utilized to increase effectiveness and success.

SCOPE OF RESPONSIBILITY

Marketing at-Retail programs are inherently complex. They involve multiple constituencies: each playing a role in the implementation of a successful program and each with a veto power that can doom a program to failure at any point in a critical chain.

Some of the constituencies involved in program implementation include: shoppers, sales floor personnel, store managers, installation crews, direct store delivery personnel, retail headquarters (marketing, store planning, planogramming, purchasing, etc.), and brand marketers, including marketing, sales, purchasing, and others. Collectively the project management team will understand and anticipate the needs of each constituency so that a timeline is developed and information shared in a manner that will result in successful implementation in store. The process is the same for multi-national companies managing a world-wide launch and regional players refreshing a program already in the field; the relative level of complexity and number of constituencies involved may change, but the tools, principles, and flow to be managed remain the same.

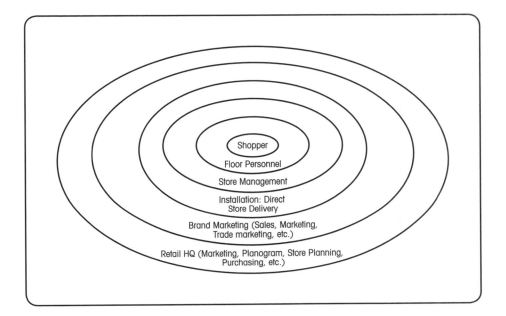

Figure 3-1 illustrates the relationship between the key constituencies in major Marketing at-Retail programs. The shopper is always at the core of a successful program; we all work to serve enlighten, inspire, educate, and delight her so she will reward us with loyalty and increased spending. Other constituencies serve as gatekeepers influencing the shopper experience in store. The broader the scope of the program, the more constituencies involved. A cursory review of the graphic makes it clear that no simple at retail programs exist and professional project management is a critical success element.

The goal of Marketing at-Retail programs is to:

- leverage conscious and sub-conscious shopper behavior combined with
- an analysis of the competitive retail environment
- to design optimal solutions that deliver
    - the right message
    - in the right place
    - in the right manner
- to drive sales and margin objectives while
- building greater shopper satisfaction and loyalty

The goal of project management is to bring this vision into reality.

CONSTITUENCY NEEDS

At retail programs involve multiple constituencies. At a minimum they involve the shopper and the retailer; most often they will involve the shopper, the brand, and the retailer. Beneath these broad categories, however, there are multiple layers that can directly impact a program. These include both intermediaries between the core constituencies and competing groups within constituencies.

Sometimes a program will be a category solution that involves multiple brands with differing visions and sometimes competitive agendas. At other times new groups, such as direct store delivery personnel or installation crews, are introduced into the equation to facilitate program implementation. At retail others work as gate keepers — including store managers, department managers and, in some cases, floor personnel — who exercise veto power over programs. Further within brands and retailers multiple groups are involved in program development and implementation.

The successful project manager:
- identifies the constituencies involved
- recognizes their role in program success
- understands their essential needs
- structures communication to provide the desired feedback
- provides the proper level of detail on a timely basis to support the program success

Let us briefly review some of the constituencies that are often involved in implementing effective Marketing at-Retail programs. This list is not exhaustive and the discussion is intended to be illustrative as opposed to precisely defining group needs and dynamics.

The shopper: the final arbiter of success

At the end of the day all successful entities involved in Marketing at-Retail recognize that they work for the shopper. If our programs work, we earn the right to continue to develop new programs; if they do not, we will cease to exist. The shopper determines the ultimate winners and losers. Good programs are built on this recognition and anchored in insights about the shopper's needs and desires. The smart project manager constructs a schedule that will fulfill the basic need of getting the at retail program in place at the right time.

The retailer at headquarters: the primary gatekeeper

The retailer owns the location for the desired interaction with the shopper. Today all retailers understand that their store is a brand in and of itself. As a brand with a set of values and expectations rooted in multi-tiered marketing that has gone on for many years at great expense, retailers consider every program in terms of its fit with their overall brand strategy and the way it supports their goals with their targeted shoppers.

For purposes of this discussion we have broken the retailer into two groups: headquarters and store personnel. In general, the headquarters group will give the approval and direction for display development, while the store personnel will be involved in the implementation phase of the program.

Depending on the size of the program and the retailer involved, a project will have one department or many departments involved in the development and approval of a program. A partial list of the departments that would typically be involved in a major program:

- Merchandising/Buying – decides what is carried in the store
- Store Planning – controls the total store layout and design
- Planogramming – controls the shelf presentation at retail
- Visual Merchandising – develops the look of the store
- Purchasing – executes purchase orders and controls vendor relationships
- Strategic Sourcing – determines supplier architecture to support the chain's programs
- Relationship Managers – control the relationship with a group of suppliers
- Special Project Groups – either temporary or permanent groups who manage the details of large programs
- Installation Managers – control the flow of information to the field installation teams and manage installation schedules for the chain

The groups that are actually involved in your particular project will vary based both on the chain and the scope of the project. In all cases, it is important to have one person designated as the traffic cop through whom all information flows and a defined decision-making mechanism for key decisions.

The store: veto power on the floor

As we found in our headquarters discussion, the store relationship with a program is multi-faceted and can be relatively simple or complex. Groups to consider in store include:

- Store management – controls the entire store; may decide that a unit will not work for his store
- Department manager – controls a department or section of the store; may decide that a program does not work for his department
- Floor personnel – works a section of the store; may be involved in display set-up and decide unit is too hard to set up or contains insufficient, wrong parts, etc.; may decide unit is annoying and deactivate critical interactive elements.

Most often store personnel are not involved in the development and approval. (A notable exception is many of the quick-service restaurants which generally have franchise boards representing the field voice in decision-making.) However, at each step of the command structure at retail, groups have veto power over the unit. Depending on the chain the exercise of that veto power may be relatively weak or strong. The wise project manager incorporates the needs of the store personnel into the design of the program.

The brand marketer: delivering their message at retail

The brand marketer has a product the shopper wants and a message they want to deliver to current and potential shoppers to increase the positive perception of their brand while inducing trial, greater usage, and brand loyalty. Today all brands recognize that their products operate within a larger retail environment. It is critical for brands to position their efforts so they work in concert with and improve the store and the category while also driving their needs.

This movement represents a significant change from the previous Marketing at-Retail model where brands created national programs that their sales force sold into retail. Today, the brands work with individual retailers to design and develop customized programs that work on multiple levels. Just as the retailers have interdisciplinary teams involved in major projects, so too do brand marketers. While the range of options may flow from a single brand marketing person driving a program with a single contact at retail through a dedicated interdisciplinary brand team that focuses their exclusive attention on a single retailer, the process and the key elements of success remain the same.

The brand marketer must first consider the role their product can play in driving the retailer's objectives. Then they must analyze the category to develop a program that will increase total category results versus moving more of their individual product. Major programs will only work if they advance the brand's objective within the context of the category and the store.

As with retailers the key to driving success is the designation of a traffic cop who controls the flow of information and a defined decision-making mechanism.

Other intermediaries: a necessary link in the process

Other groups can play an integral role in driving the success or failure of your program. Some groups that are frequently involved include:

- Store installation groups – teams focused solely on department changeover and fixture/display set-up
- Contract installation groups – engaged to set up stores, departments, or individual units
- Direct store delivery groups – internal personnel charged with bringing products and displays to the store
- Distributors – outside companies with responsibility for a group of products. Like DSD groups, they bring displays into the store with their product lines. They can be influential in placing a program at retail or can quietly exercise a veto that will doom implementation.

The producer: translating the concept into reality

It is the producer's job to translate the vision, challenge, or opportunity into reality. To do so, the producer must:

- Define and deliver a solution
- within the timeframe targeted
- for the budget specified that
- works within the constituency constraints identified

The P-O-P producer begins by understanding the issues that need to be solved or the opportunity to be maximized. The producer must then use his knowledge of production timelines and general cost parameters to define a direction that will meet the major program parameters or work to redefine the program so that later disappointment is avoided.

As the project moves through the various processes and departments within the producer's organization, project management is the glue that holds the project together. Project management is the controller of information, providing accurate timely information to all stakeholders. Information is critical to success. Without accurate timely information, disaster lurks at every bend. By making this information actionable, the project manager can ensure the program remains on track by providing early visibility to potential issues so effective, inexpensive remediation can occur.

Ideally, major projects have professional project managers on all sides – producer, brand, and retail. The key is that information flow in a timely manner against a timeline that supports success. A passive project manger on any side of a project that is not on top of details can doom it to failure; a pro-active manager who understands both the process and the environment can play an invaluable role in creating success.

What Knowledge Do Managers Need?

Managers at all levels need basic management skills; they should be able to communicate effectively, have basic computer skills, understand the needs of their organization so they can anticipate potential issues, have knowledge of the manufacturing processes involved in developing their programs, and have the ability to work on a team where they often lead others who may have titles higher than theirs. While many people may have been involved in the conception of a project, it is the project manager's job to oversee the birth. Like a superior midwife, the project manager must combine skill and knowledge to bring a program successfully to retail.

Each project manger should have a basic knowledge of all the critical elements involved in executing a major project, including production and key constituent needs. It is the responsibility of each manager to effectively represent the needs of their segment of the Marketing at-Retail mix. The successful manager will do so proactively so that they anticipate potential issues to avoid problems and increase program effectiveness.

MANAGING THE RELATIONSHIP BETWEEN CONSTITUENCIES

In a successful program, the person taking the lead in program development will switch over time so that a fluid movement among the team members develops. This is true for both the interchange between groups and within the groups themselves.

For example, a brand may take the early lead in identifying a need/opportunity; the retailer refines the program outlines and then passes it to a producer who dimensionalizes the program. The program is then passed to the retailer and brand for refinement before it is passed back to the producer who takes the lead in producing the program before one of the three assumes the lead for program implementation. The key to success is that a clear understanding of which party is taking the lead exists along with a commitment to fulfilling the team's need accurately and on time.

TRANSLATING A DISPLAY INTO FINAL EXECUTION

The need for a display program is identified by one party – usually the retailer or brand marketer. Once identified, it must be accepted by the retailers and marketers involved and then shared with a producer who will be charged with executing the program. In general, the process can be outlined as follows:

- Program Identification
- Program Acceptance
- Program Definition
- Program Assignment
- Program Ideation
- Program Refinement
- Program Development
- Program Execution
- Program Evaluation
- Program Enhancement

Program Identification

Based on knowledge of the at retail situation, one member of the marketing community identifies a need and posits a solution that will improve the at retail situation and increase sales. This identification can be led by a retailer, a marketer, or producer. In general, it is driven by a familiarity with the category, the brand, and the retail marketplace that leads to the positioning of a new program. The concept can involve a single retailer, a channel, or the entire retail distribution. Similarly, it can involve a single brand, a category, or a more general retail approach. The idea can be rough or very detailed. In any case it is sufficiently defined so that it can be discussed with others in enough detail to secure participation.

Program Acceptance

Once the concept has been identified, it is shared with the other potential partners to secure their agreement in the development and eventual implementation. Whether a rough concept or a detailed proposal, a major new program or a tweak of an existing installation, the direction must be agreed to by all parties involved in the program before it can move forward. This process can be straight-forward, involving a single retailer on a private label program, or it can be multi-faceted with many brands and retailers involved. In either case the process will include multiple parties within each channel. As discussed above, the constituencies involved are multi-layered. The concept can originate from any quarter, but will need to be endorsed by all to succeed. Detailed knowledge of the needs and restraints of all parties is critical in driving successful implementation.

Program Definition

After agreement has been reached to explore a concept, the program needs to be defined sufficiently so that additional parties can be brought in to assist with the program implementation. During this phase the parameters of the program will be set. Depending on the program and the technical and market expertise of the program originators, this phase will yield specific or general direction. The key is that enough detail is developed to intelligently identify the other resources that need to be employed and that the concept can adequately be defined to these resources so that they can develop the concept.

Program Assignment

The next step in the process is the engagement of a producer/supplier to work with the other parties in driving the program forward. The selection process is typically led by a team leader on the program. Selection is driven by either familiarity with the channel, the category, or expertise in the material chosen for the project. At this point the definition of the program can vary widely from very specific to a general direction.

Program Ideation

Once the participants have agreed to develop a program, the work of translating the concept into a workable retail solution begins. Depending on the level of detail involved in the acceptance phase of the program, this process can be long, involving multiple iterations utilizing all parties, or a quick adaptation of a fairly well-developed concept. In all cases particular attention must be paid to the manufacturability of the concept and its suitability to the targeted retailer or retail channel. The best concept will fail if it cannot be produced or if it fails within the retail environment once it is placed. A critical success element in this phase is that the decision makers and decision-making process be well-defined. Without clear definition, a program can get stuck in an endless feedback loop with no crisp decisions.

Program Refinement

Working with the information provided by the program originators, the producer/supplier will translate the broad concepts into specific proposals. The goal of this phase is to lay out options for bringing the idea to life at retail so the team can intelligently settle on the best proposal for achieving the program objectives. Typically, this process will expand the concept to contemplate a wide range of options. Through a series of concept reviews the variety of potential executions developed is eventually winnowed to a single concept. This concept is then fleshed out so it can be passed on to the prototype group.

Program Development

In this phase the idea first contemplated in the identification stage, expanded in the ideation step, and detailed during project development, is given physical form. The key considerations during this step include:

- whether the concept advances the core concept, as envisioned
- review of the shopability of the fixture
- evaluation of the proper integration of the unit into the store environment
- quality level of the unit
- suitability of the materials proposed
- potential installation issues

In some cases, this segment of the project will involve a single sample of the proposed unit. In other cases, this step will involve a series of reviews that begins with inexpensive models such as miniatures or foam core samples to test broad physical attributes that progress through a series of more defined iteration culminating in a replica of the unit to be rolled out at retail. In rare cases, participants may opt to skip this step and move directly into production. This direction is fraught with risk and opens significant exposure for disappointment with the final product. More typically, prototypes will be repeated until the unit is close enough to the envisioned product to mitigate the risk of errors in translation from sample to production.

Program Execution

After the hard work and myriad steps involved in conceiving and developing the program, the last phase is production and placement of unit in the store. Key areas to be defined in this stage include:

- The efficient production of the units
- Pack-out of displays
- Match of program components with store planogram
- Delivery options
- Installation options
- Maintenance of units in store

During this phase, the interaction of the project management team expands from the group involved in the development steps to include the teams that will lead the implementation. Depending on the program, this group may be internal, a retained service, direct store delivery teams, jobbers, agents, or some combination of the all. Success in this phase requires clear decision-making, defined communication protocols, and a command of the program details.

Program Evaluation

Using input from the installation team, shopper reaction, sales results, and feedback from all participants involved in the earlier phases, the team analyzes the key inputs to identify strengths and weaknesses in the program. During this stage, the involvement of all teams and team members is essential to maximize the impact of the evaluation process. By synergizing the points of view from all of the personnel involved in the program, improvements for future programs can be identified.

Program Enhancement

The insights gained from the evaluation phase are then integrated into a new cycle that moves from the ideation through the execution steps to yield easier execution and stronger results for future programs. This process can be very formal and detailed or informal and top-line. In the best ongoing programs it is integrated into the design of the program, creating a cycle of continuous learning and improvement.

THE TIMELINE

It is important that a realistic sense of the time needed to move through the various steps be incorporated into the project management design of the program. The timeline will vary depending on:

- the specificity of the initial ideas which will drive the ideation phase
- the clarity of the at retail needs and constraints
- the complexity of program installation
- the definition of clean decision-making protocol
- the adherence of the group to the agreed upon rules and timetables

At all stages, the competent project manager will remain aware of the overall timeline and the interconnection of decisions and actions at one stage on the total project and other inter-related steps. By effectively communicating the impact of actions today on program timing and execution down the road, a strong project manager can keep a program on track and focused on delivering the intended results.

SUCCESS ELEMENTS

Throughout all project phases the elements that drive success remain consistent:
- Knowledge of the shopper, the channel, the implementation team, and the manufacturing process
- Defined decision-making
- Mutually developed and agreed upon timeline
- Integration of unforeseen complications
- Awareness of the interrelation of program stages and impact on store execution
- Effective communication

CONCLUSION

The project manager is an integral part of all successful at retail programs. The professional manager is the glue that holds the project together ensuring that the goals established are achievable and that the program is executed in an efficient and timely manner. Successful project management requires a familiarity with all the key elements of a project, the ability to anticipate critical issues, and the ability to communicate effectively. A strong project manager can deliver tremendous benefit and drive a program to successful implementation. Project management is a critical link in Marketing at-Retail and vital to all projects.

Project Profile Questionnaire

Taken from
"The Power of Point-Of-Purchase Advertising: Marketing At Retail"
Chapter 3: Project Management
Fred Sklenar, Unified Resources
Published by Point-of-Purchase Advertising International (POPAI)

Market Analysis

Target Market

❑	Convenience	❑	Mass Market
❑	Department	❑	Mom & Pop
❑	Drug Chain	❑	Supermarket
❑	Other:		

Where are the stores located?	
Are any of these stores located outside of the U.S.?	❑ Yes ❑ No
If yes, where?	
Description of store environment:	
Is this retailer historically display friendly?	❑ Yes ❑ No

Placement in store:

❑	Aisle	❑	Gondola
❑	Ceiling	❑	In-line
❑	Checkout	❑	Lease Line
❑	Endcap	❑	Window
❑	Entrance	❑	Other:

Are any stores local to our office for a field visit?	❑ Yes ❑ No
If no, where is the nearest store location?	

Description of other displays near placement of this display:

Miscellaneous Information:

Project Profile Questionnaire

PROJECT PROFILE QUESTIONNAIRE CONTINUES ON NEXT 3 PAGES

Product Analysis

Product name(s):	
Selling points or features:	
Number of different SKUs on the display:	
Describe differences in SKUs:	
Number of total SKUs on the display:	
Product specifications:	
Samples of product available?	❏ Yes ❏ No
Pending graphics or packaging changes?	❏ Yes ❏ No
List competitor's products:	
❏ National brand name.	
❏ Private label.	

Display Criteria

Type of display desired:

❏	Banner	❏	Free-standing
❏	Connect to existing store fixtures	❏	Merchandiser (Number of sides:_____)
❏	Counter	❏	Signage
❏	Glorifier	❏	Specialty
❏	Floor	❏	Wall
❏	Kiosk		

Describe details:	
Quantity needed:	
Quantity per store:	
Budget per display:	
How long will the display be in stores?	
Special product layout?	
Merchandising/marketing goal for display:	
Will the product ship with the display?	❏ Yes ❏ No

List any special functions (e.g., movement, illumination, special engineering):	
Client-specified materials of choice:	
Client-specified materials to avoid:	
Production methods considered inappropriate:	
Graphic message to communicate:	
Placement of graphics:	
Special printing requirements (such as spot colors):	
Special colors requested:	
Are there any logos to use or will they be available?	
Will the client supply final art?	❑ Yes ❑ No
If yes, on disk?	❑ Yes ❑ No
Are there other media tie-ins?	❑ Yes ❑ No
Who will set up the display?	
Instructions needed:	❑ Printed sheet ❑ With photos ❑ Video
Will a separate company be contracted for in-store set-up?	❑ Yes ❑ No
Size recommendations or limitations:	
Is there budget available for tooling?	❑ Yes ❑ No
Does the client have existing tooling that this display must fit into?	❑ Yes ❑ No

Deliverables

What is the client expecting?

❑	Conceptual rough sketches for fax.
❑	Conceptual sketched mounted for client meeting.
❑	Renderings mounted for presentation.
❑	Renderings posted on Web site.
❑	Renderings e-mailed.
❑	Sketch models for digital photos to be posted on Web site.

❑	Sketch models for digital photos to be e-mailed.	
❑	Working prototypes.	
Delivered how and where?		
Work is needed by?		

Approvals

Who will be required to approve the program?		
❑	At the client:	
❑	At the retailer:	
Will the pre-production prototype need to be installed at the corporate offices of the retailer prior to approval for full production.	❑ Yes ❑ No	

Shipping/Delivery Packaging

Any special client specifications?	
Shipper size requirements (UPS, FedEx, other expedited delivery companies, fit in sales rep's car, etc.):	
Special printing on carton (code numbers, UPC bar codes, PO numbers, etc.):	
Where will the displays be shipped?	
What carrier is recommended by the client?	
Is floor loading acceptable?	
Special pallet considerations:	
Any previously incurred problems that need to be avoided?	

4

Sales Promotion Planning

Arlene S. Gerwin
President
Bolder Insights LLC

SALES PROMOTION PLANNING ENHANCES MARKETING AT-RETAIL PROGRAMMING

This chapter defines sales promotion and presents the various tactics and tools used to meet objectives and maximize the marketing investment. The emphasis is on sales promotion planning – the process, the timing, the tools, the pitfalls and the benefits. The chapter discusses both short and long-term sales promotion planning and how sales promotion relates to the other elements of the marketing mix.

Sales promotion and Marketing at-Retail work hand-in-hand to effectively and uniquely communicate with the consumer. Well-designed Marketing at-Retail materials such as displays, case cards, shelf talkers, banners and the like are enhanced by a consumer call to action such as cents-off coupons, recipe booklets or BOGO's (buy one, get one free).

WHAT IS SALES PROMOTION?

POPAI's P-O-P Advertising Desktop Reference guide defines sales promotions as "the use of temporary incentives by consumer goods and services companies to change the behavior of their trade (retail) consumers and/or their end consumer."[1] As such, sales promotion is an important element of the overall marketing mix. Companies develop comprehensive strategic plans that incorporate integrated marketing communications campaigns with the overall objective to build brands, enhance services or even build company equity. Thus, sales promotion is one of the building blocks of the marketing plan along with packaging, advertising, market research, public relations, consumer relationship marketing and even event planning – in essence, the holistic communication strategy to the target consumer.

As consumers ourselves, everyone is quite familiar with sales promotion tactics. Just walk into your neighborhood supermarket, pharmacy or office supply retailer and you are bombarded by promotional messages. "Save 50% Off the Suggested Retail Price". "Buy a bottle of soda at full price and get another one for free". "Buy two cans of soup and get a free box of crackers."

What do these offers have in common besides potentially confusing the average consumer? They are all promotion tactics that add value to a product and enhance Marketing at-Retail efforts. As poorly conceived as they sometimes seem, such consumer promotions encourage the customer to buy a specific brand, to buy more than one item at a time, or to buy a preferred brand and sample another. In short, they give consumers more for their money by reducing the cost or by providing something for free.

Figure 4-1 shows a selection of Marketing at-Retail displays presenting value-added consumer offers.

Figure 4-1

Value added displays for free video rentals and bobble head toys.

HOW DOES SALES PROMOTION DIFFER FROM ADVERTISING?

To begin, the objective of advertising is quite different from that of sales promotion. Advertising is usually viewed as a longer-term investment. Over time, advertising builds brand equity by establishing a consistent image or feeling for a brand—a softer sell. Current national advertising campaigns for consumer goods such as luxury cars or cosmetics, for example, are designed to build brand image and the advertising campaigns may last for several years. In comparison, sales promotions are more immediate, involving a finite time period. Sales promotions offer the consumer something more tangible. Due to the finite time period that a sales promotion runs, return on investment (ROI) can usually be calculated. The impact of sales promotions is, therefore, easier to evaluate than advertising results.

But the line between sales promotion and advertising can sometime be blurred. For example, it is not unusual to see "an ad" in an FSI (free standing inserts in the Sunday newspapers). Most pages in an FSI contain either a coupon, refund or a mail-in offer of some kind—a consumer call to action. But on occasion, a brand may run an information ad with no consumer offer for the advertising value alone. It is doubtful; however, if the consumer is actually spending time reading this ad as opposed to clipping the coupons. This type of informational ad is best run in advertising vehicles such as newspapers or magazines. Thus, marketers need to be mindful of the best use of promotion vehicles such as FSI's.

At the majority of marketing-savvy companies, sale promotion budgets are larger than advertising budgets, attesting to the desire for more immediate consumer response and quicker payback on marketing investment than that provided by investing in advertising

SALES PROMOTIONS REQUIRE CAREFUL PLANNING

Ever since retail establishments came into existence, there has been some form on in-store promotions. Carefully hand-painted signs announcing a sale or price reduction can often be spotted in 19th century photos of country general stores. Figure 4-2 shows an example of such early consumer offers.

Figure 4-2

A 1950's retail store front of Eckerd Drugs. Notice the POP signs in the window.

Sales promotion tools are used for a shorter period time, however, that does not mean that these programs can be quickly and carelessly developed. Marketers may be tempted to "shoot from the hip" and create ad hoc promotions in an attempt to quickly move product. This is a dangerous practice than can backfire in the long run. Ill-planned and poorly timed promotions can interrupt the natural consumer product-use cycle, artificially inflate sales volume and even disrupt normal seasonality trends.

For example, a consumer sees cat food on sale at a deeply discounted price. Unless the consumer is planning to feed additional cats, it is likely that her pets will still eat the same amount of cat food. The consumer's cat food purchases will likely cease until her supply runs low. The myopic marketer who analyzes only the short-term spikes in sales volume during the discounted promotion period will not see the true picture. The marketer will be disappointed in subsequent weeks when sales trends decline and profit erodes. Thus, it is crucial for the marketer to understand product seasonality, penetration, non-promotional product sales and plan accordingly for the promotional sales lifts.

The most successful sales promotions are those that are developed against a clear set of marketing objectives. For example, a campaign that succeeds in getting consumers to stock up on pet food meets the objective of temporarily removing those consumers from the market, precluding their purchase of competitive pet food brands. This strategy is extremely effective, and frequently used, as part of a preplanned campaign to defend against the launch of a competitive brand. It illustrates how sales promotion has evolved from a hastily conceived tactic to a preplanned, long-range strategic campaign.

SALES PROMOTION PLANNING IS AN EXTENSION OF THE STRATEGIC PLAN

Effective sales promotion tactics are included in the overall marketing plan and ultimately included in the company strategic plan. Marketing plans are usually developed annually and specifically detail objectives, strategies and tactics that support corporate objectives over a one to two year horizon. Equally important is the long-term strategic plan that maps out corporate goals beyond the current year, typically five years out. The marketing plan is revised annually so that it is always current and contributes to the future vision of the strategic plan. *Strategic planning* is defined as "the consideration of current decision alternatives in light of their probable consequences over time."[2]

To mitigate risk, alternative scenarios are investigated and analyzed in the strategic plan. A useful tool is the *SWOT analysis* (*strengths, weaknesses, opportunities and threats*). Strengths and weaknesses are internal to the company, whereas opportunities and threats involve the external environment including competitors. Brands and services are virtually dissected and analyzed from all angles to determine what works, what doesn't and the potential vulnerabilities. A popular approach at many companies to the *SWOT* analysis is an internal session termed "*War Games*". Basically, marketers role play and take the position of key competitors to forecast strengths, weaknesses, opportunities and threats. This encourages them to think both offensively and defensively. Using this mapping tool, smart decisions can be made to determine long-term direction, anticipate competitive actions and to develop a sound strategic plan with contingencies.

Figure 4-3 presents the SWOT analysis grid.

Strengths	Weaknesses
Opportunities	Threats

Figure 4-3

SWOT Analysis Grid

Once agreement is reached as to the strategic direction, the marketing plan details other variables that impact a brand or service. This usually includes defining the consumer target audience— those consumers who are the best prospects for the brand or service. The consumer target may be current users, past users or even competitive users. Non-users are the most difficult to bring into a franchise and most costly to do so. The consumer target is defined in both demographic and psychographic terms. It is short-sighted to only define the consumer by demographics—age, gender, geography and household income. It is more meaningful to understand the psychology of the consumer—psychographics—what motivates someone to try a product and repurchase it? What are the behavioral traits and lifestyle of the target consumer? What are the consumer's likes and dislikes? What values are most important? Consider the differences between these two consumers: each earn the same income, both live in the same town, both are married with two children. But one is a college professor and the other is a long-haul truck driver. What appeals to the college professor may be quite different from what appeals to the truck driver. And the strategies to reach these consumers should be different as well.

Additional questions that need to be addressed include: What consumer need does the product or service fulfill? How does the product fill this consumer need better than a competitive product? What are the potential markets and channels for this product or service? The more realistic and specific the plan, the greater the probability of meeting corporate objectives.

In summary, have a game plan to follow—a long-term strategic plan—usually five years out, and an annually revised marketing plan. Both planning tools must be realistic and grounded in facts with contingencies baked in.

SMART OBJECTIVES DELIVER SMART PROGRAMMING

All marketing plans should include promotion objectives, strategies and tactics. These terms can be easily confused and are not interchangeable.

- *An objective* is the end goal. As an example, increase sales by 10%.
- *A strategy* is the overall approach to meet the objective. For example, bring new users into a brand franchise.
- *A tactic* is the specific element of the strategy. For example, launch a new product to bring in the new users to increase sales.

Figure 4-4

Develop SMART
Objectives

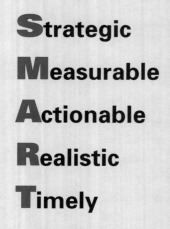

Strategic

Measurable

Actionable

Realistic

Timely

Sales promotion techniques usually fall under the definition of marketing tactics. Tactics, in contrast to strategies, are more immediate. A free coupon to sample a new flavor is considered a tactic.

Objectives, strategies and tactics detailed in the marketing plan provide a road map of action steps. A sound marketing plan clearly details how, when and why programs are planned and executed. The ability to measure results is critical to the success of a marketing plan. Setting *SMART* objectives ensures that results can be measured. A useful tool to do this is to use the *SMART* (*strategic, measurable, actionable, realistic and timely*) approach. (See figure 4-4).

The *SMART* approach also serves as a checklist when writing objectives to ensure that success is objectively—not subjectively defined.

TIMING IS EVERYTHING: THE PROMOTION PLAN SHOULD BE DEVELOPED AT LEAST A YEAR IN ADVANCE AND REFINED THROUGHOUT THE YEAR

The importance of advance planning cannot be overstressed. At the outset of a promotion, not all program details need to be finalized, but the marketer needs a road map to illuminate where to go and how to get there. There are many planning tools and software packages available to help simplify the planning process. Microsoft Project is a particularly useful project management tool. It allows the marketer to report project details, delegate tasks, obtain status updates and track costs. Simple flow charts or project templates can be utilized, like the example shown in Figure 4-5.

DEVELOP DETAILED BUDGETS AND TIMETABLES IN ADVANCE

The marketer needs to determine how company resources are allocated among the elements of the marketing mix including promotions. Promotion budgets are developed as part of the overall marketing plan. Once an overall budget is determined for the promotion plan, a more detailed promotion budget is developed for the year. The promotion budget is broken down by projects and may be segmented into seasonal time periods; for example: summer promotions, holiday promotions etc. Within these segments, the promotion campaigns are further detailed. Budget categories may include estimated costs for creative development; agency fees; coupon design and fulfillment, product and procurement costs, logistics costs, warehousing fees and distribution costs.

Early in the planning cycle when the budget is developed, many costs are only estimated. The marketer may look at previous promotion costs for similar campaigns to more accurately forecast. Obviously, the more realistic the estimates, the closer the budget will match actual costs after program execution. The wise marketer plans for contingencies and unforeseen expenses when developing the budget. Better to come in under budget than to have to scramble for additional dollars to cover actual costs. The promotion arena is not immune to the ravages of Murphy's Promotions Law: Designs that look great on paper oftentimes present unanticipated production complications, not to mention the intervention of natural disasters and ill-timed strikes.

The promotion budget is also a dynamic tracking tool. The budget template should include a method to constantly update estimated costs with actual expenditures. At many companies, marketers coordinate with financial analysts who update budgets. There are many technology solutions used at different companies for budget development, tracking and reconciliation. By constantly tracking actual costs against

Task	Week #	Description	Output Owner
Program Planning			
Program evaluation	45	Review past program evaluation	Business Analyst
Program objectives/strategies		Set goals with quantitative and qualitative measures	Promotion Manager
Concept Development, Program Design, and Program Development			
Complete creative brief	41	Inputs/approvals	Marketing Management
		Brief agency	Promotion Manager
		Budget confirmed	Promotion Manager
Concept brainstorming starts	41	Narrow brainstorm concepts to 2 or 3	Promotion Manager
		Determine channel/account customization	Promotion Manager
Concept approval	37	Marketing management	Promotion Manager
Develop program elements/prototypes	36	Program defined with visuals	Promotion Manager
Estimated costs of elements	36	Estimated budget costs for elements	Promotion Manager
		Identify long lead time items	Promotion Manager
		Issue specs for long lead time items	Promotion Manager
Program approval	30	Program elements, visuals, structure. design approved	Promotion Manager
Communicating the Program			
Communicate final program	24	Communicate program details, costs and budgets	Program Coordinator
In-Market Planning			
Begin account/channel planning	24	Retail planning	Sales Management
		Identify augmentation needs	
Ordering and Producing Materials			
Order long lead time items	24	Approve costs, select vendor	Promotion Manager
		Submit art/disks for production	Promotion Manager
Specs and drawings	20	Specs/drawings to vendors	Promotion Manager
Field inputs orders	19	Input quantity and shipping instructions	Sales Management
Bidding process	18	Sealed bids to vendors	Promotion Manager
		Bidding analysis completed	Promotion Manager
Order consolidation	18	Consolidate orders	Promotion Manager
		Review/revise items	Promotion Manager
Approve costs/quantities	17	Update promotion budget	Promotion Manager
Select vendor	17	Order materials/elements	Promotion Manager
Approve art/mech for production	17	Last chance for revisions to program/elements	Promotion Manager
Art/mech to vendor	17	Submit final art/disks and hold preproduction meeting	Promotion Manager
Start production	16	Art and disk preflight and archive	
		Production proofing	
Delivering and Executing the Promotion			
Ship materials	8	Program elements to central warehouse/collate	Traffic Managers
Promotion materials/sell sheets ship	6	To arrive at least 6 weeks before promotion starts	
Promotion in market	1	Promotion executed	

Figure 4-5   Promotion Plan Outline

the budget, the marketer can be confident that promotions are in-line with projections. When actual costs start exceeding estimate, the marketer can make adjustments accordingly.

Realistic promotion timetables are as important as accurate cost estimates, especially when a promotion includes several elements. The marketer must be sensitive to longer promotion lead times for custom-designed items and off-shore sourcing. For example, a holiday promotion may include multiple items such as a permanent wooden display with a cardboard header card, a corrugated-case display, a premium dealer loader, posters, shelf-talkers and a printed sales brochure. If the premium is custom designed and produced offshore, a minimum of six months and as much as a year may be required for the design and production process. Shipping time should also be included. It is therefore not uncommon to initiate the design and planning of complicated, multi-faceted promotion campaigns 12 to 18 months in advance. This ensures that longer lead-time items are produced and delivered on time. After all, a Christmas display delivered in February is worthless!

A COMPREHENSIVE CREATIVE BRIEF IS A MUST

Once the marketing plan is approved, a creative brief should be developed before plunging into the tactical execution of a promotion campaign. The creative brief is an invaluable tool that provides the agency or design firm with important information for developing the creative concept and recommending appropriate promotion elements to support the concept. The creative brief is just that –brief—typically one to two pages in length. Limiting information to no more than two pages focuses ideas and forces the synthesizing of the creative rationale. It helps the marketer to think very specifically and strategically about what must be accomplished.

Most creative briefs include an estimated budget. Not indicating a budget range is unwise and can lead to off-strategy promotion development. A marketer who briefs an agency and says that the budget is not included because he doesn't want to stifle the agency's creativity is only asking for trouble! Imagine if the marketer has a budget limit of $25K for the project and the agency returns with multi-million dollar concepts. That's a waste of everyone's time! The agency has to go back to the "drawing board" involving additional time and money. So, always include a budget on the brief, even if just a range.

The creative brief provides background data, strategies and objectives, timing, communication priorities, legal requirements and overall tone for the promotion. Budget parameters and a timetable should always be included. Approval sign-offs should also be clearly defined. Does a lawyer need to review before proceeding?

Figure 4-6 is an example of a template for an Agency Creative Brief.

Figure 4-6

Agency Creative Brief

Brand: _____	Initiation Date: _____
Project No.: _____	Project Contact: _____
Program Elements: _____	Program Period: _____

Background Information	
Brand Strategy	
Promotion Strategy	
Program Objectives	
Research/Analysis Component	
Communication Priorities	
Advertising/Media Campaign	
Target Audience & Mindset	
Competitive Information	
Program Requirements	
Tone	
Call to Action	
Mandatories/ References	
Program Budget	

TRADE AND CONSUMER PROMOTION OBJECTIVES ARE CLOSELY LINKED

Promotions fall under two broad classifications—trade promotions and consumer promotions. They share similar end goals but differ as to who is incentivized and how.

Trade promotions are targeted at the retail customer or at the middlemen—those responsible for getting goods and services from a manufacturer into a retail establishment. Examples of trade promotions include incentives to authorize new products, distribution-building programs, display allowances, volume discounts and shelf-expansion incentives. Trade promotions push product into the store—onto the shelf or on a display—and are therefore termed *push strategies*.

Consumer promotions, on the other hand, are those programs targeted at the purchaser or end consumer. Accordingly, consumer promotions are termed *pull strategies* because they literally motivate the consumer to pull the product off the shelf or display and out of the retail store. Trade promotions and consumer promotions should be jointly planned to maximize consumer purchase of product that has been pushed into the retail environment.

Consumer promotions usually offer the potential consumer some type of added incentive structured to meet the brand strategies and objectives. For example, if the stated objective is to generate trial of a new product, the consumer promotion tactic could offer the consumer a free coupon to try the new product. Or the promotion could provide the consumer with a free sample distributed at retail or even delivered to the consumer's doorstep.

In addition to motivating trial of a new product, consumer promotions can build demand, build brand awareness, generate an impulse buy and even motivate multiple purchases. Various consumer-directed tactics can be employed to encourage buyer action including coupons, refunds, rebates, sampling, and free items, to name just a few. See figure 4-7. These offers can be delivered via various vehicles ranging from handing the consumer an incentive in-store to using print media such as newspapers and magazines, free-standing inserts (FSI's), direct mail or electronic communication.

Figure 4-7

Coupons and rebates assist sales at the point of purchase

As part of a larger, integrated marketing campaign, consumer promotions can also include games, contests, sweepstakes, cross-promotions and tie-in promotions. Care should always be taken as to how these programs are structured as laws regulating such activities can vary by state and by country.

Loyalty programs are another consumer directed promotion concept and have been around for over 100 years. S&H Green Stamps date back to the 1930's. After making a purchase, consumers received small green stamps that they pasted into books. Filled books could be redeemed for a range of items to reward the consumer for her loyalty.

Loyalty programs are structured marketing efforts that reward, and therefore encourage, loyal buying behavior....[3] American Airlines is credited with launching the first frequent flier program. Almost all of the major hotel chains and all major airlines issue their own loyalty cards, many via rewards credit cards. Loyalty cards are now prevalent in grocery and drug chains, electronics stores, shoe stores, and even restaurants. In addition, Staples, Inc, and Office Depot (office supply chains) started issuing club cards in 2005. The consumer presents the card when purchasing an item or service and can receive a monetary discount or receive points to later redeem for free goods or services.

At-retail, displays serve as a bridge connecting trade and consumer promotions. The most powerful offers are those delivered directly to consumers in the retail environment while shopping. Well-constructed and attractive display units—temporary or permanent—showcase products for consumers with coupons in-hand. A consumer might see a wooden rack filled with wine bottles and a free recipe booklet suggesting which wines complement various foods—meat entrees, for example. If this rack is strategically placed near the meat section, the consumer need not search the store for ingredients.

When trade and consumer promotions work in tandem, the push and pull efforts reach a state of equilibrium. The trade incentives ensure that the right products are at the right place at the right time. The consumer incentives deliver motivated buyers to purchase the products. Together these efforts support the marketer's objectives by delivering projected sales and profit.

JOINT PROMOTIONS LINK BRANDS AND ENHANCE CONSUMER VALUE PERCEPTIONS

Joint promoting, also known as *co-promoting*, is the joining of two brands promotionally and sharing Marketing at-Retail merchandising materials to make the shopper's task easier—and provide twice the promotional impact at half the cost to the marketers. Two companies or brands are likely to consider co-promoting if an offer will appeal to both target audiences.

Using joint promotions, brands can communicate extended usage ideas, provide new recipes using both brands, suggest serving ideas tied to specific holidays or even promote counter-seasonality usage. During the holiday season, when floor display space is at a premium, multi-brand promotions proliferate. For example, soft-drink companies build massive in-store holiday displays, add snack products to these displays, and offer shoppers coupons for the purchase of two or more items. In effect, these displays are a one-stop snack shopping center. See Figure 4-8.

Figure 4-8

Joint Promotion

Joint promotions can also give exposure to brands or services outside their usual channel of trade. For example, amusement parks jointly promote with many types of products. Consumers might gain free admission by collecting soft drink cans. The amusement park promotes the venue in supermarkets and other retail outlets, and the free offer increases soft-drink sales. Both the amusement park and the brand benefit.

CAREFULLY SELECT PROMOTION ELEMENTS—BE SURE THEY ARE ON STRATEGY, AFFORDABLE AND CAN BE PRODUCED ON TIME

Although the marketing plan provides a road map of action steps, any road map offers several routes to reach the ultimate destination. Similarly, there is a range of promotion tactics available to the marketer to meet the objectives and strategies set forth in the marketing plan. Several major promotion tools have been discussed in this chapter. Figure 4-9 summarizes some of these tools and serves as a simple check-list.

In many cases, several different promotion tactics can all be strategically sound. If so, the marketer must determine which approach meets the budget parameters and the project timetable. Estimating costs can be a challenge. When coupons, refunds and rebates are offered, for example, forecasted redemption can vary widely. Coupon fulfillment services issue redemption reports that provide guidance, but history does not always repeat itself.

The astute marketer knows the importance of good forecasting and budgeting and of having contingency funds identified to cover unexpected expenses.

P-O-P Promotion Tools	Objectives	Strengths	Weaknesses
Displays • Permanent • Temporary	• Generate off-shelf product display • Build brand/product awareness	• Shopper convenience • Increases retail volume • Showcases consumer offers	• Retail space limited for displays • Costs • Limited time on floor
Price Reductions • Temporary markdowns	• Motivate consumer trial • Generate multiple purchase • Defend against competitive pricing	• Clears out inventory • Moves old or off-season items	• Not important factor to all potential buyers • Reduces margins
Coupons • Manufacturer • Retailer	• Motivate consumer trial • Generate multiple purchase • Build brand/retailer loyalty	• Instant gratification • Redemption slippage	• Low redemption • Limited appeal to coupon clippers • Inconvenient
Refunds/Rebates	• Motivate consumer purchase • Build brand/product loyalty	• Provides future reward	• Delayed gratification/reward • Not all retailers participate
Sampling	• Generate trial • Motivate brand switching	• Direct to consumer • Instant gratification	• More expensive promotion vehicle • High cost per consumer reached
On Packs/In Packs	• Sampling device • Generate trial of related or different product	• Free item • Instant gratification	• Retailer shelving and inventory issues
Games/Sweepstakes	• Generate consumer excitement • Tie to advertising campaign	• Generates brand PR • Big prizes	• Limited consumer appeal

Figure 4-9

Promotion Tools Grid

BUILD IN FLEXIBILITY TO REACT TO UNEXPECTED EVENTS

To summarize this chapter, flexibility is critical as relates to both time and money. Promotions can be cancelled unexpectedly when budgets are cut. Competitors may enter the market unexpectedly, forcing defensive plans to be quickly developed and executed. The astute marketer has an arsenal of tactics waiting in the wings to meet such unplanned occurrences.

ENDNOTES

[1] *P-O-P Advertising Desktop Reference Guide* (Washington, D.C.: Point-Of-Purchase Advertising International, 1999), 25.

[2] Peter D. Bennet, ed., *Dictionary of Marketing Terms*, 2nd ed. (Lincolnwood, Ill,: NTC business Books, 1995), 276.

[3] Sharp, Byron and Anne Sharp (1997), "Loyalty Programs and their Impact on Repeat-Purchase Loyalty Patterns," International Journal of Research in Marketing, 14 (5), 473-86.

5

Post Promotion
Evaluation

Martin Block, Ph.D.
Northwestern University

POST PROMOTION EVALUATION

Evaluating point-of-purchase material after it has been administered has evolved from a primarily survey research activity to an examination of retail point-of-purchase data over the last 50 years. The process of evaluating all promotion including point-of-purchase material has changed with the changing marketplace. The explosion of available data including the proliferation of point-of-sale (POS) scanning, customer loyalty programs and the now commonplace customer databases are all driving the change.

Management demands for better accountability and real measurement is also driving the change, leading to much less emphasis on traditional research measures.

The digital revolution that has swept the business world now shapes the way the impact of price changes and promotional activity are assessed, including all point-of-purchase material. The technology has made possible the collection of purchase and sales data in ways that were previously not possible, and it has greatly enhanced the ability to manipulate and analyze that data. Two factors emerge as driving forces in the move toward analysis of sales promotion. These are improved cost accounting and availability of data on sales performance, down to the level of individual items at the individual retail outlet.

Improved Cost Accounting

Improved accuracy of cost-accounting methods by both the manufacturer and the retailer now makes it possible to more accurately allocate both fixed and variable costs on a brand-by-brand, size-of-package by size-of-package basis. The proliferation of items has led to difficulty in determining if all items are justified on the basis of their contribution to profit. However, with the ever-decreasing cost of collecting and processing data, historical data on profit contribution can be kept at the finest level of detail.

Improved Data

Before POS was employed at the checkout lane, virtually no individual purchase data were available. The growth of automated checkout devices, or scanners, has been historically justified by most retailers on the basis of improved checkout productivity, that is, reduced labor and reduced error in entering prices. A by-product of POS installation is an accurate recording on an outlet-by-outlet basis of the prices charged and the sales volume for each item sold during time periods as short as one week.

A number of syndicated data services are currently using scanner-collected data to provide client manufacturers with detailed reporting of brand-sales volume, competitive pricing, and promotional activity. Most importantly, the accumulation of very detailed historical information on an outlet-by-outlet basis provides a foundation for the statistical analysis of interactions among the pricing and promotional activities, including point-of-sale, of competing brands. Also critically important is the ability to conduct experiments at the retail-outlet level to assess the probable impact of pricing and promotional activities outside the observed range of historical conditions.

A.C. Nielsen is a leader in using scanner data for tracking product sales and has one of the most consistent historical databases for examining the impact of pricing and promotion decisions in grocery product categories. The Nielsen data are collected using scanners in grocery, drug, and mass-merchandiser stores in selected markets around the country. The data have been collected for several years on grocery stores, providing a reasonably complete database on grocery product sales.

A criticism of this approach is that no psychological variables are measured or recorded. The technology measures only the overt behavior of product purchase. However, it can be argued that such variables are not particularly important given that sales, and hence revenue and profit, are so well measured. Still there is some room for the survey methods.

Promotion Decisions

Before the data and appropriate analytic techniques can be brought to bear on any promotion evaluation problem, it is necessary to establish objectives for that promotion.

1. *Setting Objectives.* The first step is always setting objectives. Objectives for sales promotion, like objectives for any marketing strategy, must be unambiguous and realistic. The objectives will be unambiguous if they provide for measurable outcomes. The objective of increasing sales by one hundred thousand units, however, is precise and measurable. Objectives may be stated in terms of volume sales, share of market, profitability, trial of product among previous nonusers, or changes in inventory position. Objectives must also be realistic in terms of their potential to be fulfilled.

2. *Price and Promotion.* In most analyses of sales promotion activity, it is best to separate the decision about the pricing of the product from any decision about using promotion. A product should have an established, normal selling price that consumers expect to pay. This price is certainly influenced by both manufacturer and retailer costs, but it is not necessarily determined by them entirely. The biggest problem for both the manufacturer and retailer is being able to estimate enough of the demand curve in order to determine the estimated sales levels at alternative selling prices. Because scanning records every purchase of a product instantly, comparisons can be made on virtually a day-to-day, store-by-store basis. Products then can be analyzed on a very short time interval, such as a day or a week, or over a very long time, such as months or years. Comparison of natural or promotion-induced price changes with sales volume will then provide a most reasonable estimate of the fundamental demand or price-volume curve for that product. By holding some of the variables constant, such as the normal selling price, the impact of promotion can be examined.

Evaluation and Research

Establishing the relationship between selling price and unit sales requires very careful study of product sales at the retail level. Obtaining an accurate measure of retail sales is necessary to properly evaluate the effectiveness of sales promotion programs, and it requires a special research effort. The research required is often best performed by external specialized research organizations.

Measuring Product Sales

Retail product sales can be measured in several ways. Various methods have evolved over the years for different product categories. The methods that have evolved and are described here are all commercial successes. They are all offered for sale by at least one commercial research service organization and, of course, are purchased by marketers.

Store Scanner Data

Using the universal product bar code, a computer-controlled bar-code reader identifies the product, the appropriate price is found in a computer-maintained database; and the customer is provided a printout receipt. Each purchase is entered into a database for later analysis. An average supermarket may record approximately one hundred fifty thousand such individual purchases in a day. The automated checkout data provides all of the characteristics of the package and brand, plus the exact price paid and the purchase quantity. The data are precisely timed so that the date and even the time of day are known. However, scanner data alone provides no information about the consumer making the purchase.

Store Scanner Panels

One solution to the consumer problem with store scanner data is the store scanner panel. By providing individuals with special cards that can be read in the store, complete recordings of all scan-able purchases can be made.

Time Period

Data must be aggregated in time. The results need to be measured on a basis consistent with the duration of the promotional event. For a weekend-special store sale, daily measurement may be required. For the typical week-long event found in many grocery, drug, and mass-merchandise stores, weekly sales are usually sufficient. The same problem of aggregation exists with data summarized over several sales outlets with differing promotional conditions.

Sales and Usage Measurement

Sales are traditionally presented in the form of market share in marketing plans. The term market share simply refers to the sales for a given product brand divided by the total sales in the product category. When one knows a product's market share, one can compare the performance of an individual brand against competing brands. This is why it is so often used as a means of expressing product sales. When used at high levels of data aggregation such as annual U.S. sales volume, it is a good indication of relative effectiveness.

A problem in using market share for short-run analysis is that competitive activity is included in the number. For example, if brand A runs a promotion and enjoys an increase in sales, and if brand B also runs a promotion at the same time and increases sales, brand A may have very little change in market share but significant volume-sales increases. Because market share also includes competitive activity, market share loses sensitivity to a given sales promotion program. A much better measure of sales to evaluate sales promotion is then sales volume. A second problem with market share is that an accurate assessment is required as to which brands or products are in the appropriate market. Many product categories such as sliced lunch meats, canned soups, salted snacks, cookies, and snack crackers have a large variety of sizes, forms, and flavors. Improper specification of the items to be used as a basis for market share may materially bias analyses.

Experiments

By coding the presence of a sales promotion program using dummy variables, historical data can be analyzed as though an experiment were conducted. The control condition becomes all of those times when the promotion is not present. The non-promotion occurrences represent the base business for the particular brand and are defined as the average business or sales. Particular care must be taken if one effect of promotion is to cause inventory stockpiling by retailer or consumers.

While the analysis has been described here as an experiment, it is not an experiment in the strict sense. The control and experimental conditions are not strictly parallel in time, and it is always possible that conditions during the time of the promotion were unusual in some way, making them different from the average of other times. This can be partially solved by conducting experiments in different markets at different points in time. Certainly the analyst needs to be aware of the issue.

UPC Codes and Product Characteristic Libraries

There is no central authority which maintains descriptions of the product characteristics associated with UPC codes in distribution. To further complicate the situation, manufacturers have some control over the usage of UPC codes assigned for their use. Codes used to identify special packages or temporary formulations may be rested for a period of time, and then re-issued on products which may be totally different brands than their previous use. Thus, the product characteristics associated with a UPC code are time dependent. This is not generally a problem for retailers, as their UPC code files contain information on the category assignment and pricing of codes in real time, and they seldom face the problem of different products carrying the same codes.

Suppliers of syndicated data maintain extensive dictionaries for the UPC codes which they cover. These dictionaries typically contain information on brand name, size, flavor, form, packaging, volumetric basis, and even the ingredient lists. Auxiliary information such as manufacturer identification, a supplier defined product category hierarchy, typical pricing, and date range covered by movement are also included to aid in editing and quality control.

Outliers

The types of systems we have been describing, whether POS based, in-home scanner based, or Internet based, cover thousands of transactions in short time. A variety of situations exist which can cause outliers. Some are software related, when infrequently occurring conditions generate extreme data or programming errors generate spurious results. Some result from redefinitions of a UPC code. Such redefinitions can cause abrupt changes in transaction counts, dollars per item, or average items per transaction.

Measuring consumer response to sales promotion has always been a difficult task. Until the availability of scanner data, measuring consumer response was limited to aggregate summarizing of coupon redemptions and consumer attitude surveys. After scanner data became readily available, actual consumer shopping behavior could be easily analyzed. For products sold in grocery outlets both the brand of product must be considered and the store itself, since not only is loyalty to a brand important, but also loyalty to a store. Additionally, the mix of items offered in a category may vary dramatically from store to store. Particularly important may be the presence of private label, or store brands, and generic products.

The term base-level business is the sales level that a brand has during non-promotional periods. It is normally the standard of comparison for the incremental sales generated by a promotion, or the level of business that would occur if no promotion or display activity were present.

Separating Promotional Effects

One of the more difficult tasks in understanding the marketing-communications mix is separating the impacts of various tactics such as changes in price, in-store displays, feature advertising, and television advertising. Not only do these fundamental tactics impact sales by themselves, they also work together synergistically, which adds to the difficulty of understanding them.

Another difficulty already discussed in this chapter is the particular personalities and characteristics of different product categories and different brands. What might be true for one brand may not be true at all for another. Geographic markets also respond differently and have different preferences for brands, flavors, and package sizes. Therefore, analysis must be done for each individual brand, as has been repeatedly stressed in this book.

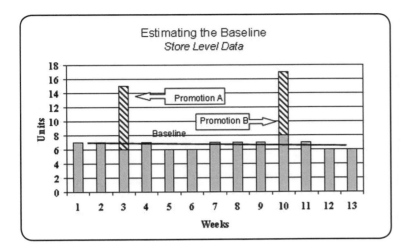

Baselining

The need to separate promotional impacts from normal sales when analyzing manufacturer shipments, and later, scanner data led to the development of time-series-based analysis methods modified to cope with the special problems associated with sales promotion. These methods are variations on the ratio-to-average methods of time series and attempt to separate weekly sales into two components: (1) *base sales*, which refer to the level of sales expected, including trend and seasonality but excluding the impact of sales promotion (including short-term carryover or loss) and (2) *incremental volume*, that extra amount of sales attributable to retail sales promotion activity.

Once the separation has been made into base and incremental volumes, analysis of many questions relating to volume sales is also simplified. Short-term promotional effects of price reduction, ad featuring, and in-store display can be analyzed using only promoted observations and studying the relation of total sales to base sales. Long-run effects such as the impact of changes in the base price, the introduction of new competitors, the impact of TV or print advertising and the general pattern of trend and seasonality can be studied using the base volume, without confounding by short-term promotional activities.

Assumptions and Problems

Baselining is an heuristic procedure and depends upon many assumptions. One of the first assumptions occurs in the flagging of observations as promoted or not. In the generally inflationary environment that has existed in the U.S. since the mid-1960s, most consumers have been conditioned to accept upward changes in price as permanent and to view downward changes in price as temporary. With this in mind, weeks with price increases are generally not flagged and removed from the baselining procedure. Weeks of reduced price are flagged as promotion weeks (temporary price reduction). Occasionally, examination of the time series of prices will reveal that a price reduction was permanent.

Seasonality

Proper calculation of seasonal indexes is difficult. Weekly seasonality indexes are generally not provided as measures, as proper generation might require a different seasonality index series for each major brand (size) included in the database. For analyses at an aggregate level, seasonality estimates are usually provided from external sources, particularly at the regional and total U.S. levels. For simple analyses at the aggregate level, moving averages of the total sales of a brand or group of related brands are usually used in constructing seasonality series. Where more precise measures of seasonality are required, an analysis of aggregated data may be used to provide a more precise series for weekly seasonal effects.

Many retail products exhibit short-term changes in sales level that are repetitive and predictable from year to year. Often these changes are related to the weather, but there are many other factors, such as social custom and traditions, which also lead to cyclic fluctuations in product sales over the months of the year. The typical analysis method was based on generating a seasonality index by month. In addition, some significant seasonality events occur irregularly from year to year, which cause problems for time series-based methods of estimating seasonality.

The quantification of retail price promotion responses and the syndicated reporting of baselines lead naturally to the analysis of financial returns attributed to the various elements of the marketing mix including any point-of-purchase programs.

Marketing Mix Models

Marketing mix evaluation models available from consulting companies and suppliers of syndicated data generally focus on evaluating short-term volume increases due to marketing activities. Estimates of intermediate and long-run effects may be added using external research, but are usually not estimated as part of standard marketing mix evaluation. Information on the costs of marketing activity may be added before or after the delivery of the volume analysis results.

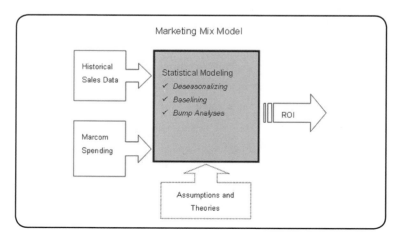

There are a variety of stand-alone models, which have been used for the evaluation of various types of marketing activity. Many of the marketing activities are aimed at changing average buyer behavior over time. While even small increases in average buyer purchasing can lead to significant product sales gains, such changes are difficult to measure in aggregated sales data confounded by competitive marketing. The design of choice for such longer run effects, such as those generated by TV and Internet advertising and by consumer promotional activity such as couponing, sampling, and informational mailing has long been designed and controlled experimentation on consumer panels. Data from these panels can be collected either by written diaries or through scanning of product purchasing by panelists. The typical experiment consists of random assignment of panelists to either a test group or a control group. Panelists may be assigned weights based on their geodemographic representativeness. Data is collected over a base period, and then one group of panelists is subjected to some alteration in the marketing mix element under study. Data collection continues, and statistical analysis methods are used to test for significant changes between the test group behavior and the control group behavior.

Among the mix activities which have been extensively studied using controlled panel experiments are:

- Advertising copy (copy A vs. copy B)
- Advertising spend levels (typically standard vs. heavy or standard vs. light)
- Long-run advertising effects
- Coupon values
- Coupon purchase requirements
- Length of time for which a coupon is valid

Controlled experiments involving trade promotion are more difficult to execute, as the experimental manipulations are available to all shoppers at the stores used in the test.

In these tests, the stores in the markets were split into two relatively geographically separated groups. Panel participation was limited to households which shopped almost exclusively in one group or the other. Each major retailer in the market had stores in each of the two groups. With this design it was possible to obtain accurate readings on pricing and promotional activities including:

- Base price over or under key price points such as round dollar numbers
- Base price differential to competition
- Promotional prices over or under key price points such as round dollar numbers
- Deep discount infrequent promotions vs. shallow discount frequent promotions
- Placement of in-store displays
- Specially constructed displays (such as display cartons coordinated with TV advertising)
- In-store self-liquidating coupons
- Bonus packs vs. price discounts

As the results of such studies accumulate, the companies providing the research panels have been able to conduct meta-analyses of the results and obtain estimates which are used in the construction of marketing mix models used on the analysis of POS sales data.

The marketing mix model system typically consists of:

1. *Seasonality.* Markets may have different seasonal patterns due to temperature, average weather conditions, and local consumption preferences. The seasonality estimation will also adjust for extreme deviations from the average marketing mix.

2. *Pricing.* Since the analysis is at the brand level, but prices are set at the brand size level, the model must aggregate prices of brand sizes in distribution into a stable brand price, which reflects the prices of various brand sizes in distribution and is relatively insensitive to short-run volume fluctuations in brand size sales.

3. *Trade Promotion.* Trade promotion activities are often executed on a subset of sizes rather than all sizes in distribution of the brand. The model must aggregate retail trade promotion on various sizes into a set of promotional variables which reflect total brand activity. Point-of-purchase material would typically be a part of this activity.

4. *Consumer promotions.* The model summarizes the impact of various consumer promotions into variables, which reflect the pattern of incremental volume expected for the week. If there are multiple sources for coupons, the model will handle the method of combining their expected incremental volume effects.

5. *TV advertising.* The model will handle the integration of TV activity delivered via national network, spot, cable, and satellite channels. It may account for multiple copy lengths and multiple copy variations.

6. *Print advertising.* If print advertising is an important element of the marketing mix then the model will integrate the expected impacts of print advertising from all major placements.

7. *Competitive marketing mix activity.* At a minimum, this model will account for competitive trade promotion, advertising, and consumer promotion.

8. *Geodemographic normalization.* This accounts for non-seasonal fluctuations in store traffic, which may be driven by retailer trade promotion outside of the product category and for store-to-store differences in customer counts. In its simplest form, the model may transform volume sales into volume sales per million ACV (all commodity volume).

Interaction and Synergy

Similarly, advertising and consumer promotion may have lead-lag relations with seasonality of category sales. The modeling system should also consider interactions and synergies among various elements of the marketing mix. For example, are point-of-purchase displays more effective when coupled with high levels of TV advertising and less effective at times of low TV advertising levels (after appropriate seasonality adjustments)? How much more or less incremental volume might be generated by the combination of in-store displays with feature advertising than that generated by separate display and feature events?

Analytical Problems

The assembly of the data and modeling system into a set of observations and variable values for those observations involves a number of key decisions. There are a number of trade-offs among model complexity, usability, interpretability, and robustness of the results.

Aggregation

There are three key aggregation decisions which influence the entire design and estimation of the modeling system. These are the levels of aggregation in the product dimension, the level of aggregation in the geographical dimension, and the level of aggregation in the time dimension. Numerous academic studies exist which demonstrate that significantly different estimations of marketing mix effects may be obtained depending upon the level of aggregation used. The authors generally feel that the best results are obtained when the observation is at a level of aggregation which does not mix significantly different levels of the mix elements to be estimated. However, if the accurate estimation of certain effects is more important than the accuracy of estimation of certain other effects, then aggregation levels may be chosen which favor the accurate estimation of highest importance effects. Brand size aggregation is a key decision. Consider a complex brand such as a major cola brand. Such brands are provided in a wide variety of sizes for ease of use on various usage occasions. Retail trade promotions are generally executed at the size level not at the brand level. In addition, within each size there may be a significant variety of product variations.

Where measurement of advertising and consumer promotion effects is the primary focus, some model systems will aggregate data to the market-week level. The primary justification here is that all shoppers within a market are exposed to the same schedule of national or local television and that consumer promotion is generally applied at the market level. By aggregating sales to the market level, any cross-retailer cannibalization due to trade promotion is averaged out, and the estimated model results for advertising and consumer promotion have minimum bias due to trade promotion differences across retailers.

Characterizing Variables

The final model may contain hundreds of different variables, with many different characteristics and functions. The dependent variable in the model usually is a (possibly transformed) measure of volume sales for a product specification at some level of geographic summarization for some summary time period.

6

Creativity in P-O-P

James Eby
Senior Vice President, Group Creative Director
Wunderman Chicago

CREATIVITY IN POINT-OF-PURCHASE MERCHANDISING

Point-of-Purchase (POP) merchandising has long been a vital tool in any effective consumer-marketing program. Used in collaboration with a strategic marketing plan, healthy brand awareness and a consistent advertising message, merchandising displays can be the ultimate consumer touch point to convert a product's sale or service.

Creative is the glue that binds a marketing program together. It's the creative that must convert consumers' perceptions, the product's relevance and the brand's essence to the point of purchase.

But the creativity doesn't stop there. So much can be lost in transition, from establishing a display program to executing that program. Creativity is needed throughout the entire process. Innovative thinking about a printing technique, a simpler construction method or even a more economical way to ship a unit, are all instances in which creativity is used to produce effective merchandising.

The creative process is only as good as the people supporting it. In all areas of marketing communication, there's none more dependent on knowledge and expertise than display production. Establishing a team in the various disciplines, such as marketing, creative and production, is imperative for its success. It's important to build an open line of communication that includes the team throughout the process. Implementing open dialogue will contribute to an environment that allows everyone to stay on course toward the ultimate creative vision.

This chapter will take you through the process of developing a traditional point of purchase display and highlight the steps in which creativity plays a critical role. These are some of the areas the chapter will focus on:

- Program objectives
- Creative brainstorm
- Beginning sketches
- Design and layout
- Developing comps
- Structure design
- Final production

Program objectives

To develop any effective point-of-purchase merchandising program, we must start with a focused strategy with clear objectives. This becomes the foundation from which the creative idea will establish itself. This strategy will initially be developed from client input based on a desired outcome. In many cases this process will be reviewed and discussed between marketing, creative, production, and then modified to maintain an even more focused assignment that all parties agree will deliver a targeted point-of-purchase approach.

How do program objectives affect the creative process? The most successful creative solutions will start with a simple set of objectives. So keep it simple. Finding the perfect balance of client information, product content, production specifications, and budget helps assure a successful merchandising program. Piles of data, consumer insights or the client's favorite color will only hinder the creative process.

Key content for briefing your creative team:

Background: Whether you're dealing with a new client or a new product, give a quick description about the project. Keep it brief and conversational.

Assignment: What do you need to do? Don't try to impress your creative department with your writing skills. Just give an overview of what needs to be done.

Assignment objectives: This is what the creative will be measured against. It's the challenge and should only list two or three key objectives. Any more and you'll risk trying to communicate too much.

Assignment strategy: This should be key marketing information that supports the objectives. Again, keep it simple. Don't overuse marketing data or industry slang. It's vital to manage and simplify the idea behind the strategy. Confirm your team understands before moving on during the briefing.

Consumer target: Who are you talking to? Provide samples of the customer. Use celebrities or fellow employees as examples for the personalities with whom you'll be communicating.

Product positioning: Advertising insight, brand positioning and point of difference in the market place. Consumers are everywhere. It's imperative to build synergies with one consistent advertising message across multiple consumer touch points. What do they already think about the product?

Competition: It never hurts to see what the other guy is doing. Provide some samples or a couple of quick bullet points. Discuss what works and what doesn't and any client insights on the client's view of the competition's work.

Specifications: These are the guidelines for production and usage. There can never be enough detail here. These are the only constraints that a creative will tolerate, and changing them is a creative killer, so double check specs to make sure they're correct.

Budget: Be clear on the dollars. Be realistic with your expectations, but be open to ideas outside the budget. Budget constraints can hurt the ideation stage. No one ever spent too much money thinking of the big idea, so don't be afraid to go big. Your client will appreciate your creativity and, better yet, might find the extra money to make that idea a reality.

Timing: Creatives need deadlines. Team members need a schedule of events on which they can all agree, starting with the kickoff meeting and moving through brainstorming, concept development and comp design, all the way to final print production. Keep in mind that the creative process takes time. When developing a schedule, be sure your creative group is comfortable with the allotted time to generate ideas before committing to any final production dates.

Starting your project with a clear and simplistic vision is a proven practice in delivering effective and exciting point-of-sale merchandising solutions.

Creative brainstorm

Brainstorm, collaborate, riff, bounce ideas, put our heads together; there are as many names as there are ways to begin the creative process. And no two creatives approach it in the same way. The brainstorm approach can change from project to project. Here are a few successful creative brainstorming techniques:

Group brainstorm

Once briefed on a project and in agreement on objectives, the creative team will assemble a meeting to start the ideation process. Members of this team can include art directors, designers, copywriters, producers, and print production specialists. Having diverse participation from different disciplines is an excellent way to brainstorm concepts with various perspectives in mind. A free-form discussion begins with random thoughts, large and small. Simple guidelines have been instituted over time with this process. Keep the objectives, timing and budget in mind, but remember there are no bad ideas. The key to creativity within a group brainstorm is the comfort to speak your mind. People in the group can start with "small" thoughts, then lead others to add to the bigger idea. Capturing the event on an easel or dry-erase board, allows ideas to stay topical. The group is allowed flexibility to move from concept to concept, build hybrid ideas or determine if a concept direction is missing the desired objectives. A brainstorm session can be as simple as one meeting or it can be a set gathering over a couple of days, as long as the idea generation is open, fresh and free flowing. A final review of the brainstorm notes is matched against the objectives to determine which ideas can be taken to the next level.

One-on-one brainstorming

This type of a session is used in many agency environments, usually pairing a copywriter and an art director together as a team that works on an ongoing basis on all projects. Throughout this process they develop a relationship with a foundation built on strong communication and design. This tactic has been successful because of the open communication and trust that comes from bouncing creative ideas off one another every day. Having a copywriter and art director together also allows the brainstorm to have a primary focus on the objectives.

- Copywriter: communication, brand awareness, message hierarchy, advertising synergy
- Art Director: graphic design, layout composition, structure design, photography

The success of this process usually leads to more defined initial concepts and sketches, making the process more streamlined. However, it is also very important to then touch base with your marketing team, and more importantly your production staff, to confirm that your concepts fit within specifications, budget, and production timelines.

Brief-and-brainstorm

As mentioned previously, there are many different processes that can be used to develop solid, creative thinking. Some individuals struggle in large group settings, others in one-on-one meetings. Or perhaps there are just not enough hours in the day to get together. This next option allows for individuals to work through their creative options on their own and at their convenience. Brief-and-brainstorm begins by gathering your team and delivering the key program objectives, and then allowing each person to ideate and develop individual concepts by themselves. Regrouping as a team provides the opportunity for each person to present his or her thoughts, similar to a group brainstorm, allowing others to comment and discuss in an open forum. In some instances this can be a better use of time than a group brainstorm, giving team members more time with the material at hand. It becomes a more creative process for critiquing the ideas, while allowing more time to absorb and understand the objectives.

These are just a few ways to ignite creativity. It is important to remember that the goal of the brainstorm is to build a solid foundation that meets the objectives defined by the group developing multiple concepts that are screened against the objectives and decided on by the team. These concepts can then be taken to the next phase in the process.

Beginning sketches

Getting concepts to a visual point is sometimes done during the brainstorm phase. As the team develops ideas in the brainstorm, art directors and designers will be quick to doodle out ideas to explain concepts. Beginning sketches are the first wave of taking a project into a 3-D vision. Sketches are used as a blueprint for understanding, sharing and communicating the creative vision. These can be simple drawings done by art directors and designers, or they can be elaborate and precise computer models set to size and scale. A couple of important functions of sketches are sharing information with the client regarding the basic construction and design that have come from the brainstorm and gaining approval that your display is on track with the objectives. Now the sketch becomes a tool that others on the team can use as a roadmap for their responsibilities along the timeline.

Design and layout

Once the sketches have been approved by the client and the budget and timing have been confirmed by production, it is time for the creative team to tighten up the concept. In this stage, the art director, designers, and copywriters will develop design and layout and define copy direction. Created by computer, these comps will be full-color, 2-D rendering examples of what the final point-of-purchase display could look like. Many options and versions will be created to decide what design best communicates the objectives.

　　Factors to consider during design:

- *Communication*: Use a call to action to quickly communicate your consumer benefit. Don't over communicate. Create simple, clean copy that meets the objectives. Use existing advertising synergies to build consumer awareness.
- *Graphics*: Use photography or visuals as eye-catching devices to attract attention to your display. Consumers will notice graphics before reading copy.
- *Colorpalette*: Use colors that complement your brand or service.
- *Typography*: Use bold fonts for headline treatments and simple, clean fonts for bullet points and body copy. Avoid creative fonts for long lines of communication.
- *Printingtechniques*: Use specialty techniques to enhance your display. Metallic inks, highlighted varnishes, embossing and die cutting are just a few examples of such techniques.

It's important to note the basics. It's even more important to stay current in design trends and creativity. Popular creative looks and feels are constantly changing over time. Colors that were popular in the '80s are now considered loud and obnoxious. Fonts have become designer playgrounds with websites dedicated to creating and sharing such fonts. Stock photography has become an outlet for award-winning photographers. Creativity should take on the best of these attributes and translate them into a message that stands out.

　　After several rounds of design and layout modifications, the concept is ready for client review. This review is crucial as the design begins to take final form on paper. All communication and objectives are continuously tracked as the next step takes the display into a more true-to-life form.

Developing comps

Now that the design of the display has been established, it is time to develop a comp. Install another contact point between production, art directors and designers to review the concept. As a layout can have a 2-D appearance, a production comp serves as an actual 3-D mock-up version of your printed display or structure. Creatively this becomes a hands-on rendition of the concept to see how the design, layout, and construction translate to the 3-D form. This is an opportunity for the design team to modify any issues that are now obvious that maybe weren't noticeable during the previous stage, possibly because up until this point the work was most likely viewed on a computer screen or a sheet of paper.

Draw on the list of factors to consider during the design phase when going over the comp. See that communication points are clear and copy points are not out of proportion. Make sure the graphics used have translated to the larger resolution size and don't require retouching. Check that all type is clear and legible. If color proofs are provided, match all colors to professional swatch books and proof all content.

Creatively, the comp stage becomes a checkpoint at which we confirm that the concept is developing on track. More often than not, issues arise that test the integrity of the concept. It is important to stay involved and engaged. Unfortunately, most art directors relinquish control around this point, when many creative decisions need to be made to uphold the concept and keep within the objectives.

Structure design

Usually as part of the comp stage, structure design can get overlooked as a creative consideration. Structure design usually lies within the production process or a production manufacturer. Unless a production staff carries a designer on staff, art direction and creative design may get overlooked. However, when production issues, budget constraints, or design flaws arise, decisions regarding design and modifications need to be made. Often these are times when the art director must do a lot of thinking on his or her feet. Creativity in this case can be considered a problem-solving technique. Staying involved through the comp stage and understanding the thought process that goes into how the structure is made, built, moved, or rebuilt will make it easier to understand issues if and when they arise. More importantly, this process can influence creativity in future designs and prove to be a valuable learning experience.

Final production

The client has approved the final comps and structures. Production has taken control of all the final art and production elements to produce the concept. All the parties involved have contributed. The last focus is on monitoring the final production. With many checks and balances in place along the way, here are a few areas where creative can keep control and add value:

- *Color*: Review press sheets for color.
- *Image*: Review graphic elements for correct trap information and reproduction value.
- *Trim*: Review all live and bleed areas for correct die-cut position.
- *Content*: Review all type and graphics for accuracy.

Creativity is more than what your display communicates. It is how the objectives are satisfied. It's the way creative translates those objectives to converse with consumers through pictures and words. It is the development of the structures and designs that are innovative and eye-catching.

The future of creativity in point-of-purchase

The use of point of purchase has a permanent place in contemporary marketing. Nothing is more evident than the use of digital signage. The practice of using screens to communicate multiple messages, target many consumers and change by day parts has proved to be a valuable option when more traditional media could only support a single communication. In addition, when marketers factor in the reality that the costs of monitors are decreasing and their life span is increasing, they tend to consider digital point of purchase over traditional paper-based display systems.

Creativity is following this trend. Expanding the principles of traditional point-of-purchase strategies, art directors and designers are learning animation programs, photography techniques and cinematography to produce these live-action segments. Applying the same rules from traditional design, here are some factors to consider when creating digital point of purchase:

- *Viewing area*: Keep viewing distances, angle of monitors and lighting in mind. Reflections, light burst and distortion will cause poor visibility.
- *Viewing time*: Use the same rules of consumer patterns for viewing time. Over communication and lengthy messages will lose consumer interest.
- *Communication*: Moving pictures and type are great for catching the consumer's attention. Don't overuse fancy techniques on type or messages that jump from screen to screen.
- *Graphics*: Live-action video and motion are imperative for this media. Use a conservative balance of moving visuals with type to convey messages.
- *Color palette*: Colors on monitors appear brighter and more vibrant. Modify brighter color values to tone down their perceived hotness.
- *Typography*: When considering type, white on a dark background is easiest for viewing. Motion type treatments can be an effective tool when used with a bolder, more legible font.

The demand for digital merchandising is high. The boom is happening. It's changing the landscape of point-of-purchase communication throughout the industry. The challenge for creative will be to capture the attention of consumers in a world of over communication.

Conclusion

Imagination is an important part of creating exciting merchandising. But creativity is more than what's printed on point of purchase. It's used throughout the entire process of producing point of purchase. The power to communicate with consumers, to affect their conscience, and, ultimately, to cause them to interact with a product is shaped by many disciplines throughout the project. Developing a system that values the creative process will produce far more superior creative and effective results, which in turn will lead to the achievement of a successful point-of-purchase solution.

7

Display Production Methods and Materials

Edward C. White, MaRC
President
Display Smart, LLC

INTRODUCTION

If you ever have the opportunity to visit a manufacturer of P-O-P advertising displays, you will be impressed at the engineering and manufacturing complexities required to construct these displays that play one of the most powerful roles in the movement of goods around the globe.

The challenge of understanding the manufacturing process of either simple or complicated displays is underscored by the vast array of different designs, production methods, and materials utilized by the P-O-P industry to build eye-catching and effective point-of-purchase advertising displays. This chapter discusses these complexities and presents the challenges faced by both manufacturers and producers of point-of-purchase advertising displays.

This chapter covers two major elements affecting P-O-P advertising design:

- Different processes and materials used in manufacturing displays
- How designers and manufacturers chose the specific process or material to produce each display

While the point-of-purchase advertising industry in not generally regarded as a high-technology industry, it is a "volume-tech" industry. It utilizes an array of different materials and industrial design methods to create P-O-P advertising displays in large quantities that are distributed around the world. P-O-P design and manufacturing teams must know how to apply various technologies and design methods in the manufacturing process to successfully and efficiently produce these displays in large quantities.

For example, it is not necessary to understand the chemical makeup of certain plastics to use them. The plastic manufacturers provide clear guidelines on the best adhesives, or the best temperature to mold plastic, or the type of saw blades to use in processing their materials. The challenge facing point-of-purchase advertising display companies today is to utilize these materials in creative and innovative ways so they can provide P-O-P clients/customers the competitive edge they need in the marketplace.

ANALYZING THE DISPLAY PROJECT

There are many ways to manufacture a P-O-P advertising display and achieve similar results. The process chosen by the manufacturer may be based on several factors:

- Quantity
- Budget per display
- Tooling cost
- Aesthetic appearance desired
- Manufacturing capabilities of the producer
- Designer's knowledge of different processes

The quantity required and project's budget will quickly start directing the producer toward the manufacturing processes that are feasible given the resources available. This would also include the tooling cost, which is amortized over the quantity of displays ordered to arrive at the total cost of the display.

Another defining factor is the aesthetic appearance specified by the client. If the desired look is soft and feminine, the processes and materials that will help achieve that look are selected to appeal to these emotions. Display producers know that some plastics, such as polypropylene, have an industrial look when processed, while others, such as frosted acrylic, can be fabricated to convey an elegant appearance.

Another reason to choose a specific processing method could be that the manufacturer has the capability to produce the display component in-house instead of outsourcing to another manufacturer. Of course, a designer may select a manufacturer and process simply because of familiarity or comfort in going in another direction.

DECIDING WHICH PROCESS OR MATERIAL TO USE

Someone once said, "Necessity is the mother of invention." Today, that statement could be restated as, "Cost cutting is the mother of invention." It is true with any of the P-O-P production processes and materials covered in this chapter. The challenge facing point-of-purchase designers today is that customers are demanding displays be produced more quickly and at a lower cost. When cars were first invented, they were cumbersome, slow, and broke down often. Now they are fast, comfortable, and may be driven 100,000 miles or more without major repair. Machines used in processing displays have progressed in the same manner; many have computerized adjustments and operations that allow quick setups and much higher accuracy.

Answering the following questions will help narrow down the type of materials and the processes used in the manufacturing of displays:

1. What is the aesthetic look desired?

The desired appearance will depend greatly upon the product, retail setting, and promotional theme. The overall aesthetic look one is trying to achieve will help to determine the materials and manufacturing processes considered in designing and producing the display.

2. In what setting will the display be used?

A department store, specialty gift store, sporting goods shop, and pet store all require different design parameters. Some retailers draw upon their experience and specify which materials they want a manufacturer to use in building their displays. In some cases, they could be concerned about durability, while in others a consistent look across stores is the objective. In situations in which multiple manufacturers are producing modular portions of the display system, coordination among suppliers and maintaining close tolerances across the "display components list" are essential.

3. What is the desired life span of the display?

To what elements will the display be exposed? Direct sunlight, moisture, heat, and cold are environmental factors that could have an impact on the effectiveness of the display. A display that looks battered or faded, suggesting that the product itself may be old or not fresh, can actually discourage a consumer from purchasing the product. How much physical contact will the display need to endure? How long will the retailer allow the display to remain in the store without requiring a "new" or fresh look?

4. What is the client willing to spend?

A display is a sales tool and must justify its existence by a return on the original investment. Will the display be used for a weekend promotion or for several years? The amount of product expected to be sold from the display will need to be calculated with these questions in mind. The percentage of advertising cost allotted to the product sold will determine how much money can be invested into the display. This budget then helps determine what manufacturing process and/or materials can be used. Determining a justifiable cost up front helps the designer and producer create a display that will meet the customer's needs within a desired budget.

5. What quantity of duplicate parts is going to be produced?

The total quantity of displays produced may not determine the manufacturing process as much as the number of duplicate parts. For example, only 500 of a certain display are going to be produced. If one of the components, such as a shelf or bracket, is used 20 times on a display, 10,000 such parts are required. A quantity of this volume may allow a more automated and cost-effective piece of equipment to be used.

QUANTITY AND BUDGET

The quantity of displays required by the client will have a large effect on what type of manufacturing process is used. Many small-quantity orders are frequently hand-fabricated and assembled. The tooling cost for small orders may not be very expensive but, when amortized over the small quantity of displays produced, tooling costs can add up to a sizable percentage of the total cost of the display. On large-quantity orders, manufacturers will utilize high-speed equipment, when possible, to save time and money. High-speed equipment can require a substantial investment in tooling. Yet when compared with a slower manufacturing process, the tooling will pay for itself with a substantially lower cost per part.

HOW VOLUME EFFECTS UNIT COST AND TOOLING COST

The examples in Figure 7-1 illustrate the effects that quantity and tooling can have on the cost of a display.

The brand marketer who needs only 100 displays and a relatively small quantity would have to spend a total of $25,000 to achieve their P-O-P advertising display requirements. Increasing the quantity ordered to achieve a lower per unit cost per P-O-P piece may just not be an option for the smaller company. National brand marketers can increase their selling margins by selling through multiple channels, thus lowering their P-O-P production cost per store.

	WIRE DISPLAY	PLASTIC DISPLAY
Quantity:	100	10,000
Tooling Jig Cost:	$150 – $300	$100,000 – $200,000
Manufacturing Method:	Spot-welded	Injection-molded
Tooling Costs Amortized over Quantity:	$1.00 – $2.00 (per display)	$1.00 – $2.00 (per display)
Cost of Unit:	$250 each	$25 each

Figure 7-1

Effect of Quantity and Tooling on Display Cost

MANUFACTURING PROCESS OVERVIEW

There are many manufacturing methods available to produce a point-of-purchase display. Most display companies build their business around one or two basic material groups and limit the scope of their manufacturing processes to developing expertise in these materials. There are only a small number of display companies that can manufacture in-house utilizing a wide variety of materials. The production processes listed in the following sections have been around for several years. Technology has helped in increasing productivity, lowering cost, and improving the quality of displays produced. Modern technology has also enabled the display producer to mass-produce complex forms that simply were not feasible previously. As production technology continues to evolve, it will offer the P-O-P industry more ways to mold, cut, glue, decorate, and assemble an advertising display.

PLASTIC PROCESSING METHODS

It would be impossible to give a detailed description of each of these processes in the space allotted to this chapter. However, after reviewing the brief descriptions of the process and guidelines on when certain processes are used, you will have a basic understanding of why a manufacturing process is used.

Following are descriptions of some of the basic methods used to mold or shape plastic:

Fabricating

Cutting, heat bending, gluing, and assembling sheet plastic into a display by hand. The plastic is formed by using a hot wire or a quartz lamp with a thin hot light directed at the area to be bent as the plastic begins to soften, the sheet of plastic is clamped in a jig and bent by hand to the proper angle. The parts can then be glued together or assembled to develop the display. Graphics can then be added by screen printing, hot foil stamping, or mounting with offset lithography labels. Hand fabricating of plastic displays is commonly limited to small quantities because it is time consuming.

Vacuum Forming

Heating either a sheet or roll of plastic until it is pliable and then formed by pulling a vacuum through the mold so that the plastic conforms to the shape of the mold. Vacuum forming stretches the sheet of plastic; depending on how much it is stretched, it will vary in thickness in different areas of the part. The mold can be made out of wood or epoxy for short runs but usually is made in cast aluminum for longer runs. Tubes are cast in the mold to allow water to be run through them to keep the mold at a constant temperature during the manufacturing process. Without the water cooling the tubes, the mold would absorb heat from each sheet of plastic formed on it, and eventually the hot mold would keep the plastic from cooling and solidifying to the desired shape. See Figure 7-2 thru 7-4.

Figure 7-2

Four-station rotary
vacuum former

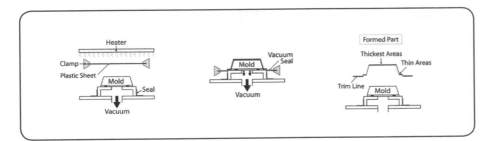

Figure 7-3

Vacuum Forming
Process Illustrations

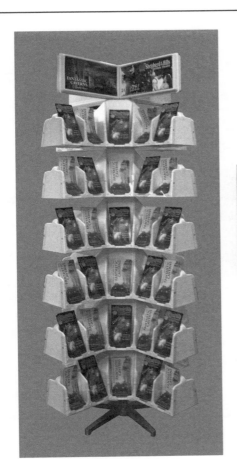

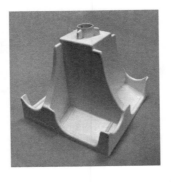

Figure 7-4

Display with vacuum
formed trays and base

Pressure Forming

Similar to vacuum forming, but with a pressure box added, to improve the level of detail and texture attainable through ambient air pressure alone. Along with pulling a vacuum through the mold, additional air pressure is applied to help push the plastic into tight corners or around text or logos for a better impression. Pressure forming can also help in maintaining the overall consistency of the thickness of the part.

Figure 7-5

Spectra 500-ton
injection molder.
Injection molding
process illustrations
are shown below.

Injection Molding

Heating pellets of plastic until they can be injected into a two-part mold under tons of pressure. The plastic is allowed to cool, and the mold is separated to remove the part. If the same amount of plastic is injected into the mold each time, the results will be identical parts that can be molded in close tolerance. Molds are usually milled out of thick, heavy tool steel. Because of the molds' cost, this process is usually used for large-volume runs. See Figure 7-5.

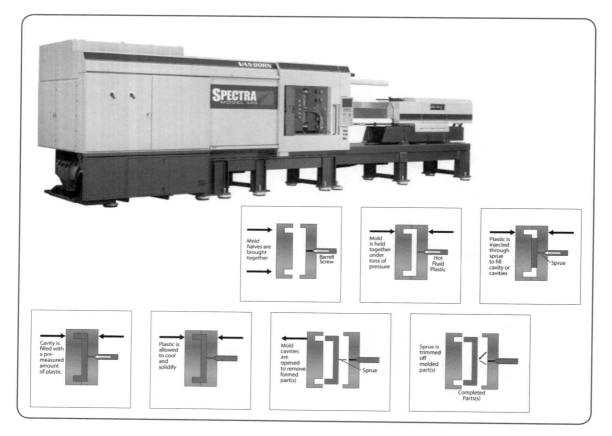

Rotational Molding

Pellets of plastic are placed in a two-part clam-style mold cavity. Usually, the machine has three or four arms with one or several molds on each arm. The arms are rotated first into a furnace where the mold is rotated slowly. The plastic pellets melt and coat the inside of the mold. The arms are then rotated. While one arm will be filled with pellets, one arm will be in the furnace and the third arm will be sprayed with water to cool and solidify the part. The arms are rotated again where the part is removed, and more pellets are placed in the mold. The most common materials used in this process are polypropylene and polyethylene. These are tough plastics that are resilient and can withstand water, chemicals, and exterior conditions. See Figure 7-6 thru 7-7.

Figure 7-6

Three station rotational molding machine and process (at left)

Profile Extrusions

Plastic pellets are heated until they are melted and can be extruded or pushed through a die in the profile shape desired. The continuous profile is then run through a water bath, sprayed with a water mist, or allowed to cool with ambient air. During the cooling process, the extruded part may be helped to hold its shape with cooling blocks. The extruded profile is then cut to the desired length. The part can be extruded to any length, but the width and height of the part is limited by the size of the extruder's barrel and how much plastic it can push out. Profile extrusions can be produced in clear or opaque plastics and in an unlimited number of shapes. Extrusions have been used as decorative trim, protective trim, support columns, shelving, shelf lips, shelf dividers, and plastic slatwall, to name a few. Figure 7-8.

Figure 7-7

Rotational molded polypropylene display

Figure 7-8

Clockwise from top left: Profile extrusion machine, process die, various extrusion examples, and plastic slatwall end view.

Flexible Mold Casting

A two-part plastic resin is mixed, which starts a catalytic reaction where the plastic begins to solidify and harden. Before the resin hardens, it is poured into a flexible mold. After the resin hardens, the mold is pulled back and the part is removed. This is a slow process used mainly for small-quantity or very complex parts. The molds are relatively inexpensive.

Which Plastic Process Is Best to Use?

Because of the flexibility of manufacturing with plastics, the options seem almost endless and sometimes confusing. Figure 7-9 offers an overall comparison of the different process costs. Note that the figures are guidelines and can vary according to the size of the part, the complexity of the part, and the material used. It is very similar to asking, "How much does a car cost?" Well, are you asking about a Volkswagen or a Mercedes? However, it is possible to give some ranges so that one has a benchmark to compare processes for choosing one over another.

Figure 7-9

Plastic Processing
Methods and Cost

PROCESS	QUANTITIES	TOOLING COST	PART PRICE	CYCLE TIME
Injection Molding	10,000 – 1,000,000	$20,000 – $350,000	$.50 – $5.00	5 – 60 seconds
Vacuum Forming In-Line or Roll	25,000 – 1,000,000	$10,000 – $35,000	$.50 – $5.00	5 – 60 seconds
Profile Extrusions	2,500 – 100,000	$5,000 – $20,000	$.50 – $5.00	10 – 30 feet/minute
Vacuum/Pressure Forming	1,000 – 10,000	$10,000 – $20,000	$.50 – $5.00	1 – 2 minutes
Vacuum Forming Sheet	500 – 10,000	$5,000 – $10,000	$3.00 – $35.00	1 – 2 minutes
Rotational Molding	500 – 5,000	$5,000 – $10,000	$30.00 – $300.00	10 – 15 minutes
Plastic Fabrication	100 – 1,000	$200 – $500 jig	$30.00 – $300.00	10 – 60 minutes
Flexible Mold Casting	100 – 1,000	$200 – $500	$5.00 – $50.00	30 – 60 minutes

Note: The above figures are very rough guidelines and can vary according to the size, thickness of plastic, complexity and type of material.

PLASTIC MATERIALS

Plastics have been developed with different characteristics to fit different needs. Acrylic looks like glass, and styrene looks like granite rock. Metallic fleck can be added, or the surface can be printed to look like wood. Described below are some of the basic plastics, which can be modified to take on several different appearances. These are general categories, without going into the chemical compounds.

Styrenes

Styrene plastics used for display components are usually opaque. Color pigments can be added to obtain almost any color, including fluorescent. There are also translucent and clear styrene plastics, which tend to be brittle. For example, some textured fluorescent light fixture covers are injection-molded out of translucent styrene. Plastic compounds can be added to styrene to increase its resilience.

- **ABS (acrylonitrile butadiene styrene)** Styrene with a "rubber"-type compound added, ABS has "very good" resistance to breakage.

- **HIPS (high-impact polystyrene)** Less expensive than ABS but less resilient, HIPS has "good" resistance to breakage.

- **Styrene** Economical, more brittle, good for low-impact uses.

Acrylics

Acrylic can be purchased in pellets or in sheet form and is often used as a substitute for glass. Acrylic is much lighter and, if broken, is much less a safety hazard in comparison to glass. Traditionally, acrylic sheets have been clear, white, or black. Now they can be obtained in a multitude of opaque and translucent colors. In the past few years, translucent color pigments have been added to achieve a neon fluorescent appearance, and a green tint has been added to acrylic to emulate the look of plate glass. Suppliers continue to develop new acrylic resin mixtures, one of the newest being a speckled acrylic with a granite appearance.

Vinyls

- **Vinyl** Vinyl is produced with different characteristics from rigid vinyl to very flexible vinyl. It is available in decorated extruded sheets and used in vacuum forming and injection molding.

- **PVC (Polyvinyl Chloride)** A resilient plastic, normally opaque, and available in a multitude of colors and textures

- **Expanded PVC – Polyvinyl Chloride** PVC with a gas injected, which adds bubbles for a less dense material. Lightweight, durable, used often in signage. Available in sheets from .010 to .5 inch thick. Produced under brand names Sintra®, Komatex®, Versacel™ and Celtec®

Break-Resistant Plastics

- **Polycarbonate** Well-known under brand names like Lexan® or Tuffak®, poly-carbonate can be opaque but has been used in a clear form to replace acrylic. It is extremely tough and resists breakage.

- **Polyethylene** A very resilient plastic used for high interaction applications, polyethylene has a low-luster surface and is difficult to glue or decorate. It has a waxy feel. Most quart oil bottles and gallon milk containers are molded from polyethylene.

- **Polypropylene** A very durable plastic that is resistant to moisture and chemicals, polypropylene has a high-luster surface and can be glued, painted, hot-foil stamped, or decorated in other ways.

- **PETG (polyethylene terephthalate glycol)** A very resilient plastic that can be clear or opaque, PETG can be sawed, drilled, screwed into, and even stapled through. It is more flexible than acrylic and may need to be formed to achieve the rigidity desired. One liter beverage bottles are produced out of PETG, which is a very similar material.

WOOD PROCESSING METHODS

Technology has also improved production efficiency in processing wood. Computer-programmable saws, routers, drills, and specialty equipment are commonly used. This automatic equipment cuts, drills, routes, rotates, and trims with great speed and accuracy. The following are some of the processes used in producing a wooden display.

Cutting/Shaping

Wood can be cut or shaped with traditional table saws, band saws, panel saws, and routers. Figure 10 show computerized saws and routers that allow for multiple sheets to be cut at one time at remarkable speeds. CNC (computer numerically controlled) equipment can often be programmed to do multiple processes. Some equipment is essentially a robot with cutting tools that can rotate on five axes. Other equipment has multiple heads that change bits or cutters automatically and can cut, shape, or drill at any angle. Instead of cutting out parts and then moving them to another workstation where holes are drilled in them, then moving the parts to another workstation where the edges are shaped, the computerized equipment will do all of this and deliver a completed display part.

In the past, to process 100 displays all the pieces would be cut and manufactured and then assembled. Now, with computer-programmed equipment, all the necessary parts for one or more displays can be quickly and efficiently cut, routed, drilled, and then assembled. Depending on the size of the order and the complexity of the display, this can be an efficient way to produce an order.

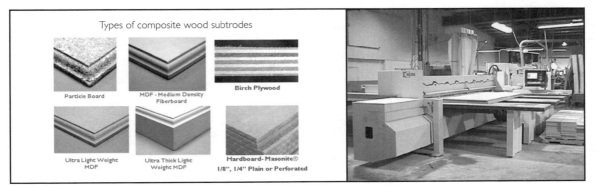

Types of composite wood subtrodes

Particle Board

MDF - Medium Density Fiberboard

Birch Plywood

Ultra Light Weight MDF

Ultra Thick Light Weight MDF

Hardboard- Masonite®
1/8", 1/4" Plain or Perforated

Figure 7-10

Computerized Panel Saw—a built in computer helps calculate the best utilization of the material.

Fabricating

Natural wood or wood composites are favored materials to work with because of the ease of fabrication. Standard wood-working equipment can be used to drill, nail, screw, and staple or glue components together. Wood can also be combined easily with other materials, such as steel and plastic, with the same fasteners.

Finishing

Wood can be stained, painted, curtain-coated, sandblasted, textured, or covered with low- or high-pressure laminate. The edges can be laminated with edge banding or covered with plastic or rubber "T" molding, or aluminum moldings, or cut with a rounded or decorative shape. "T" molding can be seen on the edges of many lunchroom or restaurant tables.

WOOD MATERIALS

Wood has been used in manufacturing displays since the late 1800s. Some of the first displays produced were the carved wooden Indians that held plugs of tobacco and cigars. Wood is a versatile material that can be obtained in a variety of formats including natural solid woods, laminated plywood, or wood chips compressed into particleboard, fiberboard, or hardboard. Today, many displays and store fixtures have their basic structure built from wood or wood composites that are either painted or covered with a high- or low-pressure laminate. The following are some of the wood and wood composites used in displays today.

- **Particleboard** Small chips of wood bonded together with a resin. The most common size is a sheet 49 × 97 inches, from ¼ up to 1-½ inches thick. Some

Figure 7-11

Display produced from MDF

mills will run sheets up to 60 × 144 inches. The surface is smooth but has very porous edges that do not paint well. Particleboard is economical and most commonly used for support structures on the interior of a point-of-purchase display. It can be obtained in low-, medium-, and high-density grades. Low-density particleboard is more likely to be used in shipping crates than in a display.

- **MDF (medium density fiberboard)** Fine particles of wood bonded together with a resin. The surface is smoother than particleboard and can be sawed, drilled, glued, and painted like regular hard or soft woods. MDF is more expensive than particleboard but substantially less expensive than natural woods. Although MDF has a higher density than particleboard, its porosity still makes the edges difficult to paint. Double-refined MDF was developed to provide an edge that accepts paint better than regular MDF. MDF is available in 49 × 97 inches up to 60 × 120 inches, in thicknesses of $^1/_4$ up to 2 inches. A very dense and heavy MDF board is made especially for producing slatwall. A lightweight MDF that cuts the weight of regular MDF almost in half is used when weight is a design issue. See Figure 7-11.

- **Hardboards** Similar to MDF but less dense and produced in thicknesses of $^1/_8$ to $^3/_8$ inch, and available in 48 × 96-inch sheets. Hardboards can be "tempered" or impregnated with a resin that hardens the board and produces a smooth surface that is less absorbent and can be painted. They can be obtained with one or both of the surfaces smooth. Hardboards are often run through a perforator where $^1/_8$ or $^1/_4$ inch holes are punched on 1-inch centers. The perforated board is then used in displays to hold peg hooks. Hardboards can be purchased with pre-laminated surfaces in different patterns from woodgrains, metalics, and textures.

- **Plywood** Multiple layers of thin wood laminated together at 90-degree angles to form a very strong board that is resistant to warping. Plywood can be purchased with a fir outer layer or with a veneer of birch, oak, cherry, special woods or pre-laminated with Melamine or High Pressure Laminate. (i.e., Formica, Pionite, Nevarmar, etc.)

- **Natural woods** Nothing beats the beauty of natural woods. Popular woods used in displays include oak, maple, poplar, pine, and birch.

SUSTAINABLE & ENVIRONMENTALLY FRIENDLY MATERIALS

With the desire to be environmentally conscious manufacturers are looking for recycled, sustainable, or environmentally friendly materials. Some of these materials are wheatboard, sunflower board, and bamboo board. There have been efforts to produce particleboard with a low level of formaldehyde, which is used in curing. Unfortunately, at this point, these materials are usually more expensive and less readily available than traditional materials.

METAL PROCESSING METHODS

Cutting

Just as in the case of plastic and wood materials, computerized equipment is helping to advance efficiency and quality in the metal-forming industry. Large computerized "nibblers" can punch holes or stamp out shapes or cut a complex pattern out of sheet metal. Lasers are also used to cut repetitive shapes, graphics, or logos in a display panel. Figure 7-12. A design that previously could have been cost-prohibitive is now affordable with the use of a computer-controlled cutter or laser. In most cases computerized equipment requires programming. As a result, the equipment is used primarily for large-quantity repetitive projects. In the future, as computerized equipment gets easier to program, it will be used for short-run orders also.

Figure 7-12

Laser Cutting Head

Forming and Fabricating

Besides the traditional punch presses, press brakes, and wire benders, computerized equipment has been developed to produce parts with little or no special tooling. Parts for a wire display with multiple bends can now be programmed and produced without expensive tooling or jigs. Metal parts can be fastened together by rivets, nuts and bolts, screws, or special fasteners. Certain metals can be bonded together by heating the parts until they melt together. This is called *spot (or resistance) welding*. Other welding methods use special gasses and/or filler materials to adhere parts together and include:

- Brazing—used on brass, copper, or bronze
- TIG (tungsten inert gas) or gas tungsten arc welding—used on aluminum and stainless steel and in close-tolerance carbon steel work
- MIG (metal inert gas) or gas metal arc welding—used on aluminum or steel, wire-fed for fast production welding
- Stick arc welding electrodes—uses a handheld welding rod for small-volume jobs

Computerized welding robots have been designed to do repetitive step welding for producing wire baskets and wire grids.

Finishing

There are several ways to finish metal displays, including plating with zinc, nickel, brass, or chrome. Parts can also be chemically etched, embossed, or textured to develop a brushed aluminum look or repeat pattern. There are several ways to paint metal parts. Parts can be dipped in paint, wet sprayed, or electrostatic powder coated.

Figure 7-13

Powder Coating

Electrostatic powder coating is the process of charging the metal part with one electrical charge and the powder with the opposite charge. See Figure 7-13. The powder paint is sprayed onto the metal component. The metal part attracts the paint like a magnet. The coated part is then passed through a heat tunnel where the powder paint melts and bonds to the part. In this process less of the painting material is lost or wasted than in a wet paint process. Depending on the part, this can be a more efficient and environmentally friendly method than spraying with a conventional wet spray system. Textures, "duo tones," and metallic finishes have been developed for powder coating to add a new look and dimension to metal displays. Wood parts can now also be electrostatic power coated.

METAL MATERIALS

Figure 7-14

Display produced with side panels and components

Metal used for display components comes in all shapes and sizes. Basic metal components include

- Sheet metal—plain, coated, textured, or perforated
- Flat stock—bars of steel
- Wire—purchased precut to length or in coils, a few thousands in diameter up to ¼-inch diameter
- Rod—¼ inch in diameter and larger
- Tubing—round, square, D-Shaped, or special formed

Most of the above metal components can also be purchased with baked-on enamel, pre-primed to accept paint, or plated with several coatings. See Figure 7-14.

PAPER PROCESSING METHODS

Temporary displays are produced with a wide range of manufacturing processes. The first stage is usually to print or mount a preprinted label to the paper substrate. Next, the printed parts are die-cut, folded, and glued or stitched. Some displays are partially or fully assembled and packed into a shipping carton. Other displays are shipped out unassembled, to be assembled either in the store or at a fulfillment center.

The following paragraphs describe different processes used to produce a fiberboard or corrugated paperboard display.

Printing Methods

Printing presses are divided into two major categories—sheet fed or web. Sheet-fed presses print on precut sheets loaded into the press. Web presses print on a roll of paper and then either cut it into sheets at the back end of the press or rewind the paper into a roll again. This roll can then be processed and made into corrugated board.

- **Offset Lithography** Offset lithography is the method used to print books and magazines. The same presses print graphic sheets that are glued to paperboard or plastic for display signage. The printed sheet is often referred to as a "Litho Sheet," or as a "Litho Label", if it is to be laminated to a substrate. Graphics for displays are generally printed on 60# to 80# paper or on an SBS (solid bleached sulfite) board from .010 inch thick to, for some presses able to handle it, up to .030 inch thick. Offset lithography is based on the fact that water and oil do not mix. Water is applied to the printing plate with a roller. An oil-based ink is applied to the plate with another roller. The image on the plate repels the water but attacks the ink. The ink on the image is transferred to the paper. To print a full-color image, four translucent colors are used; cyan, magenta, yellow, and black. The translucent colors are printed in overlapping dot patterns. The result is thousands of shades of colors. The dots are so small (330 dots per inch) that they are very difficult to see without a magnifying glass, blending together and perceived by the eye as a full-color image. This method is referred to as "four-color process" printing. Most sheets printed for displays are "overprinted" or coated with a varnish or clear coat to protect the ink. Without this protection the ink can be scuffed or marred when transported or handled. Ultraviolet (UV) light inhibitors are often added to the clear coat for added protection against fading due to sunlight. See Figure 7-15.

Figure 7-15

Display using offset printed lithography sheets laminated onto corrugated paperboard

Figure 7-16

Direct Print with water based Flexographic ink onto corrugated paperboard

• **Flexographic** Flexographic printing uses a water-based ink with pigment suspended in it. There are both sheet-fed and web flexographic presses. The ink is pumped from a reservoir up to an ink fountain. The ink is transferred by rolls to either a raised image or an etched roller and then to the paper substrate. See Figure 7-16.

• **Rubber Letterpress** Letterpress ink is a paste about the consistency of whipped butter. The ink can be an oil, glycol or soy base material. The ink is transferred from an ink fountain by rubber rolls to raised image printing plates and then transferred onto the paper stock. Printing plates were initially cut or molded from rubber. Today, many plates are produced from a light sensitive photo-polymer compound. Light hardens the area exposed and areas not exposed to light are washed away leaving a raised image.

• **Ultraviolet** UV inks are cured or dried when exposed to an intense UV light. The ink can be applied on a letterpress or screen printer. See Figure 7-17.

Figure 7-17

UV Silkscreen Printer with micro adjustment

• **Screen Printing** Screen printing was originally called "silk screening" because it was done with silk. Today, nylon or another synthetic fabric is attached tightly to a rectangular wood or aluminum frame. The fabric's pores are coated with a light-sensitive gel. After the gel dries a negative or positive film image is laid on

the screen and exposed to an intense light. The gel hardens except in the area of
the image. Water is used to wash out the gel in the image area, leaving the porous
fabric. A rubber squeegee is used to pull thick ink across the screen. The ink is
forced through the porous graphic areas and onto the substrate.

- **Digital Printing**   Digital Printing is a rapidly evolving printing process. Wide
  Format Printers that operate very similar to the ink jet printer are printing large
  sheets faster and more economically than imagined. The image is transferred
  directly from a computer file to the substrate without film or printing plates.
  These new printers may have 16 print heads and print over 63″ wide and virtually
  endless length. Wide format digital printers were initially used for producing banners and posters. With new printing and ink technology material substrates now
  include cloth, vinyl, sheet plastic, glass, tile, wood and corrugated paperboard.
  Flat bed presses can handle materials up to 1 ⅝″ thick. Some inks are solvent
  based and air dried others are cured with a UV (Ultra Violet) light. Due to the
  cost per square foot digital printing at this point is used mainly for lower volume
  projects.

Die-Cutting Methods

Die cutters are basically large cookie cutters with sharp-edged steel rule used to cut out the
display components. They are divided into two basic systems—flatbed and rotary. Sharp
cutting rule is used around the perimeter to cut out the object. Smooth scoring rule is used
to create scores or creases where the material will be bent. Small, sponge-rubber blocks are
glued to the die board. In the cutting process, the sponge-rubber blocks are compressed.
As pressure is released, the sponge rubber blocks help push the material away from the
die after it is cut.

- **Flatbed Die Cutters**   Cutting and scoring rules are embedded into a flat sheet of
  plywood in the shape of the part to be cut. The die board is then bolted to the die
  cutter. The material is positioned on a platen or flat sheet of steel. The cutting die
  is pressed through the substrate with tons of pressure while in contact with the
  steel plate. This creates a cookie-cutter effect, cutting the display part out of the
  material.

- **Rotary Die Cutters**   Cutting and scoring rules are embedded into a preformed
  round plywood cylinder. Rotary cutting rule has serrated teeth and acts as scissors. The cutting die cylinder is bolted onto a rotating shaft of the die cutter.
  Another cylinder is brought into contact with the cutting rule. As the material is
  fed through the rotating cylinders, the material is cut with a sheering action.

Folding/Gluing/Taping/Stitching

Display components often must be folded and then held in that position. Display bases are folded into a tube, and the seam or "joint" is glued, taped, or stitched. There are wide ranges of machines to automatically or semi-automatically fold display parts. Some folding machines apply cold adhesives, "hot melt" glue, or tape to paperboard.

PAPER MATERIALS

Cardboard

The word "cardboard" is used as a generic term, but actually refers to a category of papers. These papers, initially designed for specific industries (e.g., automotive, soft drink, folding cartons, or packaging), have been utilized by the display industry. Figure 7-18 is a short list of some of the paper boards used in producing displays.

BOARD TYPE	THICKNESS RANGE	MATERIAL	COMMON USES IN P-O-P DISPLAYS
Chipboard	.010 – .060	Recycled newsprint	Easels, backs of signs
Beverage board	.010 – .030	Recycled newsprint with a white clay surface	Easels, backs of signs
Solid bleached sulfite	.008 – .030	Virgin paper, bleached white and calendered	Die-cut signs, table tents, countertop displays, standees (a smooth surface that is printable)
Poster board	.030 – .125	Recycled Kraft paper with different top layers	Signs, standees
Solid fiber	.020 – .125	Recycled industrial-grade paperboard, laminated to desired thickness	Standees, signs, support parts (often laminated with an offset-printed label)

Figure 7-18

Common types of paperboard used in POP displays

Corrugated Paperboard

Laymen often refer to corrugated paperboard as "cardboard," as in a "cardboard box." The word "corrugated" comes from the fluted inner liner that gives the board thickness and strength. Corrugated paperboard, also referred to as "corrugated" or "corrugate," can be constructed in many ways. There are different combinations of paper types, flute sizes, and multiple layers to achieve different characteristics.

Figure 7-19 lists the major types of corrugated paperboard used in displays. "B" flute is the most commonly used board for displays. It is strong enough to hold most products, yet still has a good surface for printing. To obtain an even better printing service, "E, F, and G" flutes were invented. However, as the flute becomes thinner, much of the strength is lost and the designer is limited to the size of the display that can be constructed from it without adding more material. The different flutes can be combined to produce special boards. Standard combinations used in displays include B/C, B/E, and E/F. The smaller of the flutes gives the best surface for printing. The larger flute gives the board more rigidity.

FLUTE	THICKNESS	COMMON USES
A flute	$1/4$	For heavy-duty shipping cartons
C flute	$3/16$	For regular shipping cartons
B flute	$1/8$	For most displays
E flute	$3/32$	For small countertop displays and product cartons
F flute	$1/16$	Also called "Micro Flute," for signage and product cartons
G flute	$3/64$	For special effects, can be offset-printed and embossed

Figure 7-19

Common corrugated paperboard flute sizes

CONCLUSION

Although several manufacturing processes and materials have been reviewed in this chapter, only the basic methods and materials used in display design and construction have been discussed. It is important to realize that most displays are manufactured out of multiple materials, utilizing multiple manufacturing processes. To better anticipate the ever-changing demand of the consumer for something new and different, display producers must constantly research new materials or new ways to combine existing materials to catch the eye. In the time it takes to read this chapter, someone will have developed a new way of producing a display or combining new technology with current productions methods to manufacture point-of-purchase displays more quickly. Or, a designer will have discovered a new way to use an existing material. The challenge for you—whether you are a display buyer, a producer, or are in P-O-P display sales—is to understand the entire spectrum of the point-of-purchase display manufacturing process so that you can make better decisions to meet your customer's needs.

POPAI's Outstanding Merchandising Achievement Awards Contest

The Global Association for Marketing at-Retail

POPAI'S OUTSTANDING MERCHANDISING ACHIEVEMENT AWARDS CONTEST

This section showcases a variety of point-of-purchase advertising displays that received POPAI's prestigious Outstanding Merchandising Achievement (OMA) award in 2007. The brand clients and companies that produced the displays, are listed with their award levels–gold, silver, or bronze.

Since 1959, POPAI's OMA awards contest is the premier award for recognizing the most innovative and effective marketing at-retail displays that lift sales and make products memorable and enticing to consumers. The entries are judged by a prestigious panel of brand marketers, producers, and retailers. The first round of judging is done online, where judges review submitted images and case history forms, and the second round of judging is done in person, where judges evaluate the actual displays to formulate a final score. Scores are based on the display's ability to increase sales, obtain retail placements, and work strategically to position the brand at the point of sale. Over 700 cutting-edge P-O-P displays vie each year for OMA awards in over 25 categories. This is the industry's largest and longest running awards contest.

The displays shown here illustrate the wide degree of creativity, design, and function for P-O-P displays. More detailed information, including a list of materials used and brief case histories for each of these displays— plus thousands more—is available in the POPAI Creative Gallery online at www.popai.com.

Displays of the Year

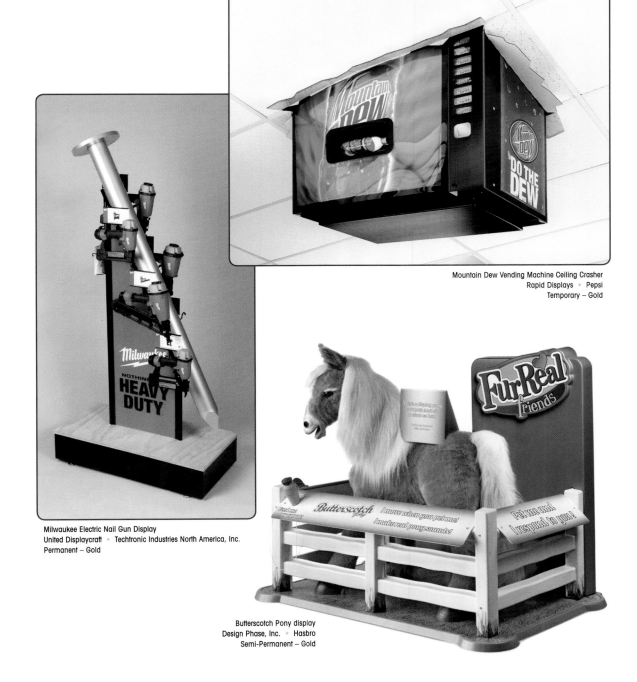

Mountain Dew Vending Machine Ceiling Crasher
Rapid Displays • Pepsi
Temporary – Gold

Milwaukee Electric Nail Gun Display
United Displaycraft • Techtronic Industries North America, Inc.
Permanent – Gold

Butterscotch Pony display
Design Phase, Inc. • Hasbro
Semi-Permanent – Gold

Beer

Coors Light Silver Bullet Train
The Integer Group • Coors Brewing Company
Permanent – Gold

Tiger Lager Rickshaw
The Strive Group • Anheuser-Busch, Inc.
Semi-Permanent – Gold

Bud Family Oversized Flip Flop
Anheuser-Busch, Inc. • Anheuser-Busch, Inc.
Semi-Permanent – Bronze

Widmer Hefeweizen Beer Rack
Grand & Benedicts, Inc. • Craft Brands Alliance
Permanent – Silver

Redhook ESB "Defy Ordinary" 12-pack Stacker
Grand & Benedicts, Inc. • Craft Brands Alliance
Permanent – Silver

Miller Super Party Spectacular
Baird Display • Miller Brewing Co.
Temporary – Bronze

Books, Newspapers, Magazines, Stationary and Office Supplies

Endymion Spring Floorstand
Chief Display Group • Random House
Temporary – Gold

Connections from Hallmark Genesis Fixture System
Hallmark Cards, Inc. • Hallmark Cards, Inc.
Permanent – Gold

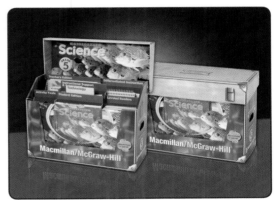

Science Tool Box Kit
Alliance, a Division of Rock Tenn Company
Macmillan/McGraw-Hill
Permanent – Silver

Disney Fairies Floorstand
Chief Display Group • Random House
Temporary – Silver

Staples U.S. Writing & Stickies Display
Artisan Complete • Staples Inc.
Temporary – Bronze

Computers

Bose Companion Triplet Display
Darko, Inc.   •   Bose Corporation
Permanent – Silver

Symantec Corporation – The DaVinci
Rapid Displays   •   Symantec Corporation
Temporary – Gold

TurboTax 40X48 CE and OSS Pallet Display
Rapid Displays   •   Intuit
Semi-Permanent – Silver

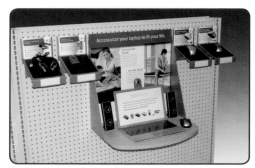

Logitech Staples Mobility End Cap
Rapid Displays   •   Logitech
Permanent – Bronze

Symantec Back to School '06 Shipper
Rapid Displays   •   Symantec Corporation
Temporary – Bronze

Cosmetics

Clarins – General Tester Stand
D3 LLC • Clarins
Permanent – Silver

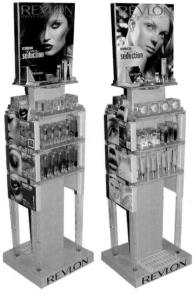

Revlon Limited Edition Collection Floorstand
Techno P.O.S., Inc. • Revlon Canada
Temporary – Bronze

Max Factor Spring 2006 Promotion
Alliance, a Division of Rock-Tenn Company • Proctor & Gamble
Temporary – Silver

L'Oreal ProManicure Nail Trays
POP Displays Inc. • L'Oreal
Permanent – Gold

Digital

Sealy Touch
Wireless Ronin Technologies
Sealy, Inc.
Permanent – Silver

Entertainment

Flushed Away Theatre Standee
The Gemini Group
DreamWorks Animation and Paramount Pictures
Temporary – Gold

Nintendogs Dalmation Standee
Wetzel Brothers, Inc. • Nintendo of America
Temporary – Bronze

Running with Scissors
Drissi Advertising, Inc. • Sony Pictures Entertainment
Temporary – Gold

Pirates Pre Pack
Cornerstone Display Group, Inc.
Buena Vista Home Entertainment
Temporary – Silver

Bibleman PowerSource Series Relaunch
U.S. Display Group
Thomas Nelson Publishers
Semi-Permanent – Silver

Zune Interactive Flipbook Kiosk
DCI Marketing • Microsoft
Permanent – Bronze

Fragrances

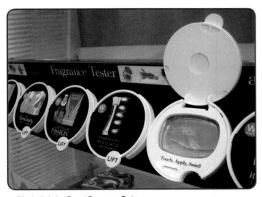

Elizabeth Arden Target Fragrance Tester
Mechtronics Corporation • Elizabeth Arden
Permanent – Bronze

JLo Live & Baby Phat Plug-In
The Strive Group • Coty, US
Temporary – Gold

The Healing Garden Organic Plug-In
The Strive Group
Coty, US
Temporary – Bronze

Elizabeth Arden Britney Spears Fantasy Wal-Mart Endcap
Chief Display Group
Elizabeth Arden
Temporary – Silver

David Beckham Fragrance Tester Unit
The Strive Group • Coty, US
Permanent – Gold

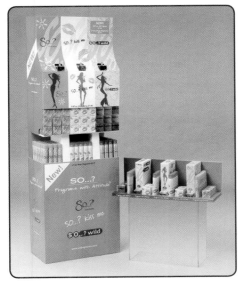

Elizabeth Arden So...? Fragrance Launch Endcap
Sonoco CorrFlex • Elizabeth Arden
Temporary – Bronze

Grocery

Clorox Disinfecting Wipes Retail Dispenser
Clorox Company • Clorox
Permanent – Gold

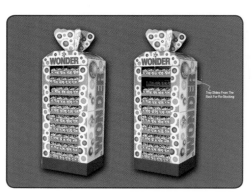

Wonder Plus Shroud
Protagon Display, Inc. • Weston Bakeries Limited
Temporary – Gold

Kellogg's Snacks 2006 Back-to-School Modular
Smurfit-Stone Display Group • Kellogg Company
Temporary – Silver

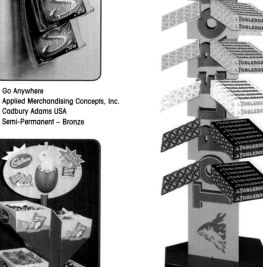

Go Anywhere
Applied Merchandising Concepts, Inc.
Cadbury Adams USA
Semi-Permanent – Bronze

Toblerone Tower
Harding Display Corp • Toblerone
Permanent – Silver

Easter Floor "Birds Nest"
Harding Display Corp. • Cadbury Adams
Temporary – Gold

Kellogg's Pirates of the Caribbean Displays
Baird Display • Kellogg Company
Temporary – Bronze

Hair and Skincare

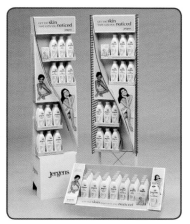

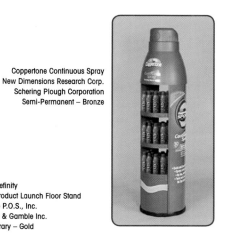

Coppertone Continuous Spray
New Dimensions Research Corp.
Schering Plough Corporation
Semi-Permanent – Bronze

Olay Definity
New Product Launch Floor Stand
Techno P.O.S., Inc.
Procter & Gamble Inc.
Temporary – Gold

Kao Brands Company 2006 JergensA EMO Displays
Sonoco CorrFlex · KAO Brands
Temporary – Silver

Garnier Skin Care Display
Summit Manufacturer · Maybelline-Garnier New York
Semi-Permanent – Gold

Pantene Parhenon
MZM (A Leggett & Platt Co.) · Proctor & Gamble Mexico
Permanent – Silver

Frizz-Ease Floor Display
Smurfit-Image Pac Display Group
KAO Brands Canada
Temporary – Bronze

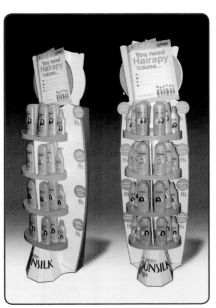

Sunsilk Floorstand
Smurfit-Image Pac Display Group
Unilever Canada
Semi-Permanent – Silver

Healthcare

Listerine Agent Cool Blue Floorstand Powerwing
Rand Display International • Johnson & Johnson and Logistics, LLC
Temporary – Gold

McNeil Consumer Healthcare – Tylenol Tower
Artisan Complete • McNeil Consumer Healthcare
Semi-Permanent – Gold

Prilosec 42ct Senior Pallet
Sonoco CorrFlex • Procter and Gamble
Semi-Permanent – Bronze

Benadryl Floor Display
Smurfit-Image Pac Display Group
Johnson & Johnson Group of Consumer Companies
Semi-Permanent – Silver

ACCU-CHEK Lancing System
Techno P.O.S., Inc. • Roche Diagnostics
Temporary – Bronze

Crest Spinbrush Mixed Pallet Display
TimBar Packaging & Display Point of Purchase Division
Church & Dwight Company
Temporary – Silver

Home and Garden

36 Volt Launch Endcap
for Lowe's Alliance,
a Division of Rock-Tenn
Company • DeWalt
Semi-Permanent – Gold

Ryobi One+ Project Center
E-B Display Co., Inc.
Techtronic Industries North America
Permanent – Gold

Scotts Liquafeed Demonstrator Endcap
Smurfit-Stone Display Group • Scotts Company
Semi-Permanent – Bronze

Black & Decker Lithium Ion Holiday Pallet Display
Weyerhaeuser Retail Experience Network
Black & Decker
Temporary – Bronze

Lutron Marquee Showroom System
The Niven Marketing Group
Lutron Electronics Company
Permanent – Silver

Raid Outdoor Ant Spikes Sidekick/Floor Display
Great Northern Corporation
Consumer Packaging and Display
SCJ "A Family Company"
Temporary – Silver

Liquor

Rex Goliath Island
ICON Design and Display
Pacific Wine Partners
Permanent – Gold

Martini & Rossi Sparkling Wine & Fresh Flower Merchandiser
Bish Creative Display, Inc. • Bacardi
Semi-Permanent – Silver

Red Guitar Display
ICON Design and Display
Pacific Wine Partners
Permanent – Silver

Heaven Hill Distilleries, PAMA Launch
Inventive Display Group • Heaven Hill Distilleries
Permanent – Bronze

Shakka Rack
Array • ABSOLUT Spirits Co.
Permanent – Bronze

Multinational

Pantene Parthenon Pallet
Techno P.O.S., Inc. • Procter & Gamble Mexico
Temporary – Gold

Samsung – Z5 Column
Leggett & Platt Display Group • Samsung Electronics UK
Permanent – Bronze

Ponds Beetle Roller
Boomerang • Unilever de Mexico
Permanent – Silver

Ariel Sancy Tunnel 2X
MZM (A Leggett & Platt Co.) • Procter & Gamble Mexico
Semi-Permanent – Gold

2006 Back to School
Lobby Display
Smurfit-Stone Display Group
Kraft Foods
Temporary – Bronze

Personal Products

Back-to-School Window
Kroll Salkin Corporation • Champs Sports
Temporary – Silver

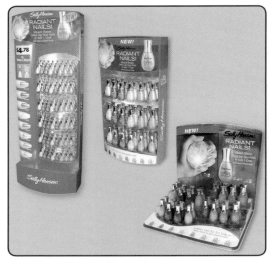

Sally Hansen Fire Opals Nail Glaze Family of Displays
Shorewood Display • Del Labs
Semi-Permanent – Gold

Disney Mobile Phone Display
Frank Mayer & Associates, Inc.
Disney Mobile
Permanent – Bronze

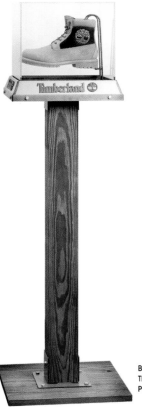

Boot Cube
The Timberland Company • The Timberland Company
Permanent – Silver

Quick Showcase
Grupo Rubrica • Radiomovil Dipsa Sa De Cv
Permanent – Bronze

Service, Signage and Sales Promotion

Hewlett-Packard Holiday Toolkit
Leggett & Platt Display Group
Hewlett Packard
Semi-Permanent – Silver

Burger King Xbox Lobby Dispenser
Rapid Displays • Burger King Corporation
Temporary – Gold

Beneful Prepared Meals
and Merchandising Program
Smurfit-Stone Display Group
Nestle Purina Petcare Company
Temporary – Silver

Leinenkugel Fiber Optic Sign
Array • Madden Communications, Inc. on behalf of Miller Brewing Company
Permanent – Gold

Retail Stores

Drug Stores, Mass Merchants and Super Markets

CVS Top of Checkout Rack
POP Displays Inc. • CVS
Permanent – Gold

Abreva 8pc Sidekick/Counter Launch Display
Packaging Specialist, Inc.
GlaxoSmithKline
Semi-Permanent – Bronze

40 Count Amour Heart Displayer
C&B Corrugated Containers, Inc.
Lindt & Sprungli (Canada) Inc.
Temporary – Silver

Tylenol Seasonal Relief Center
Smurfit-Stone Display Group
McNeil Consumer & Specialty Pharmaceuticals
Semi-Permanent – Gold

Listerine Agent Cool Blue Holiday
Wing Unit
Rand Display International
Johnson & Johnson and Logistics, LLC
Temporary – Bronze

Wal-Mart Interactive Game Cabinets
Frank Mayer & Associates
Wal-Mart
Permanent – Gold

Sketchers Real Life Merchandisers
Rapid Displays • Sketchers USA
Temporary – Bronze

Coca-Cola Drink It Down, Start It Up Display
Arc Worldwide • The Coca-Cola Company
Semi-Permanent – Gold

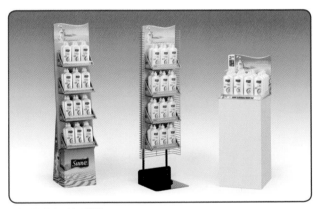

SUAVE 18z Ltn 24pc FS/SK
Smurfit-Stone Display Group • Unilever HPOC-NA
Semi-Permanent – Bronze

Kodak/SuperValu 4-Way Island Digital Print Station
Mechtronics Corporation
Eastman Kodak Company
Permanent – Gold

Gillette Fusion Expandable Brand Frame
Mechtronics Corporation
The Procter and Gamble Company
Semi-Permanent – Silver

Goody's Cool Orange Endcap
Packaging Specialist, Inc.
GlaxoSmithKline
Temporary – Bronze

Snacks

Diet Pepsi Box Office End Aisle Display
Innomark Communications • Pepsi-Cola
Temporary – Silver

Hershey Canada – Lenticular Rack
Artisan Complete • Hershey Canada
Permanent – Gold

Coca-Cola North America – Dasani Cascade
Leggett & Platt Display Group
Coca-Cola of North America
Permanent – Silver

Red Bull Hybrid Cooler
PFI • Red Bull North America, Inc.
Permanent – Silver

Hershey Canada – Generic Dump Bin
Artisan Complete • Hershey Canada
Temporary – Bronze

PowerBar Pria Permanent Rack
Alliance, a Division of Rock-Tenn Company
Nestle USA
Permanent – Bronze

Coca-Cola My Coke Rewards Summer Spectacular
Arc Worldwide · The Coca-Cola Company
Semi-Permanent – Gold

The Drink of the World Cup
Marka Diseo'o Y Produccion · Coca Cola North America
Semi-Permanent – Bronze

Cape Cod Lighthouse
The Inflatable Marketplace (Small Wonder), Inc.
Cape Code Potato Chips
Temporary – Silver

Hershey Canada – Mauna Loa Palm Tree
Artisan Complete · Hershey Canada
Temporary – Bronze

24ct. Reese's Cooler Pack
Menasha Display Group · The Hershey Company
Temporary – Bronze

Kellogg's Snacks – 2006 Holiday Modular
Smurfit-Stone Display Group
Kellogg Company
Temporary – Bronze

Sports Equipment

PING Golf Fitting Cart
Trans World Marketing • PING Golf
Permanent – Gold

MacGregor Golf Modular Display Family
Process Displays, Inc. • MacGregor Golf
Permanent – Silver

TaylorMade TP Red/TP Black Tower Display
The Carlson Group, Inc. • TaylorMade-adidas Golf
Permanent – Bronze

Tobacco

British American Tobacco –
Kent 10's – Counter Display
Artisan Complete
British American Tobacco CA
Temporary – Bronze

Camel/Kool Horeca Glorifier – Dual rotating
ImageWorks Display & Marketing Group, Inc.
R J Reynolds Tobacco Company
Permanent – Silver

Camel PlexiNeon Enhanced Focus Fixtures
ImageWorks Display & Marketing Group, Inc.
R J Reynolds Tobacco Company
Permanent – Gold

Toys and Accessories

Trixieville
Menasha Packaging Company
Manhattan Toy
Semi-Permanent – Silver

Fisher-Price Preschool Electronics Shelf Display
Darko, Inc. • Fisher-Price
Permanent – Silver

Mattel HotWheels Racetrack Interactive Display
Design Phase, Inc. • Mattel, Inc.
Permanent – Gold

Energizer Titanium Counter Display
Trans World Marketing
Energizer
Permanent – Bronze

Mega Bloks – Pirates of the Caribbean Feature Island Display
Artisan Complete • Mega Brands Inc.
Temporary – Bronze

Transportation

Gates/Car Quest Wiper Stand
Great Northern Corporation Consumer Packaging and Display
Gates Corporation
Permanent – Gold

Honda VTX Standee
Rapid Displays • Honda
Semi-Permanent – Silver

Garmin Modular Display System
Rapid Displays • Garmin
Permanent – Bronze

Star Motorcycle 20' Display
RP Creative Display, Inc. • Yamaha Motor Corporation, U.S.A.
Permanent – Bronze

Lighted Accessories Display
DCI Marketing
Harley-Davidson Motor Company
Permanent – Silver

8

Evaluating Retail Technologies

Jeff Sandgren
Principal
Sandgren Consulting LLC

REFLECTING AND REFORECASTING

In the 2004 edition, this chapter considered the accelerated pace of technological advancement, and took the position that any attempt to provide a state-of-the-art appraisal of retail technologies would be outdated in relatively short order. Instead of attempting a comprehensive appraisal of all new retail technologies, we considered a framework for evaluating them, illustrating that approach with relevant examples.

Looking back, that was a prudent approach. What seemed an accelerated pace in 2004 pales by comparison today. Looking ahead, the hot new technologies of 2008 will undoubtedly be old news before the next edition of this book comes to press. As with the previous analysis, some solutions will achieve significant adoption, others will struggle in seemingly perpetual trial, and some will simply fall by the wayside either failing to deliver real value or by being themselves replaced by even more innovative solutions.

So in this chapter we will revisit previous predictions, in the hope that this will provide us with some lessons for interpreting the current crop of emerging retail technologies. Next we will review and update the central topic at hand, that being not the technologies per se, but the methodology of evaluating them. Finally, we will apply the insights of past predictions with the latest refinements in assessment, and (boldly or foolishly) offer a forecast of top prospects for the next few years.

THEN AND NOW – REVIEWING PAST PREDICTIONS

First, here is a quick recap on the status of technologies that we cited in the previous edition. Note that most of these are still viable solutions, although some are being adopted more slowly.

Technology in 2004	Status in 2007
Radio Frequency Identification (RFID)	Supply chain adoption lagging expectations, but selected item-level solutions surprise hits
Thin Display Technology	More solutions from more vendors, but focus on consumer electronic devices has meant slower M-A-R adoption
Collaborative Planning Technologies	Widely adopted by retail merchants planning print advertising, but not yet well integrated with display planning
Digital Printing	Key technology for affordable versioning, allowing more co-branded and strategically targeted content on displays
Digital Displays	Lots of action in improved placement, content, and communication. Focus forward appears to be on smaller devices and tighter adjacency to merchandise
Shopper-Interactive Technology	Shoppers, accustomed to controlling their own experience online, embrace at-retail interactions, ranging from simple voice boxes to 'magic mirrors' and socialized gift list kiosks
Payment Technologies	Biometrics and RFID payment technologies widely adopted, and self check-out past the tipping point

THREE KEY TESTS OF EMERGING MARKETING AT-RETAIL TECHNOLOGY

While retail technologies continue to evolve, the basics of evaluation remain much the same. While proof of concept tests focus on verifying that the underlying technology performs as specified, the business value still requires that three key tests – the People Test, the Pull Test, and the Payback Test – be passed to ensure successful adoption. These tests have proved to be consistently useful for evaluating new offerings. To fully evaluate a new Marketing at-retail technology, many factors must be considered. The list at right shows 10 examples. While all of these considerations are important, this chapter outlines three essential tests that any new technology must pass—those focused on shoppers, problem-solving, and financial performance.

Technology Evaluation Considerations

1. **Priority of Problem**
2. **Potential End-User Benefits**
3. **Whole Solution Cost**
4. **Return on Investment**
5. **Competitive Advantage**
6. **Proof of Performance / Value**
7. **Compatibilities / Synergies**
8. **Workaround / Best Practices**
9. **Criteria for Success / Metrics**
10. **Process Change Impacts**

I. The People Test: Improve the In-Store Experience

Manufacturers control funding, retailers control real estate, and shareholders direct priorities—but consumer preference drives all. At the end of the day, it is the properly engaged shoppers, responding with their purchasing dollars, who determine what works and for how long. As a result, the most promising opportunities often are those intended to improve the consumers' shopping experience.

'Experiential Marketing' is the common term for connecting consumers with brands in a personally relevant and memorable way. The at-retail world remains a unique and powerful venue for communicating the essence of a brand via direct personal experience, even more so as media fragmentation erodes the power of traditional advertising vehicles. Much insight has been gained in the past few years toward understanding the different missions shoppers may have on different trips, as their in-store needs and desires differ significantly based on the type of mission. In one view, Information Resources Inc. (IRI)1 proposed that four primary types are Quick Trip, Special Purpose, Fill-In, and Pantry Stocking. Accordingly, technologies that distract the shoppers from their current mission will detract from that experience, while those that assist and enrich the fulfillment of the mission will add to it.

Whether it is discovering exciting new products, special offers, bargain prices, or simply the reassurance of a trusted brand, the key events that add up to a positive in-store experience form the essential foundation for customer preference and loyalty—to brands and to retailers. As such, these same elements of the in-store experience represent to their retailers and brand marketers a potentially sustainable source of competitive advantage. The power of Marketing at-retail derives directly from the sensory and functional presence of the media at that precise moment in time when the shopper decides to trade money for selected goods.

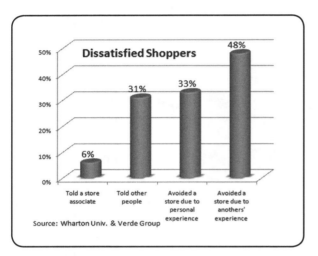

Source: Wharton Univ. & Verde Group

It is also worth noting that, while Marketing at-retail typically focuses on providing positive in-store experiences, it can sometimes help avoid bad experiences. Electronic pricing displays can ensure shelf price accuracy, for example, and RFID and other technologies can help improve in-stock levels. This is significant because of another key aspect of experiential marketing: people who have bad experiences tell other people. A 2006 study by Wharton and the Verde Group2 concluded that for every 100 shoppers who have a bad experience, a retailer stands to lose between 32 and 36 current or potential customers.

Example: digital signage goes IP and eye-level

Perhaps the best-known type of technology-enabled Marketing at-Retail is 'In-Store TV', with the best-known example being 'Wal-Mart TV' operated by Premiere Retail Networks, touted as being the third-highest viewed broadcast network in the world with over 6,000 locations (including other retailers). In 2006, test known as 'Project Mustang', in-store monitors were replaced with flat-screen panels and dropped to eye level in aisles and other key locations, instead of hanging several feet overhead. Testing showed that awareness levels for ads were "significantly higher" when screens are at eye level, in some cases almost doubling sales. Besides physically moving the digital displays, communication was also improved by shifting to Internet Protocol TV (IPTV) in which content could be easily targeted to each individual location, rather than having the same ads playing on all monitors. The targeted content was location specific, and resulted in some cases in sales increases that were 'close to double'. The reformatting has since been implemented chain-wide.

The next logical step will be small digital shelf signs that integrate more easily into the merchandising without displacing too much product. In another poll of Brand Manufacturers of IRI, these received the top vote for technologies with "the greatest potential to transform in-store marketing", with 44% of the respondents anticipating this type of solution.

Sources: Nielsen Business Media, 2006, "Wal-Mart Takes Its Ads to the Aisle", and Information Resources, Inc., "CPG Merchandising Trends 2007"

II. The Pull Test: the problem should 'pull' the solution

'Technology for technology's sake' has rarely been a compelling argument for retail adoption. But when retail problems happen to overlap technology-based opportunities, it is easy to become infatuated with the "cool factor" of the technology and lose sight of the whole solution. In this situation, the technology may be 'pushed' down to end users – like pushing a square peg into a round hole. As someone once observed when viewing a new technology, "That's a great cure. Too bad there's no disease." With numerous challenges, such as cost pressure, supply chain management, poor at-retail compliance, media undervaluation, and increasingly demanding consumers to consider, the industry simply does not have the time or resources to dabble in the technology du jour. The most effective and successful implementations come when the dynamic is reversed: the high-priority business need instead 'pulls' a best-fit technology to resolve the problem. So the second test for considering a new technology has to be: what important problem will it solve, and is it the best technology to solve that problem? To illustrate, we will consider the example of retail out-of-stocks, which costs millions in lost sales annually.

Example: persistent problems with Out-of-Stocks

One of the most intractable retail problems remains out-of-stocks. This problem has been scrutinized in a number of studies, including those by the Food Marketing Institute (FMI), the Grocery Manufacturers of America (GMA), and the Comité International d'Entreprises à Succursales (CIES – International Committee of Food Retail Chains) cited in the previous edition, which have revealed the following:

- Out-of-stocks averaged 8.3 percent overall in a 2002 study, up slightly from 8.2 percent in 1993. Sales losses from out-of-stocks average 4 percent.
- Shoppers often respond by switching brands, or stores, to acquire the desired items. Retailers lose the sale 43 percent of the time; manufacturers, 31 percent.
- Promoted items have twice the out-of-stocks of non-promoted items. (P-O-P displays contribute to—and suffer from—this problem.)

Since these conditions all contribute strong negative effects to the shopper's in-store experience, out-of-stocks clearly passes The People Test. The next question is: what solutions should this problem pull? First, let us eliminate the obvious nontechnology solution of simply increasing overall inventory levels. This is a poor solution because it would increase inventory carrying costs, which in turn would mean either lower profit to the retailer or higher prices to the consumer.

To determine potential technological remedies for out-of-stock losses, we must first examine the primary causes. According to the FMI and GMA studies referenced above, the primary causes of out-of-stocks are (1) poor ordering and/or forecasting, (2) upstream supply chain factors, and (3) having the stock in-store but not on the shelf/display. The table below presents possible solutions and the technologies that might be "pulled" into service as remedies.

CAUSES & POTENTIAL SOLUTIONS FOR OUT-OF-STOCKS			
Cause	**% of Problem**	**Possible Solution**	**Potential Enabling Technologies/Knowledge**
Poor ordering or forecasting	47%	Better reporting and forecasting tools	Analytic Software Systems, CPFR[1] Systems, Supply Chain Management Systems
		More accurate promotional lift data (to enable better peak demand forecasting)	Lift Studies (e.g. POPAI), Compliance Monitoring, Demand Analysis Systems
		Improved order support systems	Automated reorder systems, Improved mobile scan/order applications, Improved Syndicated Data
Upstream supply chain factors	28%	Improved supply chain management	RFID supply chain tracking, Warehouse Management Systems
		Remediation alert systems	POS Velocity Monitoring Compliance Monitoring, GPS Distribution Tracking
In-store but not on shelf/display	25%	Fully-integrated space management, combining shelf & POP display data	Lift Studies, Compliance Monitoring, CPFR Systems
		Better in-store inventory management	Perpetual Inventory Systems, RFID Receiving Systems
		POS scan movement alerts	Intelligent POS Velocity Monitoring
		Better POP inventory monitoring	Shelf/Display Stock-Level Sensor Networks
		Better labor forecasting	Workforce Management Systems

[1] CPFR: Collaborative Planning Forecasting and Replenishment, systems which extend resource planning across the trading partners in an enterprise. Wal-Mart's Retail Link system is an example. POS: Point Of Sale. GPS: Global Positioning Satellite, systems which geo-locate items in transit

With the size of the problem so large, the customer impact so significant, and so many emerging technologies arising as potential solutions, why is it still a problem? The three commonly cited reasons are (1) a lack of commitment to solve it, (2) a constantly changing environment, and (3) payback on the solution cost. The latter is especially important, and leads us to the third test.

III. The Payback Test: Quick Payback of Whole Solution Cost

So far we have specified the 'People' test, favoring those technologies that enhance the shoppers' in-store experience, and the 'Pull' test, focusing on solutions where appropriate technologies have been implemented to solve significant business problems. These two tests should pave the way for the final, 'Payback' test, by building on solid value propositions that can be operationalized to yield measurable benefits for retailers and brand marketers…if and only if they can do so affordably. Even companies with intractable problems rarely have the option of throwing money at their problems. Capital is always precious, so any solution—especially a technology-based one—is typically expected to pay back the investment quickly, so as to replenish the capital pool for other opportunities and quickly create a long-term enhancement to profitability. In other words, buyers don't expect to pay for solutions; they expect the solutions to pay for themselves—quickly. For retail technologies, the desired payback is rarely more than two years, most commonly under one year, and sometimes less than six months.

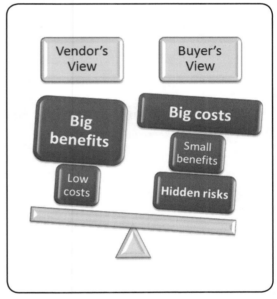

The problem of determining payback for a technology is sometimes complicated by the ambitions of those doing the analysis. All too often this leads to a benefit analysis that is seen as a prelude to price negotiation, and therefore is biased by the vendors' and buyers' conflicting positions on desired solution price. In these cases the vendor wants to maximize the potential benefits, but discount the potential costs, while the prospective buyer wants to pull the numbers in the opposite direction. The result, unfortunately, is a flawed Return On Investment (ROI) analysis. Fortunately, there is a growing trend toward adopting a more collaborative, navigational ROI analysis in which buyer and seller proceed through a phased process that evolves the business model around a mutually accepted set of economic and operational principles, and which identifies key decisions to implementation that can significantly impact the payback.

'Whole solution cost' is an important consideration in this analysis. It refers to the fact that the acquisition cost of the technology is often just one part of the total solution cost. When calculating payback, it is essential to consider the whole cost structure in the way that accountants look at "total cost of ownership." The sticker price on a new car, for example, is just one part of the whole solution cost. Finance charges, insurance, fuel, maintenance, and toll charges all figure in to the total cost of ownership.

The same approach holds true for point-of-purchase advertising solutions. Electronic displays with changeable content, for example, offer numerous applications for in-store communications with customers, but the whole solution cost will be more

Whole Solution Cost Considerations

1. Ancillary software costs
2. Annual Maintenance
3. End-User training
4. Insurance impacts
5. Wiring and infrastructure
6. Power and communication
7. Content development/acquisition
8. Program administration
9. Cost of capital
10. Increased retail theft

than just the acquisition of the displays. Electricity and communications hookups must be factored in, as will retailer charges for the use of valuable space. Moreover, the changing content itself has to be developed, or sourced and repurposed, and coordinated carefully with the overall promotional campaigns. All of this takes time and money.

This same approach needs to be implemented in any evaluation of a new technology. No matter how promising the shopper enhancement is, and no matter how perfectly matched the technology is to the business problem, the overall solutions still has to be affordable, with all related costs considered. A sample of cost considerations is provided at right; additional factors may apply depending on the solution.

Example: selling more while losing less

Last but not least on the list of solution costs is the consideration of increased retail theft. Sometimes the theft is from casual shoplifters, or even from store associates themselves; but increasingly theft is occurring from organized retail theft gangs, 'professional' thieves who operate in carefully coordinated and highly effective ways to steal items that have street value by reselling them to less scrupulous small operators. A common technique of these thieves is to steal not one or two items, but an entire shelf or display full of merchandise in what is known as a 'sweep'.

Special displays regrettably make an opportune target for this type of behavior. Store managers have reported that placement of retail displays, especially near the front of the store, can result in higher rates of theft. Retailers want the extra sales lift that comes from displays, but they also want to avoid an increase in retail theft. Accordingly, innovative display designers have introduced 'anti-sweep' mechanisms into selected displays that allow for easy removal of one or two items, but restrict rapid removal of several items at a time. Razor blades, ink cartridges, and baby formula are but a few examples of items that have seen significant theft control from these types of features.

'THREE KEY TESTS' IN ACTION: RFID AT RETAIL

Now that we have reviewed the concepts of people, pull, and payback, let us illustrate this approach with a prominent example of an emerging technology, RFID, and evaluate the solution's viability.

Hot on the technology list in the last edition were Radio Frequency Identification (RFID) enabled technologies. Radio frequency (RF) technologies use radio waves in certain wavelength bands to effect wireless communication between objects. RF technologies have been important in many retail solutions for many years, notably performing the following tasks, among others:

- Enabling greater productivity with wireless handhelds for better-informed employees
- Protecting against loss with Electronic Article Surveillance (EAS) tags
- Enabling quicker checkout with RF payment, like the Exxon-Mobil SpeedPass™
- Achieving shelf-price integrity with wirelessly updated electronic price displays

Additionally, since the previous textbook, concerns over perishable food and pharmaceutical safety has resulted in some cases in RFID tags being used to tag livestock and to provide an 'electronic pedigree' on medicines to provide early detection of counterfeits in the supply chain.

The heart of RFID is the combination of RF and Auto-ID technologies into small tags, consisting of a printed circuit and an antenna, programmed with identification codes, to enable objects to be identified when they pass within a prescribed proximity to an RF reader which detects the tag's identification code.

The RFID tags currently receiving the most attention are Electronic Product Code (EPC) tags, which extend the idea of a printed UPC barcode to an electronic implementation with more digits – enough digits, in fact, to give every single tag its own unique ID. The EPC initiatives sought to use non-battery-powered 'passive' RFID tags and an identification schema endorsed by a global consortium, EPCGlobal, to allow unique identification of merchandise at the pallet, case, and item level. Initial applications have been targeted at improved product availability, enabling stores to keep better track of inventory so items can be restocked faster and more products are on the shelf when shoppers want them. Future applications are intended to help shoppers find products in the store more easily, speed check out, allow for faster returns, protect against counterfeit products, and monitor the freshness of goods with expiration dates.

The standardization is, of course, key to global adoption; and in this case it is keeping pace with the technological development. Shortly after this book's last edition, the standards for 'Gen 2' labels were ratified, allowing for better performance and easier manufacturing (i.e., cheaper costs). As of this writing 'Gen 3' is nearing ratification, carrying the Gen 2 protocol forward into implementations with active (battery-powered) tags, which will have much longer communications ranges and even more potential applications.

Update: EPC results at Wal-Mart

The University of Arkansas' Information Technology Research Institute worked with Wal-Mart in an extensive study in 2005, conducting 'almost daily' audits of 4500+ SKUs over a six-month period, to measure the improvement of stores using Electronic Product Code (EPC) RFID labels to reduce Out-Of-Stocks, and concluded that RFID reduced OOS at store level by 16% over non-RFID based stores.

While this is a significant improvement, skeptics argue that much of this benefit could be obtained from properly implemented Point-Of-Sale transaction data integrated with a Perpetual Inventory System. Still others find that Out-Of-Stocks could best be addressed by reallocating store personnel. In a 2007 study published by Wharton, researchers found that a "modest reallocation of the payroll budget among stores" in one particular chain could yield a 2-3% increase in sales with no increase in cost.

RFID AND DISPLAY MONITORING

One scenario with which to illustrate the People/Pull/Payback Test approach is the likely near-term point-of-purchase use of RFID with an application targeted against poor compliance in retail execution. As many studies, including ongoing POPAI studies, have documented, P-O-P promotional compliance remains dismal. Audits typically show execution in the 30 to 40 percent range. Solutions based on human audit have not been widely accepted; concerns focus on speed, accuracy, and reliability. Many industry leaders see a fully automated implementation as a more desirable and valuable solution.

Not surprisingly, RFID provides an excellent technological foundation for such a solution. One Chicago-based company, GOLIATH Solutions, worked closely with POPAI and a number of manufacturer and retail industry leaders, has led the field in solutions of this type, including securing the first nation-wide retailer rollout with Walgreens. Additional solutions from providers such as Oats Systems leverage EPC tags to provide a less-specific monitoring by noting when displays move from the backroom to the sales floor, and off again. And other providers, including GOLIATH, are working the other end of the spectrum to sense display placement all the way down to a shelf-specific level. How does RFID compliance monitoring stack up against the three key tests?

People: The almost-invariable sales lift associated with P-O-P advertising clearly establishes it as a plus for shoppers. Therefore, better-executed in-store point-of-purchase advertising clearly enhances the overall shopping experience.

Pull: Numerous studies have confirmed the long-standing vexation that manufacturers feel when a large portion of their precious promotional funds is used to purchase chain-wide P-O-P that ends up largely unused. Human audit services have been proffered but never fully assimilated. Clearly this is a problem in need of an automated solution.

Payback: Pricing and payback for RFID are yet to be demonstrated, but early indications are positive. First, the value proposition is significant. Cost savings from reduced waste offer a desirable hard savings; incremental sales and margin from improved execution add enormous potential value for both retailer and manufacturer; and the analytical value of finally being able to accurately attribute improved sales to actual execution should deliver tremendous strategic benefits. Second, the investment itself appears affordable. Design emphasis on low infrastructure and tag cost should enable pricing that provides a quite favorable return on investment against the potential value.

ADDITIONAL NOTABLE EMERGING TECHNOLOGIES

Retailers' romance with retail technologies continues at full throttle. In 2007, retailers spent $7.9 billion on information technology (IT) goods and services, and they are predicted to spend more than $10 billion on Business Intelligence offerings alone by 2013. Against this continued spending the following is a brief look at additional significant trends in emerging solutions.

'Merged Channel' Combinations: Boomerang Technologies Close the Loop

In the past, retailers and brand managers have had concerns about 'channel blurring' as the proliferation of consumer touch-points – in-store, on-line, by call centers, catalogs, and even cell phones – have posed challenges in communication and brand messaging. Turning problem into opportunity, leading companies have mastered the orchestration of these various technologies and real (and virtual) places of purchase into what it now called the 'merged channel'. Best implementations achieve what is called the 'boomerang effect,' driving shoppers from online to in-store and back again.

Promotional Price Optimization

Communicating price remains a key, and sometimes difficult, element of point-of-purchase messaging. Retailers of all types are implementing price and promotion optimization systems. These systems help ensure optimum synchronization between price and promotion communications. POS-synchronized electronic price displays remain challenged by payback in the United States, where most retailers would require the cost of implementing the technology to drop to the point where it can be paid back more quickly by simple labor savings (from reduced price change activities). Adoption is accelerating more rapidly in Europe, with retailers like the Metro Group, as evidenced in their "Future Store" Initiative.

Digital Printing Technologies: Anything, Any Size, Anywhere

Digital printing has had a revolutionary effect on the printing industry, reducing setups, improving throughputs, and creating new efficiencies. Advances continue in wider formats, higher speeds, more varied substrates, and improved image quality. New inks continue to expand the print horizon. Additional advances should be expected in image capture devices, image processing software, image output devices, media, inks and toners, and finishing systems.

Digital Display Technologies: Improving Visual Interaction

Electronic displays of visual images and item-specific information are becoming increasingly prevalent. Dynamic display technologies will continue to enhance the in-store experience as new capabilities are pulled in and leveraged to better serve end-customer needs and preferences. Static print imagery is not going away in our lifetime, but its virtual monopoly over in-store visual communications will increasingly yield to more dynamic and effective visual tools. Plasma displays should continue to become more affordable solutions for selected in-store advertising applications. As noted in the example on Project Mustang, these technologies have matured into full-fledged digital advertising networks.

Thin Display Technologies: Squeezing Digital into Small Displays

Thin displays with new, electronically driven inks are appearing in more places. Today the leading technology has been electrophoretic, a form of encapsulated electronically-drivable pigments from companies like E Ink. But these will be joined over the new few years by organic LEDs (OLEDs), and by an even newer technology, photonic crystals or 'p ink' from companies like Opalux. Taking it one step further, solutions are now available which project digital images on fine sheets of mist, dispelling the need for any solid physical substrate whatsoever.

Shopper-Interactive Technologies: Personalizing the In-Store Experience

Kiosks, while not as widely implemented as once expected, continue to find niche applications in areas like photo, cosmetics, and home improvement. Personal shoppers have evolved from early designs that were primarily shop-and-scan applications, into systems that allow shoppers in supermarkets to receive customized promotional offers while they shop, or even receive notification when photos, prescriptions, and deli orders are ready.

Hypersonic sound technologies allow audio marketing to be pinpointed to smaller areas. Combining with the previously mentioned growth in digital displays, a company called LocaModa is working to allow shoppers' own cell phone to locally control the content on in store digital signage, personalizing these dynamic displays. And in perhaps the most narcissistic of technologies, 'magic mirrors' combine the shoppers own reflection with digital displays and tag sensors to allow time-starved apparel shoppers to see themselves in various outfits without actually having to try them on.

Retail Forensics: Monitoring Behavior at Retail, Mining Shopper Insights

Ground-breaking explorations like POPAI's Marketing at-retail Initiative (MARI) and others are leveraging a host of technologies to harvest a mountain of shopper behavioral observations. Some retailers are even combining surveillance cameras that look for thieves and in-store accidents to capture information on the nuances of shopper-display interactions. Add to this the evolution of sophisticated data-mining techniques, and the prospects for understanding shoppers at a level of intimacy akin to e-commerce tracking and analysis are encouraging—or frightening, depending on your perspective.

Planning Technologies: Enterprise Optimization

Collaborative design and versioning applications are enabling faster, more efficient, more predictable, and more effectively tailored design development. Image asset management systems have evolved into enterprise-collaborative planning and execution systems for Advertising, Merchandising, and Promotion (AMP) processes, now with integrated predictive analytics and workflow management, from providers like Connect3 Systems. This level of technical integration will help enable better business process integration and so help give manufacturers a more consistent marketing approach across the whole marketing mix.

Payment Technologies: Merging P-O-P and POS

Changes such as self-checkout and SpeedPass™-type payment options are becoming increasingly common, both in number of stores deployed and in percent of shoppers using, demonstrating shopper willingness to adopt new technologies in order to streamline their in-store process. Biometrics has become mainstream, with shoppers using their thumbprints as payment ID and even as frequent shopper loyalty cards. Cell phones are also becoming payment devices. As customer payment options grow, especially through the utilization of wireless communication devices, the traditional delineation between the tender-oriented focus of traditional POS and the merchandising-oriented focus of traditional P-O-P may blur—or it may sharpen into a hybrid of the two: a consumer-oriented point-of-response, strikingly similar to online retailing in which selection of products and tender of payment are accomplished at the same place and virtually the same time, like the final example, Amazon's Kindle.

Exhibit Z: Amazon blurs the boundary

As this chapter is being written, Amazon, an indisputable leader in online retail technology, has just launched Kindle, their e-reader which combines electronic paper by E Ink with high-speed wireless communication technology used in smart phones, to essentially 'virtualize' retail. The Kindle user becomes, in real time, the Point-Of-Purchase, Point-Of-Sale, and Point-Of-Consumption – in this case for content for the book. While retailers have been struggling with channel blurring between different classes of trade, Amazon's Kindle has just blurred the boundary of 'clicks v. bricks' that hitherto defined the 'online' and 'offline' retail worlds. You don't have to be on an internet-connected computer; you don't have to be in a book store. While reading one book, no matter where you are, you can – within one minute – acquire virtually any other book (or newspaper, magazine or blog)…for less money than you would spend buying a physical book.

Is this the model of all retail for the future? Fortunately, no – but it is another signpost on a dynamically changing landscape. Is this relevant to the Marketing at-Retail industry? Unfortunately, yes, because, like the internet shopping experience in general, it continues to raise the bar on experiential marketing, making it more difficult to effectively engage shoppers with the traditional at-retail displays.

TECHNOLOGY EVALUATION: KEY TAKE-AWAYS

In conclusion, one last argument for the importance of the three key tests deserves mention. Virtually any company has three groups of people to please: customers, employees, and shareholders. The three proposed tests align closely to those groups:

- The People Test focuses on satisfied, loyal customers,
- The Pull Test looks toward productive, unhampered employees, and
- The Payback Test is directed at ensuring happy, well-rewarded shareholders.

Although numerous other considerations may be made, a poor evaluation in any of these three key areas is likely to result in problems and disappointments.

Finally, this chapter would be incomplete without noting that all of these technologies will add to P-O-P's slice of the pie. Well-designed, well-implemented, technology-based solutions will continue to be a source of process improvement, positive customer differentiation, and competitive advantage. As these technologies continue to enable point-of-purchase advertising to mature into an even more viable and cost-effective media, forward-thinking companies will continue to reap the rewards.

ENDNOTES

[1] Information Resources Inc., 2007, "Shopping Trip Missions: A New Avenue for Growth"

[2] Wharton, University of Pennsylvania, and Verde Group, 2006, "The Retail Customer Dissatisfaction Study"

[3] AMR Research, 2007, "Retail Software Market Sizing Report"

9

Trade Practices and Intellectual Property

Paul W. Reidl
Attorney-at-Law
Modesto, California[1]

OVERVIEW

This Chapter examines the rules, laws and regulatory principles that apply to point-of-purchase ("P-O-P") advertising. It is written for business people, legal assistants, and attorneys with limited experience in this area. Because specific rules vary from state-to-state and country-to-country, it is always prudent to consult with an experienced lawyer. Nothing in this Chapter is intended to be, nor should be construed as, legal advice.

TRADE PRACTICES

"Trade practices" are the specific legal rules, customs, and industry codes of conduct that govern advertising media, whether broadcast, print, outdoor, or P-O-P materials. Compliance with these trade practices can be compulsory (i.e., statutory rules and regulations) or voluntary (i.e., industry codes of conduct and recommended "best practices"). Note that while the Internet is largely unregulated, it is good practice to apply the trade practices rules of the "bricks and mortar" world to Internet advertising, as applicable.

Legal Restrictions

All countries have laws and regulations governing advertising. Some of these are general rules that apply to all advertising. For example, some countries ban or severely restrict "comparative advertising," i.e., advertising that mentions a competitor and compares the products being promoted directly to the competitor's product. Other rules are specific to a particular industry. For example, in some countries it is illegal to promote tobacco products, alcoholic beverages, or pharmaceuticals. Others place conditions on the manner in which the products are promoted. For example, in the United States it is lawful to do certain promotions for tobacco products, but they must contain the mandatory government health warning. Someone who is involved in distributing P-O-P materials should familiarize themselves with the laws of each country in which the P-O-P materials are to be distributed.

In the United States, both federal and state governments have laws that govern trade practices – and both can apply to the same P-O-P piece. These laws typically provide both a public and a private remedy. A public remedy is one in which the government can take action against the distributor of the promotional piece. The federal agencies responsible for enforcing these laws are the Federal Trade Commission and the United States Department of Justice. The comparable state agencies are usually the state's Attorney General's office or consumer protection office. The actions could range from a letter of inquiry to a civil enforcement action.

Private remedies are those sought by a competitor or by a consumer. These are legal actions brought under various federal or state unfair competition laws. For example, a competitor could bring a false advertising claim under Section 43(a) of the Federal Lanham Act. A consumer could also bring a cause of action under various state consumer protection laws such as the Connecticut Unfair Trade Practices Act. The available remedies vary by jurisdiction, but generally include damages and/or injunctive relief.

Trade Association Codes

Industry trade practices codes are developed and maintained by the various trade associations, such as the American Association of Advertising Agencies, the National Association of Broadcasters, and Point-Of-Purchase Advertising International ("POPAI"). They also can be developed by trade associations for a specific industry, such as the Distilled Spirits Council of the United States (spirits) or the Beer Institute (beer.)

These industry trade practices codes are a form of self-governance for the industry and the profession. Although there is no direct financial penalty for non-compliance with these codes, a member company that finds itself in violation of its association's code of conduct may find itself censured by that association. The censure could include the following: (1) loss of certain membership benefits for a specified period of time, for example, voting rights, committee privileges, and trade show exhibition rights; and (2) notice in the media — including industry publications — of the violation. Some trade associations have internal committees that review complaints about a member's advertising and publish the results. Some also offer a mediation or dispute resolution service to resolve complaints between members about a particular claim in a piece (e.g., a claim that "four out of five doctors recommend brand x").

For these reasons, someone who is involved in creating or distributing P-O-P materials should familiarize themselves thoroughly with their industry's code of conduct as well as that of any trade association in which their company or client is a member.

Point-Of-Purchase Advertising Trade Association

The P-O-P advertising industry's professional association is Point-Of-Purchase Advertising International, headquartered in Alexandria, VA. Founded in 1936, POPAI is one of thousands of trade associations located in the metropolitan Washington area.

Like many trade associations, one of POPAI's stated goals is to serve as an advocate for its particular industry while promoting the highest level of professionalism within that industry. POPAI's elected leaders and professional staff often serve as resources for government agencies and congressional committees. Continuing education programs for its members, including a formal Certified Point-of-Purchase Professional ("CPP") program, are an example of the association's commitment to higher professional standards.

POPAI has established industry ethics and expects its members to comply with the following standards:

- Abide by all federal and state laws while maintaining the highest level of integrity and honesty;
- Communicate clearly and comprehensively all relevant company policies prior to entering into a business relationship, including pricing and ownership issues; and
- Possess awareness of and adhere to P-O-P industry trade practices and standards as issued by POPAI.

POPAI maintains a number of committees and task forces that meet throughout the year, including one that deals solely with trade practices and intellectual property.

INTELLECTUAL PROPERTY

The term "intellectual property" generally refers to rights owned by an individual in something that they created. In general, there are five kinds of intellectual property rights: copyright, trademark, a right of publicity/privacy, patent, and trade secret. Since advertising materials and P-O-P materials are, by definition, things that have been created, they are fraught with intellectual property issues.

Intellectual property is, for the most part, a privately-held right.[2] This means that while government agencies may grant or affirm an individual's rights, the government does not enforce them on behalf of the owner.[3] Instead, the owner must enforce its rights by bringing a lawsuit against those who use their intellectual property without permission. This is called an "infringement" action. As a remedy, the owner of the intellectual property right can obtain an injunction (i.e., a court order prohibiting the further use of the offending piece) and/or monetary damages. In the United States, it may be possible in exceptional cases (such as deliberate infringement) for the plaintiff to obtain enhanced damages (i.e., a multiple of the original damages award) and reimbursement for the attorneys fees incurred in bringing the action.

Most intellectual property rights are "territorial," i.e., they are defined by the laws of each country. The owner of the rights must affirmatively establish its rights in each particular country, and its ability to enforce those rights will depend on the law of each particular country. Thus, the person distributing the P-O-P piece must understand the legal situation in each country in which it is to be distributed.

While a P-O-P piece inherently constitutes at least in part a work protected by copyright, it may also implicate trademark rights (if it promotes a specific brand), patent rights (if it uses a specific kind of display stand, equipment, or design), and rights of publicity and privacy (if the piece features the likeness and image of a person). The publisher of a piece should consult with knowledgeable legal counsel and understand the ramifications of each of these before publishing the piece.

Each of the various types of intellectual property is discussed below in more detail.

Copyright

General

Copyright law protects the creative expression of ideas. Copyright is a form of protection provided by the laws of the various countries, including the United States, to the authors of "original works of authorship," including pictorial, graphic, and sculptural works. It is also governed by an international treaty. This protection is available to both published and unpublished works.

In the United States, Section 106 of the Copyright Act of 1976 generally gives the owner of copyright the exclusive right to do, and authorize others to do, the following:

1. To reproduce the copyrighted work in copies or digitally;
2. To prepare derivative works based upon the copyrighted work;
3. To distribute copies or digitizations of the copyrighted work to the public by sale or other transfer of ownership, or by rental, lease, or lending;
4. In the case of literary, musical, dramatic and choreographed works, pantomimes, and motion pictures, and other audiovisual works, to perform the copyrighted work publicly;
5. In the case of literary, musical, dramatic, and choreographic works, pantomimes, and pictorial, graphic, or sculptural works, including the individual images of a motion picture or other audiovisual work, to display the work publicly; and
6. In the case of sound recordings, to perform the copyrighted work publicly by means of a digital audio transmission.

The following categories of works are protected by copyright in the United States:

1. Literary works;
2. Musical works, including any accompanying words;
3. Dramatic works, including any accompanying music;
4. Pantomimes and choreographic works;
5. Pictorial, graphic, and sculptural works;
6. Motion pictures and other audiovisual works;
7. Sound recordings; and
8. Architectural works

These categories should be viewed broadly. For example, computer programs and most "compilations" may be registered as "literary works;" maps and architectural plans may be registered as "pictorial, graphic, and sculptural works." P-O-P advertising is obviously covered in the above descriptions and includes not only sketches and designs of point-of-purchase materials, but models and prototypes as well.

The author of a work automatically owns a copyright in it the moment it is created. The author is entitled to put the © copyright symbol and the date of creation on it, e.g., "© 2007, Jane Doe. All Rights Reserved." If a work is subsequently modified slightly, the author's rights relate back to the date of the original creation and the copyright line should reflect this.

A work not made for hire (see below) is normally protected by copyright for the life of the author plus 70 years. This means that the author and his heirs have the exclusive right to prevent others from using the work, in whole or in substantial part.[4] It also means that at the expiration of the copyright the work enters the "public domain" and can be used by anyone. Thus, for example, Leonardo Da Vinci's famous "Mona Lisa" painting could be used by anyone because Da Vinci died nearly 500 years ago.[5]

An author is not required to obtain a registration of the copyright from the Library of Congress Copyright Office. Self-designation is sufficient for giving public notice of the claim of authorship. However, a registration is required in order to bring an infringement action. From an international standpoint, a registration in the country-of-origin is required in order to assert rights under the relevant treaty and corresponding national law.

Many designers and artists will use previously published works as "inspiration" for their designs. The laws recognize that designers and artists do not work in a vacuum and there is nothing inherently wrong with this practice. It is fraught with risk, however, because the copyright laws prohibit a third party from using a work that has been derived substantially from a work protected by copyright. Determining what is permitted and what is not often requires a qualified lawyer to draw fine distinctions. A savvy brand marketer who hires a third party to create a work should require a written warranty that the work is "original" to the author as well as an indemnification against costs and attorneys fees for any claimed breach of that warranty.

Work for Hire

The laws of the United States recognize that, under some circumstances, the actual owner of the work may not be its original author. This is called the "work for hire" or "work made for hire" doctrine. A work for hire is described in Section 101 of the Copyright Act as: (1) "a work prepared by an employee within the scope of his or her employment;" or (2) "a work specially ordered or commissioned for use as a contribution to a collective work, as a part of a motion picture or other audiovisual work, as a sound recording, as a translation, as a supplementary work, as a compilation, as an instructional text, as a test, as answer material for a test, or as an atlas, if the parties expressly agree in a written instrument signed by them that the work shall be considered a work made for hire." When a work is made for hire, the person for whom the work was prepared is the owner of the copyright.

The term of copyright protection for a work made for hire is 95 years from the date of publication or 120 years from the date of creation, whichever expires first.

Essentially, this doctrine recognizes the modern commercial reality that companies create and manufacture promotional materials in a variety of ways. Some companies have their own in-house design staffs and others use outside, independent contract designers.

The application of the work made for hire doctrine has important legal consequences. Many brand marketers mistakenly believe that when they hire a non-employee to design P-O-P materials the ownership of that design automatically belongs to the brand marketer. This is incorrect. The ownership of the copyright belongs to the designer (author) of the P-O-P materials unless the brand marketer has obtained a written agreement that assigns ownership to the brand marketer.

The work made for hire doctrine is a creature of United States law. It is not widely applied in other countries. In most countries the copyright in the work will remain with the author, even if the author is an employee, unless assigned by agreement to the brand marketer.

Further information on copyright law can be obtained from the Copyright Office of the Library of Congress, www.loc.gov/copyright.

Trademarks

A trademark is a word, phrase, symbol, or design, or combination of words, phrases, symbols, or designs, that identifies and distinguishes the source of the goods and services. Trademarks are commonly referred to as brand names or logos. Examples of trademarks include fanciful words (XEROX), common terms used in an uncommon way (APPLE for computers), surnames (GALLO), slogans ("Just do it!"), designs (the NIKE "swoosh" symbol), and some kinds of ornamentation (the Mercedes-Benz hood ornament.)

Not all terms can become trademarks, however. Terms that are "generic," such as "vino" for wine or "gin" for spirits can be used by anyone on those goods. Similarly, terms that describe a characteristic of the goods generally do not function as trademarks. Examples include "red" for red wine or "dark" for beer.

The overall shape, "look and feel," or "get up" of the goods can also function as an identifier of source. This is referred to as "trade dress." An example of protectable trade dress might be the "get up" of a McDonald's restaurant. Like trademarks, trade dress is not protectable if it is generic (an ordinary Bordeaux wine bottle with a leaf on the label) or functional (the shape of a handle on a piece of luggage).

Trademarks are territorial in the strictest sense of the word. The owner of the trademark must affirmatively establish its rights in each country of interest. There are two basic ways to establish rights. In the vast majority of countries, rights can be established only by obtaining a registration from the national trademark office. These countries apply a "first to file" rule, i.e., rights are awarded to the first person who applies for the rights and satisfies all of the requirements for a registration.

The second way to establish trademark rights is the "first to use" rule. This is followed in most of the English common law countries, including the United States. In these countries the rights go to the person who first uses the trademark in that country – at least in the geographic area in which the trademark was used. The registration of the trademark merely affirms the rights and makes them national.[6]

A person who claims trademark rights in a word or symbol may use a TM subscript or superscript adjacent to it. This reflects merely that the person claims that the word or symbol is a trademark. The person is entitled to use the ® subscript or superscript for the trademark only after it has been registered.

In most countries, the initial term of a trademark registration is 10 years. It can be renewed an infinite number of times, even though the trademark has never been used in that country. In the United States and several other countries, however, a trademark registration may be maintained only if the owner demonstrates use of the mark at regular intervals, such as at the time of renewal. The laws of most countries allow interested third parties to petition the trademark office to "cancel" a registration on proof that the trademark has not been used in that country for a prescribed period of years (typically three or five consecutive years).

Most companies have a lawyer "clear" a potential trademark prior to its use in each country. This process involves a review of the trademark registry(ies) and other materials to determine whether anyone is using an identical or similar mark on identical or similar goods. If a third party such as an advertising agency or consultant is retained by a brand marketer to develop a new trademark or logo, the parties should have a written agreement that specifies which party is responsible for the clearance process. Such agreements should contain an indemnification provision against costs and attorneys fees incurred in the event of an infringement claim.

Further information on trademarks can be obtained from the United States Patent and Trademark Office, www.uspto.gov/main/trademarks.htm, or the International Trademark Association, www.inta.org.

Rights of Publicity and Privacy

Most countries and some states in the United States have laws that protect a person's rights in their name, likeness, and image. These laws prohibit a third party from using a person's name, likeness, or image to promote goods or services without first obtaining permission. Some of these laws apply only to living individuals; others also apply to deceased celebrities.[7]

Thus, a brand marketer who uses a living person's name, likeness, and image in a P-O-P piece must make sure that there is written permission. If the individual is a deceased celebrity, the brand marketer must make sure the P-O-P piece is not distributed in a jurisdiction that gives the celebrity's heirs a cause of action for unauthorized use.

A written permission should cover the period of time that the P-O-P piece will be used and each country in which it will be used. As with works protected by copyright, a savvy brand marketer that hires a third party to prepare a P-O-P piece will require a written warranty that appropriate permissions have been obtained and an indemnification against costs and attorneys fees for a claimed breach of that warranty.

Patents

Whereas copyright law protects the expression of ideas, patent law protects ideas themselves. All countries recognize protection for such "inventions." If an inventor can demonstrate that its invention is useful, novel, and non-obvious over the existing art, then it is entitled to a "patent" on the claimed invention. The patent gives the inventor the exclusive right to practice the invention for a fixed period of years. Unlike trademarks, the patent does not have to be used during its term.

A patent is, in effect, a contract between an inventor and a government. In return for disclosing everything the inventor knows about its invention in its patent application, the government gives the inventor the exclusive right to practice the invention for a fixed period of years. Thereafter, the invention enters the "public domain" and can be practiced by anyone.

Like trademarks, patents are territorial in the strictest sense of the word. In order to protect an invention in a country, the inventor must obtain a patent in that country. There are complex legal requirements for filing global patent applications. A treaty administered by the World Intellectual Property Organization facilitates such filings.

The territoriality concept can have important practical consequences. If an inventor seeks and obtains patent protection in only one country of the world, its competitors can freely practice the invention in every other country because the inventor's patent does not apply there. The only way for an inventor to have stopped its competitors in those countries was to have filed patent applications and obtained patent protection there.[8]

In the United States, a designer may also obtain a "design patent" for new, original, and ornamental designs for an article of manufacture. The objective of a design patent protection is to encourage the decorative arts by giving certain new, original, and ornamental appearances to an article of manufacture to enhance its commercial value and increase demand for it.[9]

There is a relationship between trade dress protection and patent protection in the United States. Trade dress protection may cover the same designs as patent protection, but trade dress protection is not for a fixed period of years; it can continue into perpetuity, provided the trade dress continues to be registered or used. The Supreme Court has decided, however, that in almost all cases the holder of a patent cannot enjoy the protections of trademark or trade dress law for the invention after the expiration of the patent unless the portion of the invention that constitutes the claimed trademark is non-functional.[10] The determination of what is functional and what is not can be made only by an intellectual property lawyer.

There is no "work for hire" concept in patent law. Inventions are always owned by the inventor and, in the United States, must always be filed in the name of the inventor. Subsequently, the invention can be assigned to a third party. An employer must make sure that there is a written agreement that requires the employee to assign the rights to any inventions to the employer. Similarly, the designer or developer of a P-O-P piece will own any patent rights arising from their work unless there is a written agreement with the brand marketer that requires the assignment of those rights.

Further information on patents and patent law can be found on the web site of the United States Patent and Trademark Office, www.uspto.gov/main/patent.htm.

Trade Secrets

A trade secret is competitively sensitive business information that is generated and maintained in confidence. A trade secret may be a process, technique, program, device, pattern, formula, or compilation. Generally known information, when uniquely combined with confidential business information, can also qualify as a trade secret.

As long as a trade secret truly remains a secret, the owner has the exclusive right to use or sell it. If the trade secret is discovered through "proper means," including reverse engineering, the trade secret loses its protection. Confidentiality agreements are generally used to ensure that trade secrets stay secret. Perhaps the best example of a trade secret is the formula for Coca-Cola.

There is a tension between patent protection and trade secret protection. Both cover competitively sensitive business information. A trade secret is protected forever as long as it is kept secret. Because patent applications eventually become public documents, an inventor who seeks a patent is making an irrevocable decision to disclose the invention and the best mode of practicing it to the public in return for the benefits of having the exclusive right to practice it for a fixed period of years. For example, the active ingredient in BOTOX was publicly disclosed by the inventor in its patent application. Every pharmaceutical company now knows what it is and how to make it, but they cannot lawfully do so because they would be sued for patent infringement. At the end of the term of the patent, however, the invention will pass into the public domain and anyone can make and use the active ingredient.

As might be suspected, marketers will, if possible, sell the patented product under a brand name such as BOTOX, which can be used before and after the patent expires. Thus, while a third party could sell a product containing the active ingredient in BOTOX after the patent expired, they could not use the trademark BOTOX to describe or market the product.

POPAI's Role in Protecting Intellectual Property

In 1997, POPAI produced the first edition of the "Point-of-Purchase Advertising Industry Standards of Practice Manual," which was updated in 2001. The manual was produced not only for association members, but also for nonmembers, since many producers/suppliers, brand marketers, and retailers are unfamiliar with the laws that define intellectual property. Copies have also been shared with other advertising, marketing, and retail trade associations.

POPAI assists members in protecting their intellectual property in several additional ways. For example, POPAI has developed "spec label" language serving to educate business partners on both sides of the producer/client equation, about which a company asserts ownership over the particular design in question. Obtainable from the "Members Only" section of www.popai.com, this language can be downloaded and affixed to a proprietary design and serve to educate the reviewing party on the participating company's assertion of ownership.

Another example of POPAI's work to assist members in protecting intellectual property is the establishment of POPAI's Intellectual Property ("IP") Registry located on www.popai.com. The IP Registry serves as a repository for proprietary designs. Any company wishing to protect proprietary designs that they own can register a design in the IP Registry where the design's image will be both time- and date-stamped. In the event that there is a subsequent dispute over ownership of the design, the registering company can download the image from the IP Registry—complete with the date and time at which the design had been registered—thus being able to demonstrate the company's original assertion of ownership.

Over the years the POPAI Intellectual Property Committee has met with the United States Justice Department, the United States Patent and Trademark Office, the United States Copyright Office, and with federal and state officials familiar with trade practices and intellectual property issues. The purpose of these meetings has been: (1) for POPAI officials to understand clearly the different jurisdictions between these government agencies, as well as the differences between a patent, copyright, and trademark; and (2) for government officials to better understand why the registration of P-O-P advertising intellectual property is important.

The "Point of Purchase Advertising Standards of Practice Manual" is also a good resource. A copy of the United States manual is included on the CD-ROM that accompanies this book. Individuals wishing to obtain a copy of manuals developed by chapters in other countries can do so by contacting www.popai.com.

ALLOCATING RISK AND RESPONSIBILITY

As explored above, there are many different kinds of trade practices and intellectual property issues involved in the preparation and distribution of P-O-P materials. The easiest, quickest, fastest – and most irresponsible – way to address these issues is to ignore them. This simply postpones their resolution until a time when there is a live issue on the table, such as an infringement claim, which is the worst time to start thinking about allocating responsibility and risk. While P-O-P producer sales personnel are understandably reluctant to address these sensitive issues too early in the process for fear of upsetting the client, it is far better to address these issues sooner rather than later.

The smartest way to handle these issues is to anticipate them before they arise, preferably at the outset of the professional relationship. To this end, the producer, designer, and brand marketer should develop a written agreement that clearly establishes the parameters under which the work will be done. This agreement should include provisions that address:

- Responsibility for understanding the trade practices rules in each country of interest;
- Responsibility for compliance with the relevant trade association codes;
- Ownership of the copyright in the works produced;
- Responsibility for registration of the copyright for the works produced;
- Responsibility for clearing and registering the trademarks and trade dress used on the works produced;
- Ownership of any patents arising from the works produced;
- Responsibility for registration of the patents for the works produced;
- A confidentiality provision;
- Responsibility for securing any necessary permissions for the names, likenesses, or images used on the works produced;
- Appropriate warranties;
- Appropriate indemnification provisions for a breach of a warranty; and
- Responsibility for enforcing the rights in the works produced.

There is no "one size fits all" agreement. The parties are free to allocate risk and responsibility as they see fit. The parties who take the time to address these sensitive issues at the outset of their relationship will always be better off when issues arise than those who do not.

HYPOTHETICALS

The following hypotheticals examine the kinds of issues that can be raised in this area. There are no right or wrong answers.

Hypothetical 1

Company A is a long-time client of your design firm. A brand marketer with Company A, fresh out of business school, asks for your help on a new brand of potato chips product called PATRIOTS that will be launched nationally in January. The brand marketer tells you that the chips are made from "authentic Idaho potatoes grown in Mexico." She wants to leverage the launch of the brand with the Super Bowl, and she asks you to design a mass display with a Super Bowl theme. She wants the display to depict the Lombardi Trophy, a photo of Vince Lombardi, logos of the AFC and the NFC, and the tag line: "It's the real thing!" What are the issues?

Discussion

Since Company A is a client of your firm, the first thing you should do is to check your agreement to determine who is responsible for dealing with the issues. Then you should discuss the issues with the brand marketer. They are, in no particular order:

1. The terms SUPER BOWL, LOMBARDI TROPHY, and the AFC and NFC logos are trademarks of the National Football League. They cannot be used without the league's permission. Who is responsible for getting this? What is Company A willing to pay for this license?

2. The likeness and image of Vince Lombardi is that of a deceased individual who was a celebrity at the time of his death. Since this is a national program, you will need the permission of his estate in order to use his likeness and image. Who is responsible for getting this? What is Company A willing to pay for this consent?

3. The concept of "authentic Idaho potatoes grown in Mexico" is troubling because it is arguably misleading. How can Idaho potatoes be "authentic" if they are not grown in Idaho? This raises trade practices issues. Is this consistent with your trade association code of conduct and suggested best practices? Is there a risk of being sued for false advertising by a trade association of Idaho potato growers?

4. The tag line, "It's the real thing" is a well-known tag line used by Coca-Cola. Would use of this tag line constitute copyright infringement or trademark infringement? Who is responsible for determining this?

5. The trademark PATRIOTS is also the name of the NFL team from Boston. Would use of this trademark constitute trademark infringement? Who is responsible for determining this?

6. Assume you raise these issues with the brand marketer. She tells you that permissions are unnecessary and she orders you to do as she says or she will take the business elsewhere. What do you do?

HYPOTHETICAL 2

This is a variation on the first hypothetical. Assume that under the agreement with the brand marketer you are responsible for obtaining all of the permissions. There is a warranty and indemnification provision. You think you have obtained all of the consents for your client's SUPER BOWL program; you are assured by the brand marketer that the trademarks are cleared and the display is designed and sent out to stores. You get a fax from the brand marketer consisting of a complaint filed by the estate of Vince Lombardi in Superior Court for San Francisco County, California, demanding $1,000,000 in damages for the use of his likeness and image without his permission. You investigate and learn that the person responsible for obtaining the permission of the Lombardi estate had dropped the ball and, in fact, there was no permission. What do you do?

Discussion

Unfortunately, mistake, reasonable good faith effort, or the absence of bad intent are not defenses to an intellectual property claim. Since California has a very tough statute protecting the likenesses and images of people who were celebrities at the time of their death, and since Vince Lombardi was fairly well-known at the time of his death, this is a serious legal problem. Since you warranted that you had obtained the permission and agreed to indemnify the brand marketer in the event of a breach of that warranty, you should refer the matter to your insurance carrier.

HYPOTHETICAL 3

Brand marketer B is a global company. P-O-P Supplier A sees a display in the United Kingdom that has been developed and produced by a competitor, P-O-P Supplier B. The display is a unique design that incorporates various multimedia and Internet services that provide on-demand information to the consumer about the product from the web site of Brand marketer B. Sensing a business opportunity, P-O-P Supplier A approaches Brand marketer B and offers to make an identical display in the United States. Brand marketer B has not used the display in the United States, but it knows that P-O-P Supplier B has applied for a patent in the United Kingdom. It likes the price quoted by Supplier A and tentatively agrees to negotiate a national agreement with P-O-P Supplier A to provide the displays in the United States only. You are an employee of Brand marketer B and are asked to work with P-O-P Supplier A on the agreement. What are the issues?

Discussion

You first need to identify and review the agreement with P-O-P Supplier B. If the agreement assigns all rights in the display to Brand marketer B and it is non-exclusive, then you are free to do business with P-O-P Supplier A. If there is no agreement, you should consider the following issues before moving forward:

1. A patent application in the United Kingdom does not cover the United States because patent rights are territorial. It is possible, however, that P-O-P Supplier B filed a patent application in the United States. If so, and if the patent is issued, the use of the display would infringe on the rights of P-O-P Supplier B. You should consult with counsel on whether there is a way to minimize the risk.

2. The multimedia content being used on the display originates from your web site, so you probably have permissions to use it to promote your products. This should be verified internally.

3. Because there is no written assignment of the copyright, P-O-P Supplier B owns the copyright in the display. Absent an agreement, you do not have the right to reproduce it.

HYPOTHETICAL 4

P-O-P Supplier A makes a proposal to a brand marketer for a comprehensive national campaign in the United States for a new product. This proposal includes displays that were developed by P-O-P Supplier A for the brand marketer and this program. It also includes merchandising equipment proprietary to P-O-P Supplier A. The brand marketer agrees to the proposal, incorporates it into the brand promotional plan, and directs its field sales team to start selling it into stores. He signs a written agreement with P-O-P Supplier A that gives them the exclusive rights to produce the displays. A retailer reviews the brand marketer's proposal and loves it, but the buyer's brother-in-law runs his own P-O-P company and the retailer wants him to produce the displays or he will not accept the proposal. The retailer's brother-in-law calls his counterpart at P-O-P Supplier A to brag about the new business and tells him that he and the retailer intend to drive him out of business.

Discussion

This is an easy one. The brand marketer cannot honor the retailer's request without breaching the agreement with P-O-P Supplier A.

But assume that the brand marketer did not have a written, exclusive agreement, and that the displays and equipment were simply purchased and paid for as invoiced. Would the result be any different? Consider the following:

1. P-O-P Supplier A developed the displays for the brand marketer's program in the United States. Does this make it a work made for hire such that the brand marketer would own the copyright in the work? Not unless there is a written agreement that either designates it as such and/or assigns the rights to the brand marketer. If there is no written agreement, P-O-P Supplier A owns the copyright and the display cannot be reproduced without its permission.

2. The equipment was "proprietary." What does this mean? If it is not covered by one or more patents, it could be reverse engineered by the retailer's brother-in-law.

3. Is there a trade practices issue with the retailer having his brother-in-law make the displays? An ethical issue? Are either of these a concern of the brand marketer? P-O-P Supplier A? P-O-P Supplier B? The retailer?

4. Is there a trade practices issue arising from the brother-in-law's braggadocio toward P-O-P Supplier A? That depends on whether the retailer and his brother-in-law actually have the power to drive P-O-P Supplier A out of business and have taken steps to do it. Based on the facts, this appears to be nothing more than rough and tumble lawful competition.

From a business standpoint the hypothetical raises significant business issues for the brand marketer because accommodating the retailer's request risks the ongoing business relationship with P-O-P Supplier A, and refusing the request risks the ongoing relationship with the retailer.

HYPOTHETICAL 5

A brand marketer in the United States commissions a design from P-O-S Supplier A and obtains a bid from P-O-P Supplier A. It pays for the design. The brand marketer is shocked at the amount of the bid and shops it to competitors of P-O-P Supplier A. One of the bids is significantly lower than the initial bid. The brand marketer takes the low bid to P-O-P Supplier A and demands that it do the job for the lower price. What result?

Discussion

1. While P-O-P Supplier A may decide for business reasons to produce the display at the lowest-priced bid, it is under no legal obligation to do so.

2. Could the brand marketer have given the project to the low bidder? Under the hypothetical, the answer would be "no" because there is no agreement recognizing this as a work made for hire and/or assigning the copyright to the brand marketer. P-O-P Supplier A still owns the copyright in the design and it can not be used by the brand marketer without permission.

3. What if the brand marketer had a confidentiality agreement with P-O-P Supplier A? Could it have solicited bids from other P-O-P Suppliers? If the design was "confidential" under the confidentiality agreement, disclosing it to third parties would have been a breach of that agreement.

ENDNOTES

[1] The author is a 1980 graduate of The George Washington University Law School, a member of the State Bar of California, and a former President and Chair of the Board of Directors of the International Trademark Association. This Chapter is adapted from a Chapter originally authored by David W. Schultz, Past Chairman, POPAI.

[2] An example of a quasi-governmental, publicly-held right might be a geographic indication, i.e., a term with a unique goods-place association such as Napa Valley (for wine), Parma (for hams and processed meats), or Feta (for a type of cheese from Greece.)

[3] Of course, a government can own and enforce its own intellectual property rights. For example, the University of California holds many patents and aggressively enforces them. Colleges and universities own thousands of trademarks related to their athletics programs (e.g., the University of Texas "Longhorn" word mark and "Longhorn" logo.) These are also aggressively enforced.

[4] There are statutory exceptions that are not relevant here, such as for news reporting, where a third party may use a work without the permission of the copyright holder.

[5] It is possible to convert a work in the public domain into a trademark for goods or services through use or registration. For example, a cigar company that adopted a MONA LISA and design trademark for cigars could prevent others from using the name and design on cigars in the geographic area in which it had trademark rights.

[6] Although the United States allows the filing of an "intent to use" application, a trademark registration cannot be issued until the applicant demonstrates that it has used the mark in commerce in the United States.

[7] The State of California provides strong protection for deceased celebrities. The licensing of the names and images of deceased celebrities (e.g., Marilyn Monroe, James Dean, and Elvis Presley) is a very lucrative business for their heirs.

[8] The inventor's dilemma is compounded because the laws in most countries require patent applications to be filed before the invention is first disclosed to the public. Thus, unlike trademark or copyright law, the inventor cannot wait and see whether the invention is a commercial success before formally seeking rights in multiple countries. Instead, the filing decision must be made before the product is even on the market.

[9] The European Union also provides protection for unique designs. This is known as the "Community Design" registration.

[10] The specific case involved the shape of a stand for holding a type of traffic sign. The owner of the expired patent claimed that the shape of the stand was distinctive and functioned as an indicator of source, i.e., a trademark. The Court ruled that because the shape was functional (it was claimed in the patent as part of the novel design,) the policy behind the patent laws trumped the trademark laws and, therefore, the shape had irretrievably entered the public domain.

10

Global Trends in Marketing at-Retail

Robert Liljenwall
The Liljenwall Group

GLOBAL TRENDS IN MARKETING AT-RETAIL

If you could travel to the world capitals and visit the leading shopping centers and retailers, the one conclusion you would immediately reach is this: They all look the same. They feature many, if not most, of the world's most popular brands. The centers and retail designs reflect a sophistication that you are used to seeing anywhere in the United States. You are struck by the wide use of LCD screens throughout the center. The signage and point-of-sale displays look disarmingly similar to those back home. There is a seamless transition between old and new, and you realize – as a marketing professional – that the world has "caught up". Globalization hits home.

Regardless of whether you are in Dubai, Bangkok, Mexico City, London, or Los Angeles, the challenges, however, remain the same: extracting money from customer wallets. That is the goal, isn't it? It is not so much a matter of putting product on the shelf as it is getting it off the shelf. We call it sell-through.

The challenge has not changed wherever you are – marketing at-retail has become the battleground to win the hearts and wallets of consumers. The Marketing at-Retail industry is a $30 billion worldwide business, growing at the rate of seven percent annually.[1] New technologies, new alliances, and aggressive retailers and brand marketers are influencing a global change in how products and goods are sold at retail. Consumers have become more sophisticated, smarter. They make their brand choices based on a wide variety of influencers, whether it is price, value, quality, brand knowledge, convenience, or "just out of habit." And "habit" (i.e., brand loyalty) is what every retailer and brand marketer is counting on: make the buying decision automatic.

Competition for the consumers' wallet has also intensified outside of the retail store. The Internet and mobile communication devices have taken on greater influence and dominance in our lives. We spend more time on the Internet than ever before. We wear our cell phones as personal body devices and hands-free and WiFi are as much a part of our day as reading the newspaper once was.

Globalization intensifies. The big retailers are getting bigger and more powerful in their globe-trotting ways. The Big Five remained the same for the past four years (since 2004) – Wal-Mart, Carrefour (France), Home Depot, Metro (Germany), and Tesco (UK). And Sears Holdings (Sears and Kmart) has re-entered the Top 10 after being absent for a decade.[2]

The global economy experienced a 60% growth rate from 2003 (2.7%) to 2005 (4.3%). What is even more impressive is that over the last 10 years, developing economies have grown faster than in any period since 1965 – even faster since 2000 according to the World Bank. While the global picture is dominated by developing countries such as Brazil, China, India, Russia, and South Africa, more are doing well and suffering less, thereby raising the average growth rates.[3]

What is amazing to witness is how 'developing countries' (with oil resources especially) are changing the global stage, especially in Dubai. Dubai has already laid claim to one of the world's most important business centers with its incredible growth and attraction of major corporate offices. Abu Dhabi, Dubai's sister emirate, is competing for world attention with a brand-buying spree unprecedented in world history – paying $520 million for a brand relationship with The Louvre and $150 million for the Guggenheim Museum. Dubai paid Tiger Woods $45 million for his first branded golf course.[4]

What is happening on this fast-moving global platform is the transference of knowledge and technology. Third-world countries – who have the resources – can hire the best architects and planners, build infrastructure, and attract business and visitors by transforming their countries with unprecedented speed. Dubai, Abu Dhabi, Kazakhstan, India, China, and Russia are examples of this rapid growth.

And nowhere is it more apparent than in the retail environment. High standards for retail environments, set throughout the developed countries such as in the United States, UK, France, and Hong Kong, for example, can be easily replicated anywhere there is a market for quality shopping environments. The major retailers follow the money. Establishing a global infrastructure to service these brands and retailers then becomes a priority.

Within this context, brand marketers, retailers, and at-retail vendors continue to face challenging tasks for servicing a demanding global market. New technologies provide user-friendly solutions, but their attendant development and implementation expenses are not always as friendly.

Global Trends

In a survey of at-retail leaders around the globe, nine significant trends were prominent in the major industrial markets of North America, Europe, and Asia. These trends reflect the volatile nature of technology, industry consolidation, and global building by retailers and brand marketers. While varying in importance and prominence from market to market, these trends reflect the fast-paced growth of all retail segments and categories. Retailers and brand marketers scramble to keep pace with competitors in the battle to win consumers who have become more sophisticated and demanding shoppers.

The nine major trends are:
- Shopper engagement
- Technology explosion – at all levels
- Global retail expansion
- Private-label growth
- Internet and social media
- Controlling the retail environment
- Outsourcing
- Improved measurement
- Partnering

All three stakeholders – retailers, brand marketers, and at-retail vendors and suppliers – are major players in each of these trends, and they must be constantly sensitive to the trends that are shaping their ability to survive. Staying competitive means staying ahead of the curve, whether it is buying smart in China or managing your business better at home. The stakeholders, as you will learn, are all under attack from competitors.

Shopper Engagement

It is all about the customer. The buzz term in retail is 'shopper engagement' – engaging the shopper at a variety of levels – experiential, self-directed, and/or staff interface. Why so? Retailers have come to realize that they are also in the entertainment business – not just to sell stuff or provide service, but to create a pleasant, engaging environment where customers feel comfortable. Where they can browse, 'try on' products, and 'hang out.' There is another term for this growing and important phenomenon that is not new: Brand loyalty -- creating customers who are so loyal to the brand that they love to just 'hang out.'

Apple has created the quintessential shopper engagement paradise where customers can 'play' with every device on display. There is the Genius Bar where technicians are at your disposal (make your online appointment) to help you fix or learn about your new Mac, iPod, or iPhone. There is a child's play area where kids have their own Mac Playroom and learn how to use real Macs! The stores are sleek, engaging, and functional. Their flagship in Manhattan, New York is open 24/7 – every day of the year. It never closes. And it is jammed all the time. The result? Apple has the highest sales per square foot in retail in the world today, more than $4,000 sq. ft.[5]

But there are other ways that retailers are engaging the shopper – from Build-A-Bear to the famous 'demo-queens' at Costco, where one can literally have lunch or dinner by just roaming around picking up samples of their latest faire at the more than 20 stands located throughout the store.

There is nothing more powerful, however, than the customer loyalty card found at supermarkets, restaurants, or casinos. These are differentiated from store credit cards (Macy's for example), in that the cards are issued to customers at no cost. In the gaming industry, where the loyalty card programs provide a wide range of potential benefits -- from free hotel rooms and meals to shows and merchandise, they become a win-win for the casino and gamer.

Harrah's International's Total Rewards program has more than 42 million card-carrying members worldwide. Approximately 8 million are active at any one time. Total Rewards' benefits are based on the amount of money wagered in any of their casinos around the world. All slot machines and table games are linked to Total Rewards; Harrah's knows exactly how much you spend (gamble), your wins and losses. And the more you gamble, the greater the benefits. By tracking customer behavior and spending, Harrah's knows who their best customers are and reward them accordingly.

Total Rewards, according to Gary Loveman, Chairman and CEO, is the prime reason they have built their global brand to the prestige level and accounted for their financial success.[6] Every major casino in the world has some type of loyalty program, which is the ultimate shopper engagement.

Technology Explosion – At All Levels

The goal of the retailer, brand marketer and at-retail vendor is to get closer to the customer, to grandualize down the selling proposition to the individual consumer so that the retailer can easily extract more money from the customer's wallet. This is accomplished by giving customers what they need and want, and that is accomplished by knowing them better through shopper engagement.

One of the continuing trends in retail technology is the development of interactive shopper systems that enable stores to get closer to customers. Utilizing a combination of touch screen and signal transmission technologies, retailers are able to connect with each customer via a "smart touch screen" located on the shopping cart. These new customer-focused systems bring together radio frequency identification (RFID), infrared (IR), WiFi, Bluetooth, and loyalty programs that utilize the data mined from the customer's previous purchases (via the loyalty club tracking programs).

Using a variety of devices either on the cart or carried by the shopper, the technologies allow the store to immediately connect with the shopper and offer discounts and promotions for the items "the customer historically purchases." All of these systems use a variety of RFID, WiFi, IR, and data mining technologies being tested.

Self-Checkout

The drive to reduce retailer costs, especially labor, has resulted in the development of self-checkout systems, to which supermarkets and big box suppliers such as Home Depot are turning. One of the systems, USCAN (developed by Magellan), is being distributed through Kroger and its U.S. subsidiaries Ralph's and Fred Meyer. The self-checkout stations are composed of scanners where customers can self-scan bar-coded products, weigh produce, and do their own bagging. For example, at a Fred Meyer store in Astoria, Oregon, one station processed 33 percent of the grocery customers, which represents 47 percent of the revenues.[7] As supermarkets strive to reduce overhead to better compete against mass merchandisers, self-checkout systems are expected to increase their penetration.

The self-checkout technology is just another example of how retailers are finding ways to get as close to the customer as possible to facilitate choice, service, and efficiency, thereby reducing the retailer's expense and improving the shopper's ability to buy cheaper and buy more.

Presentation Technology

There continues to be an influx of presentation technology into the market place at an unprecedented pace. Interactive kiosks and plasma and LCD screens are the most noticeable technologies that are seen by us all, and the trend is being rapidly adopted by retailers around the world.

This hasn't always been the case. When large LCD screens were introduced by ad-based media companies, retailers and brand marketers argued over who would pay for it. Retailers were unwilling to fork over the high cost for these brightly lit TV panels even though there were valid lift studies that proved their value (up to 160% increase in sales). This at-retail medium was a proven winner, but retailers simply didn't want to invest the money, especially for a large-store format.

Gradually, however, retailers who sought to differentiate their store environments from competitors installed the large panels throughout the store, greatly improving customer length-of-stay and increasing sales with category-specific advertising (part of the store's co-op program to pay for the equipment).

The influx of LCD screens across the world is now in full swing. It was amazing to see LCD screens in Istanbul's Grand Bazaar, the oldest shopping center in the world started in the 15th century. They featured brand advertising and English as the primary language.[8]

Retailers have also embraced the large-format printers because they can reproduce high-quality graphics for a fraction of the cost of screen printing from preset templates, making the medium easy to use at the regional or, even, store level. Carrefour (France) is the master at putting up large-format P-O-P signage throughout their stores to promote items that go on sale the very same day.

Digital signage made a big splash several years ago (E-Ink and Mag-Ink were two of the prominent players), and this technology is slowly finding a foothold in the industry with improved graphics combined with their relatively low-cost display options.

Interactive kiosks continue to penetrate the retail world, and they work well in certain business models. The business model of selling tickets or products through kiosks that are dependent on advertising revenues has not been historically successful. However, interactive kiosks that provide information to customers work extremely well, especially airport-based kiosks utilized by the airlines to dispense boarding passes and tickets.

The challenge with most presentation technologies is determining who will pay for the medium. Retailers are reluctant to share co-op dollars with outside vendors that want to install presentation technology and tout brand marketers to customers already in the store. But research has more than demonstrated that these presentation technologies, in fact, work and improve sales.

Global Retail Expansion

From a pure economic point of view, Wal-Mart continues to pull away from the field, remaining the largest, most dominating retail entity on the planet. Where Wal-Mart lacks in market penetration (currently in only 10 countries), it makes up for in raw global power—ranking as the world's second largest corporation. Wal-Mart's annual sales for FY 2006 were $315 billion, more than three times its closest competitor Carrefour (France) at $92.7 billion.[9]

The other major retailers—The Home Depot (US), Metro AG (Germany) and Tesco (UK) — continue their global penetration march. Ahold (Netherlands) has slipped out of the Top 20 and is in the process of selling off its operations.[10]

What makes Wal-Mart such a force is its drive for dictating the rules by which vendors and P-O-P suppliers must play the game to get a share of its business. They have reduced by some 60% the amount of at-retail displays in their stores and are in the process of mandating RFID tracking for their vendors, which will surely have a trickle-down effect for the rest of the retail industry, thereby spurring the integration of this identity technology.

In terms of the challenges ahead of the global retail environment, retailers and brand marketers are faced with matching the fast-growth period of 2000-2006 where retail stocks outperformed the S&P 500 by a stunning 135%. However, since then, the robust economy in Europe and in the US has slowed, and as consumers retrench and government spending grows, multi-national companies are facing receding retail sales, thus affecting their stock levels (that includes US, UK and Europe-based firms).[11] Another factor that will affect global expansion is outsourcing which is facing a backlash at home, and as a result many overseas manufacturing jobs are returning to their home country where quality and timing can be better controlled.

Private-Label Growth

Retailers have discovered the power of private labels and the added profits they bring to the bottom line. Private labels have always lured retailers because of the edge they bring in generating higher margins than national or regional brands.

Notable private-label brands such as Marks & Spencer (UK), Sam's Choice (Wal-Mart), President's Choice (Loblaw, Canada), and Kirkland (Costco) reflect the fast-expanding role private brands have in today's retail market. In the United States alone, private labels accounted for more than $51 billion in sales among supermarkets, mass merchandisers, and drug outlets in 2007. Private-label sales have been growing at a four percent annual rate according to the Private Label Manufacturers Association in just the United States.[12]

The statistics in Figure 10-1 indicate the power of private labels as tracked by Nielsen for PLMA. Advanced markets of Western Europe grew despite strong competition from the major brand marketers. Private labels account for more than one of every three products sold in the UK, Germany, France, Spain, Belgium and Switzerland.

Figure 10-1

Private-Label Market Share (percent)

United Kingdom	43%	Netherlands	22%
Belgium	42	Finland	25
Germany	39	Spain	35
United States	21	Italy	16
France	34	Sweden	28
Switzerland	53	Czech Rep.	27

Source: PMLA 2008

Retailers are devoting more space and resources to their private label programs by taking advantage of existing vendors and their learning curve. Private-label design has improved, and retailers are beginning to think like brand marketers using loyalty programs and their power of merchandising to drive customers to their in-house brands. Because retailers control the selling environment, they can effectively place their own brands in advantageous shelf positions.

Are private labels a threat to national brands? According to William Smith of Procter & Gamble and past chairman of POPAI, "If you're in the top three brands, private labels will not be the threat that they are to brands in fourth or fifth position."

The lure of increased profits will continue to drive this global trend, and the PLMA predicts that more than $55 billion in retail sales in the US will shift to private labels by 2017. That is a seismic shift for brand marketers and retailers.[13]

Internet and Social Media

Since 1995, when the first widely marketing web browser was introduced (Netscape), our world has changed dramatically. The Internet (via our computers, PDAs, and cell phones) has transformed our way of communicating, informing, educating, and most importantly, selling. For many categories, the point of sale has shifted from traditional retail stores to the Internet, especially in web-friendly categories such as computers, software, books, toys, flowers, and travel. As much as 90% of retail sales has shifted from some traditional retail channels to the online channel. This is especially true in air travel. In fact, air travelers are penalized by making a plane reservation via a 'live operator.'[14]

Retail sales on the Internet have enjoyed a 25% annual increase until 2007, when sales growth slowed down to 21% over the previous year. Consumers in the US spent more than $175 billion online, and a projected $30 billion will be added to this total every year for the next five years according to Forrester Research.[15]

Savvy retailers, who have adopted and adapted the Internet's best practices, have seen a dramatic increase in online sales. The e-tailing trend will continue as retailers learn the advantages and adapt their marketing strategies to multi-channels. One of the compelling trends has been the extensive use of search engines (key words) which have enabled retailers to intercept web surfers to attract them to their online offering. Search engine marketing is the clear leader in delivering new customers to online retailers, which was responsible for delivering 43% of the overall customers to their sites.[16]

Not only are online efforts designed to drive e-commerce sales, retailer web sites use their online presence to drive customers into the store with multi-channel promotions centered on gift cards, in-store promotions, and coupon redemptions.

On a global basis, the Internet penetration is exploding.

World Internet Usage 2007

Figure 10-2

World Region	Internet usage	% Penetration	Usage Growth
Africa	44.3 million	4.7	882.7%
Asia	510.5 million	13.7	346.7
Europe	348.1 million	43.4	231.2
Middle East	33.5 million	17.4	920.2
North America	238 million	71.1	120.2
Latin America	126 million	22.2	598.5
Australia	19.2 million	57.1	151.6

Source: Internet World Stats, 2008

What we learn from these statistics is that by the end of 2007, the average world growth of the Internet was 265.5%, with more than 1.319 billion Internet users. There is no medium in history that has achieved such phenomenal penetration, which is led by the United States, Australia/Oceania, and Europe. Asia has more than 510 million on the Internet.[17]

But the Internet also plays another important role in the point-of-purchase industry. The power of broadband enables all of the technologies we have discussed to exist and function in real time. Beyond the presentation technologies of retail television networks (e.g., LCD screens, interactive kiosks), the Internet is the data conduit that feeds the retailer's and brand marketer's thirst for instant knowledge. The Internet provides the engine to communicate with far-distance retail locations and servers that drive the information where it is needed.

Social Media

Another important trend is the growth of 'social media' – which is best described as the online technologies and practices that people use to share content, opinions, insights, experiences, perspectives and media themselves. More importantly, social media is the "me" medium of this decade. You own your own website (Myspace or Facebook) or web broadcast station (YouTube). A growing list of other 'hot' sites, such as imeem.com, lets you share music playlists. These 'personal' sites are sweeping through the younger demographics.

As this web-based world grows, entrepreneurs are learning how to use the 'Net to merchandise products and services. These social media sites become the hub of viral marketing, and as such, play a critical role in creating word of mouth and 'buzz' marketing campaigns. This trend will continue to expand as the Internet continues to grow.

The Brand Explosion

Not only has technology exploded in recent years, so have brands. Combined with the proliferation of private labels and brand marketers' accelerating market segmentation, there are new brands hitting the shelves everyday — each targeted at new or growing niche markets.

Brand marketers, armed with research generated by mining consumer buying behavior data, are creating new products to not only reach better defined niche markets but also to respond to changes in lifestyle, such as the diminished demand for high-carb foods and increased emphasis on "heart-healthy" diets. As baby boomers hit 65 (some 80 million came into retirement age in 2007), there is an increased demand for segmented new products to meet the senior needs and wants.

The brand explosion, however, is not confined to baby boomers. It is happening across a broad spectrum of categories — consumer electronics, entertainment, media, automobiles, travel, and household products.

Figure 10-3 illustrates the explosion of choice that occurred in the United States between 1970 and 2000.

Figure 10-3

Explosion of Brands in U.S. Consumer Market, 1970–2000

	1970	2000
Vehicle styles	654	1,212
Frito-Lay chips	10	78
Breakfast cereals	160	340
Radio stations	7038	12,358
Amusement parks	362	1,174

Source: Jack Trout, 2001

This chart, compiled by Jack Trout – who co-invented the brand positioning strategy with Al Ries in 2000, represents the trend that continues today. While the brand explosion has created more opportunities for the point-of-purchase industry, it has also created more communications clutter and intensifies an already competitive environment for valuable retail space. Retailers are retaliating by seeking more control over their selling place.

The shifting roles of retailers and brand marketers

One of the more notable global trends is that retailers are becoming brand marketers (creating and promoting their own brands) and brand marketers are becoming retailers. Retail has become the battleground for retailers seeking to increase profit margins by increasing private-label programs (as discussed above), and brand marketers, feeling squeezed at retail, are flexing their brand muscles by creating their own stores within earshot of existing channel supporters.

Major consumer brands such as Apple, Pioneer Electronics, and Sony have established their own signature stores, usually in upscale regional centers where they do not compete with established channels.

Pioneer Electronics, a new retail concept that features only Pioneer products—was designed to build the company's brand and feature their high-end LCD and entertainment products. The first store, located at South Coast Plaza, CA, was so successful that they are now launching similar stores across the US.[18] Like the Apple stores, Pioneer is interactive, allowing customers to sample all products.

These brand stores, of course, feature permanent and temporary P-O-P displays, each one fitting to the overall store design. Environments are tightly controlled at corporate, and there is little or no clutter.

The World's Top Brands

In the world of brands, there is constant movement of global brands that cross all borders. Interbrand, one of the world's foremost brand consultancies, tracks consumer brand preferences, and historically, major brands such as Disney, Marlboro, McDonald's and Mercedes have enjoyed premier recognition in their global brand survey. However, the last Interbrand survey released in late 2007 shows that Coca-Cola is again the world's number one brand and many of the previous top brands have slipped in the consumer poll.

Figure 10-4

Top Ten Global Brands

#1 Coca-Cola	#6 Toyota
#2 Microsoft	#7 Intel
#3 IBM	#8 McDonald's
#4 General Electric	#9 Disney
#5 Nokia	#10 Mercedes

Source: Interbrand Brand study, 2008

What this chart is telling us is that the 'major' brand marketers continue to do their job – giving customers what they want and need; delivering on their promises; staying ahead of the competition; and using their global brand power to keep the loyalty of their customers. Superior performance is the foundation for these top brands.

The Top 100 brands, as compiled by Interbrand, include many former Top 10 brands such as Apple, Marlboro, and Sony. These brand lists (interbrand.com) reflect a certain fickleness on the part of consumers, especially in the high-tech field. Apple, with only five percent market share, ranks ahead of PC leader, Dell. Apple, in particular, has carved out entire new categories – including iPod, iTunes, and iPhone – which are the market share leaders in their categories.[19]

Brands are a company's most important asset, and protecting the brand on a global basis continues to be the Number One priority for every brand marketer (and retailer). It is a difficult task – managing brands in more than 180 markets.

Controlling the Retail Environment

Retailers are no longer satisfied to give their stores over to brand marketers who want to buy their way in. Retailers across the board are installing more permanent point-of-purchase displays, while reducing the number and size of these displays to meet new design standards.

For example, Wal-Mart decided several years ago to reduce the average number of at-retail displays in its stores, which numbered approximately 700 per store on any given day. Citing the glut of displays and amount of management time to supervise this activity, Wal-Mart reduced the average number of displays to 300.[20]

When Blockbuster redesigned its stores, it converted all in-store signage to a new brand identity system and eliminated all movie displays. The company soon discovered it needed studio-provided displays to hype the latest DVD promotion, and so it allowed a limited number of displays back in to boost sales. Blockbuster also uses its at-retail displays to promote its online DVD business – Total Access – and this represents the perfect cross-promotional, cross-functional marketing program.

Movie chains, the historic centerpiece for movie P-O-P business, saw a major drop in business when theater executives decided to "clean up" their lobbies. But the perceived benefit of cleaner lobbies did not make up for the pre-release promotion provided by the often-dramatic P-O-P movie displays, and movie displays are now prominent in theaters once again.

Retailers have sought to upgrade their store designs by reducing clutter, creating more permanent fixtures and providing a branded experience. For example, Costco and Sam's Club spice up their warehouse look with demonstrations "food queens" who provide free samples of everything from cherry pie to the latest coffee.

Starbucks, with nearly 15,000 outlets worldwide, maintains a rigidly controlled selling environment that features attractive, permanent P-O-P displays, "living rooms" that feature large couches and chairs and the latest hot technology—WiFi capabilities that allow customers to access the Internet.[21] While some retailers have made efforts to reduce clutter and gain better control of their selling environments, supermarkets, super drugstores, mass merchandisers, and "big box" retailers continue to be the primary venue for P-O-P displays. Retailers with aggressive private label and loyalty programs are purchasing more P-O-P at the expense of brand marketers' desire to increase their retail presence.

Outsourcing

Perhaps the most notable global trend in the past 10 years has been the transfer of P-O-P manufacturing to China and other Asian countries. "Made in China" symbolizes the acceptance and awareness that all P-O-P manufacturers must reduce costs. Of course, this is not news to anyone in the display manufacturing business, or to anyone striving to reduce costs. The landscape, however, is littered with companies who naively moved manufacturing projects to China only to discover they made a costly mistake.

Outsourcing overseas has been the trend for the past 15 years in the United States, and many companies have established solid relationships with Chinese firms for a variety of goods and services. This trend will continue.

But in recent years, a resurgent trend has emerged with many companies in the at-retail manufacturing business. Brian McCormick, vice president, Rapid Displays, Chicago, points out that "…it is not always a given that we are going to ship a project to China or out of the country." [22]

What Rapid has discovered, painfully in some cases, is that the best-laid plans do not necessarily work out. McCormick points out that customers who have tight deadlines and require precise quality performance are candidates to keep the business 'onshore.' "We cannot afford to take chances with projects that if something could go wrong, and then it does."

According to McCormick, Rapid Display can better manage the project in-house than sometimes relying on sources outside their control. "Clients are happy when you meet deadlines, budget, and quality expectations."

Mexico and Central and South American nations, which recently saw an influx of manufacturing from the United States, Canada, and Europe, have seen jobs disappear and shipped to China and other Asian nations. Mexico has launched marketing programs to keep manufacturing in the country by offering incentives and seminars on how to compete with China.

Improved Research Performance

One of POPAI's major initiatives has been its drive toward getting point-of-purchase advertising accepted as a measured medium along with radio, television, print, the Internet, and outdoor advertising. This challenge was answered when POPAI announced the MARI (Marketing at-Retail Initiative) project, being conducted in the UK and Germany.

POPAI-sponsored research undertaken for the MARI project is designed to provide the marketing and media planner with all the tools they need to evaluate the effectiveness of the at-retail program – not just the gross rating points (GRPs).

While the results of the MARI project are being tabulated as this Edition is going to press, the project is designed to:

- Increase awareness of the medium and its value
- Include marketing at-retail advertising in media planning, forecasting, and tracking
- Make informed decisions about media alternatives and
- Increase focus on executional excellence

The results of the research will demonstrate that marketing at-retail has a measurable impact on retail sales. Retailers gain the benefit of these sales lifts in more ways than just increased sales; they do not pay for the displays and in fact often receive added promotional fees and discounts for letting the brand marketer install the display.

It is a win-win situation for both parties. Beyond these measured media studies, such as MARI and other research done by many of the POPAI chapters around the world, brand marketers and retailers are convinced now that point-of-purchase advertising is effective. Research in all countries will continue to demonstrate that point-of-purchase advertising is the one medium that works in the selling environment. Brand marketers and retailers alike rely more heavily today on pre- and post-promotion research than ever before.

Partnering

The authors have emphasized the theme throughout this book – teamwork between stakeholders (P-O-P supplier/vendor, brand marketer, and retailer) has become a necessity for all to succeed. Each stakeholder must become intimately involved in the planning, execution, and implementation process of achieving the maximum potential for every marketing-at-retail opportunity.

This is not a new trend. It's been placed in practice by every successful retailer, brand marketer, and at-retail vendor or supplier. "Partnering" is an appropriate description of what has to happen between the client and vendor, on every level.

With globalization of retailers and brand marketers, the marketing at-retail industry faces worldwide challenges in serving its clients. As a result, P-O-P vendors and advertising agencies continue to consolidate to serve this global economy.

Throughout the research for this Third Edition, the authors are unanimous in their emphasis on partnering with the customer. This transcends the retailer/brand marketing and at-retail vendor. It extends to the end-user – the customer.

In the final analysis, shopping engagement only occurs when the shopper wants to be involved. Remember, the customer controls your revenue stream. And as such, understanding how the end-user 'feels' about your project/display in the store environment determines how successful you will be extracting money from their wallet.

In order to achieve that, you have to understand the needs and wants of all the players in the marketing food chain, starting with the ultimate end-user, the customer.

THE GLOBAL SHOPPER

The most important member of the global P-O-P perspective is not the retailer, the brand marketer, or the P-O-P provider. It is the customer.

Since 1995, POPAI has sponsored and continues to sponsor research to determine the effectiveness of at-retail advertising by analyzing customer behavior. The POPAI-commissioned studies reveal one universal fact: More than 70 percent of purchase decisions made by shoppers in these studies were made after they entered the store. Results reflect statistics from each country. Shopping patterns vary by country, and the studies clearly reveal the tremendous marketing opportunity of point-of-purchase advertising in the retail environment – no matter where you are in the world today.

We are providing research results from POPAI studies conducted in the UK, France, Belgium, Holland, USA, and Brazil (see Figures 10-5 to 10-12, on pages 194 to 197). While these studies were conducted in the mid- to late-1990s, they reflect existing data that has been assembled through recent research conducted by the various global POPAI chapters.

Figure 10-5

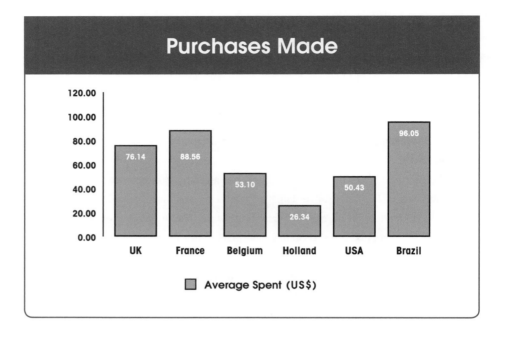

Figure 10-6

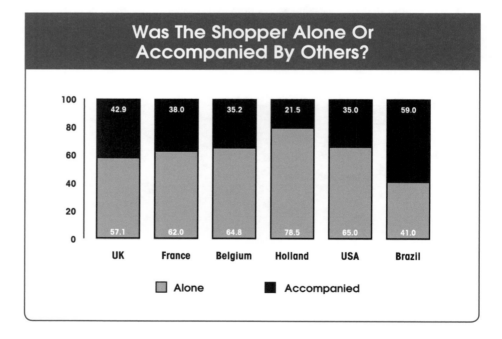

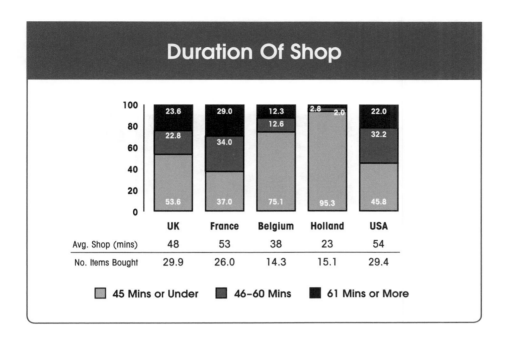

Figure 10-7

Duration Of Shop

	UK	France	Belgium	Holland	USA
Avg. Shop (mins)	48	53	38	23	54
No. Items Bought	29.9	26.0	14.3	15.1	29.4

45 Mins or Under   46–60 Mins   61 Mins or More

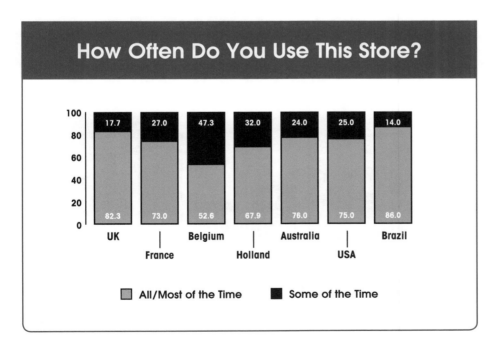

Figure 10-8

How Often Do You Use This Store?

All/Most of the Time   Some of the Time

Figure 10-9

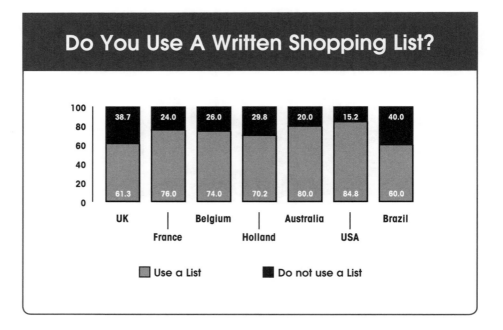

Figure 10-10

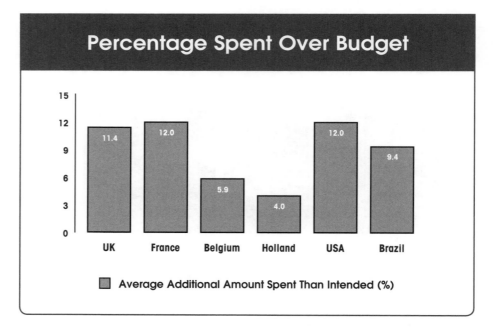

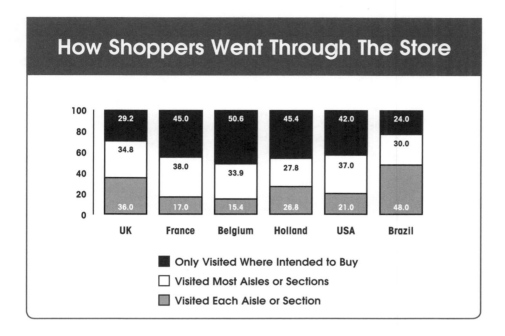

Figure 10-11

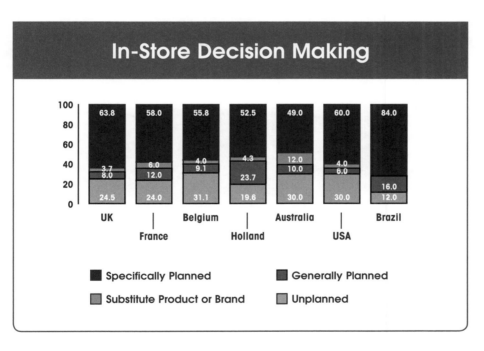

Figure 10-12

ENDNOTES

[1] POPAI, 2007, marketing statistics

[2] AT Kearney Global Retailing Report, 2007

[3] World Bank, World View, 2008

[4] Interbrand, Global Brand Report, 2007

[5] Apple, www.apple.com, 2008

[6] Harrah's 2006 Annual Report

[7] Fred Meyer, interview by author, 2007

[8] Grand Bazaar, Istanbul, site visit, 2007

[9] AT Kearney, Global Retailing Report, 2007

[10] ibid, 2007

[11] AT Kearney, 2007

[12] PLMA, Annual Report, 2007

[13] ibid, 2007

[14] e-Commerce Times, 2008

[15] World Internet Usage, Annual Report, 2007

[16] ibid, 2007

[17] ibid, 2007

[18] The Eddy Company, 2008

[19] Apple, 2007 Annual Report

[20] Wal-Mart interview, 2006

[21] Starbucks 2007 annual report

[22] Brian McCormick, interview, 2007

11

Global Reapplication and Market Adaptation: A Case Study for Anheuser-Busch, Inc.

Kurt Witzel
Senior Manager, Global Retail Marketing
Anheuser-Busch, Inc.

GLOBAL REAPPLICATION AND MARKET ADAPTATION: A CASE STUDY FOR ANHEUSER-BUSCH, INC.

Case Study: The conception, development, and implementation of the Communication And Promotion System (CAPS) as a beer merchandising tool for Anheuser-Busch, Inc. and their family of wholesalers in the United States.

In 1876, Adolphus Busch founded the company that is known today as Anheuser-Busch, Inc., with his father-in-law, Eberhard Anheuser. Mr. Busch, then 37 years old, had been a soap salesman in the city of St. Louis prior to his marriage to Lily Anheuser in 1861. Being quite the salesman, young Busch concentrated on the sales and marketing of the local beer products the new company produced, and Mr. Anheuser spent his time in the brewing cellars focusing on making the best beer products in the city of St. Louis. Mr. Busch would spend his days traveling from account to account, talking with both retailers and consumers, hearing what they had to say about his products, and taking those comments back to his father-in-law for consideration when brewing the next batch of a new product they had created called Budweiser. For the remainder of his life, Mr. Busch was in love with "the art of the sale and promotion," and as a result, he developed the first line of Marketing at-Retail materials seen in the beer industry in the Midwest area of the United States. He would produce and distribute materials used to serve and market beer products, such as round metal serving trays, metal signs, and small giveaway items to all the retailers in the area. Of course, area retailers were happy to accept and use the free merchandising pieces to promote the sale of Mr. Busch's products as it would make money for them as well.

Early Anheuser-Busch Marketing at-Retail materials

Over the years, following the early lead of Adolphus Busch, Anheuser-Busch company executives saw the wisdom and foresight of Mr. Busch in producing in-store marketing materials to be used in both on-premise accounts (bars, restaurants, dining establishments where beer was consumed in the establishment) and off-premise accounts (grocery, liquor, convenience stores, etc., where the consumer would purchase beer products and take them home to consume).

For more than 150 years, Anheuser-Busch has set the standard at retail for the marketing and selling of beer through the use of temporary and permanent materials placed in the retail accounts throughout the United States and the other 142 countries where Budweiser is distributed and sold.

But as the retail marketplace began to change in the '80s and '90s and the retailer became more influential, the types, styles, quality, and amount of M-A-R materials that were placed in their business establishments, Anheuser-Busch was required to re-examine the tools they had used for more than 150 years and to evolve those materials to fit the in-store needs of the retailers and also to fit the more demanding eye of and skepticism of the consumer.

**Point of Sale material
1960–2003**

The wine and liquor industries also found that, in order to create a high-end image at retail in order to continue to compete in the alcohol category, they needed to upgrade their retail marketing materials as well.

The Brand Creative Services department, responsible for development and production of these materials at Anheuser-Busch, decided to put together a group to investigate the current market situation at retail, and as a result, they came up with several interesting discoveries:

While our point-of-sale graphics were good to excellent, the manner in which these graphics were delivered in the retail environment left much to be desired. Flat printed counter cards, convenience poles, and stand-up were visually exciting as long as you stood directly in front of the display; however, very few consumers saw only the front. As they journeyed up and down the aisles at retail, the saw the unattractive side of the POP materials and the grey easel back piece that held the front graphics print in place. Ultimately this was not the image that we wanted to portray to consumers at retail.

As a result, in 2004 we developed what came to be known as 'Image POP.' This new line of POP featured four-sided boxes that were printed with dimensional options for customization. They were double UV coated, printed on 16 point board and were meant to stay in the retail marketplace for several weeks as opposed to a week or two at most, as with the counter cards and convenience poles. While more expensive, we thought this line did indeed elevate our image at retail and, by being four sided, it gave our sales personnel a chance to 'turn' the box on the display periodically to give the display a new look, although we were using the same POP piece, just displaying a new side every so often.

Image POP 2004–2006

In 2004, this line of materials grew to more than 20 percent of our total orders from A-B wholesalers throughout the system, and was declared a 'win' for our products when other competitive beer companies (SAB Miller and Coors Brewing) followed our lead in producing their own line of 'Image POS" materials.

While effective in the short turn, one of the downsides of offering POP materials that were strictly image oriented was the lack of opportunity for pricing on the piece. This is a big issue when dealing in the beer industry and it created unwanted clutter as our sales people produced other materials to communicate the sale price of the products that sat right along side the Image POS and again took away from the quality, clean, high-end image that we were attempting to portray in the retail marketplace.

We utilized the Image POS pieces until late 2006, when we knew that we needed to once again try to take our retail marketing program to 'the next level.' Our group met to review our current state of retail look, and under the leadership of Vice-President of Brand Creative Services, Dan Hoffmann, our group came up with some additional findings. We found that:

- Our current approach to retail merchandising was somewhat varied and inconsistent. As a result of the evolution of customized POP, and the introduction of the Image POP line, we had all kinds of creative pieces with all types of design in the marketplace.
- The initial concept of having the Image POS as stand-alone pieces that would enhance our image at retail was being compromised by the wholesalers producing custom POS piece with pricing to augment the Image pieces.
- We had to question the functionality of some of our pieces that were correct in a strategic sense, but lacking in tactical practicality.
- The multitude of sizes and varieties that we need to produce in order for the Image POS to fit every retail channel was adding to the clutter and inconsistency in the marketplace as well as hurting our ability to gain efficient pricing due to short runs of multiple pieces.

Image POS usage

Knowing that we had to redesign the manner by which we were delivering Marketing at-Retail materials going forward, we set out the following objectives that our group had to consider when redesigning our materials:

Retail Execution Objectives

1. Drive and merchandise floor displays – Floor displays are the primary space at retail, and if we want to expand our sales going forward, we had to make this placement a priority.

2. Optimize secondary display opportunities store-wide – utilize the complete brand portfolio

Retail photographic survey

As our brand offerings have grown exponentially over the past three years through development and acquisition, we needed to develop some system by which all our brands, from the largest selling to the smallest niche brand, could utilize a vehicle to deliver our marketing communication at retail. And we knew that if we were going to compete with other products and categories for placements around the store environment, we would have to develop pieces that had a small enough footprint not to be intrusive, but also big enough to hold enough product to be effective as secondary displays in aisles other than the beer and alcohol sections of the store.

3. Merchandise Cold Beer – A great percentage of beer sold in the off-premise channels is sold cold, meaning out of the cooler or around the cooler. We needed to work on developing merchandising vehicle that could be placed and utilized in this area of the store.

4. On-premise: Prominent Brand Presence and Merchandise Drink Opportunities

One of the most challenging aspects of beer marketing involves how you can connect with the consumer in an on-premise (where beer is actually consumed) account, like a casual dining establishment. They generally do not want a lot of advertising hanging form their ceilings or on their table as they are trying to create a pleasing and non-threatening atmosphere for their consumers. How do we promote our products in a clean and consumer friendly manner in these types of establishments?

The second set of objectives we needed to address was that of retail image for our brands. What would be our objectives for this new marketing delivery device that would address these objectives?

1. Reinforce/elevate brand image at retail – Like the Image POP, we wanted to make sure that as we evolve our marketing at-retail that we kept in mind the desire to show our products in the most favorable light possible.

2. Connect brands to beer occasions and local properties/events – Make sure that we consider the aspect of our customized POS program when developing this vehicle and make it complimentary to what we are trying to do in terms of pre-printed brand image in-store. These pieces should be able to be used to promote local events and properties with which the local wholesaler may have a partnership.

3. Consistency of brand image positioning and graphic identity – It is important to remember that all of our pieces must adhere to the personality and profile for each individual brand. Therefore, the delivery vehicle for these marketing at-retail pieces must be somewhat generic in nature and cannot make a marketing statement on their own.

4. Flexibility to accommodate customization – We must remember the size of our signmaking templates (customized POS) and the format they are delivered in when making decisions regarding how these new marketing vehicles will be designed and deployed in the retail marketplace.

After several months of meetings, discussions, designs, and redesigns, we were ready to put our new concept to the design test and brought in several design agencies and manufacturers to consider the project. VP Dan Hoffmann had a vision for what this program could and should be, and his concise direction provided ample information for the suppliers to work with.

Again, after several months of design comps, we were able to being developing what we were ultimately to call the 'Communication And Promotion System,' or CAPS program.

The CAPS program did many things for us:

- It provided wholesalers throughout the country with a new standardized, modular system to merchandise beer at retail
- Featured a universal Frame System to accommodate brand marketing at-retail material inserts, including our core brand imagery, program thematic imagery, and packaging imagery
- The multi-use aspect of the 'frame system' accommodated wholesaler signmaking and pricing inserts
- This program featured 'universal' display racks, display bins, and other retail tools to help display beer at retail. All pieces were customizable and were able to be utilized by all brands within the Anheuser-Busch system.

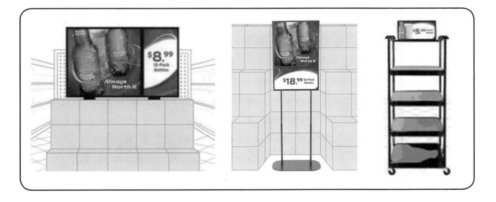

C.A.P.S. Elements, left to right: Small Frame, Pigtail Stand, and Vertical Rack

The program featured several 'retail material frame systems' that utilized both large and small frames in many different applications. The large frame was 39 inches by 27 inches, the small frame was 29 inches by 18 inches, and both featured channels by which the cardboard marketing materials could be slid into. Thus the frames were able to be used over and over again with any A-B brands, and there were sturdy metal frames that could withstand the retail environment for at least at year and maybe longer. These frames featured metal feet that could be easily put on or taken off with metal thumbscrews. This way we could utilize the frames vertically as well as horizontally, and in a set frame stand from the floor or hanging in an account via wires attached to the hanging clips.

The beauty of the system was that all the materials were dimensionally the same format (the large square image inserts were either 18″ by 18″ or 27″ by 27″, and the corresponding pricing inserts were 9″ by 18″ or 13″ by 27″ respectively).

Each frame can be used either horizontally or vertically, stood up on a display using the feet provided, hung from the ceiling via the hanger clips, or used on the in front of a standing display by using the metal frame stand that has telescoping and adjustable 'legs' that can be raised or lowered depending on the display.

We developed the vertical and horizontal racks for use as secondary displays around the retail footprint.

C.A.P.S. Elements,
left to right:
Verticle Frame and
Side by Side Frame

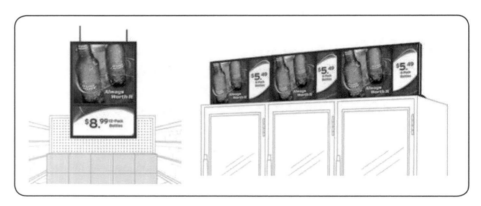

The horizontal display has shelves that can be moved up or down, depending on the size of the packaging that was being displayed on the rack and its use was primarily in areas that you could slide up against the display. Good examples of this might be in front of the deli counter, the seafood section, the bakery, or the meat department. This low profile gave it the ability to be an 'add on' in front of a counter without having to obstruct what was behind the glass in the display.

The vertical display is tall and slender and likewise has shelves that can be moved up or down on the display. This slim profile can be used in aisles to showcase new or niche products that might not get initial shelf or cooler space in the beer section and allows us the ability to get additional product on floor. If the product moves off this slim line display, then a case can be made with the retailer to give it shelf space on the warm beer shelf or in the beer cooler.

Two other elements to the program that are the only two temporary pieces of the CAPS program are the Bin Display and the Cross Merchandising Bin Display. Both of these corrugated pieces are meant to be used for displays lasting only a few weeks, and their inexpensive price confirms these pieces are designed for 'lack of longevity.'

The Bin Display is black in color and is not logoed in any manner so that any A-B product can be displayed in this small 5 case bin display. Utilizing one of the 18″ by 18″ square brand cardboard graphic pieces, the wholesaler can use this piece for quick in and out package or for use with a promotional primary package that may only be in the market for a short time.

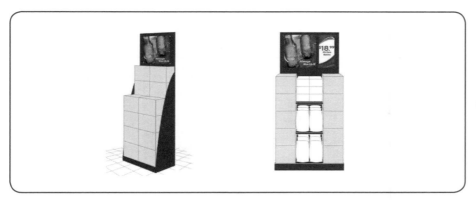

C.A.P.S. Elements,
left to right:
Bin Display and
Cross-March Bin Display

The Cross Merchandising Bin Display is bigger and sturdier and can not only hold up to 10 cases of product, but the middle shelves have extra support in order to allow for the display of varied cross merchandising partner products. This can be salsa, chips, charcoal, or any number of cross merchandising partner products. Like the smaller Bin Display, the 10 case Cross Merch. Bin Display is not logoed with any brand, but can use both the 27″ by 27″ Image square and the 13″ by 27″ pricing insert.

Again, flexibility is such an important part of these bin displays as well as this overall program, and that flexibility is one of the reasons the program has met with such success with both the A-B wholesaler family and our retail partners.

The last two pieces that were part of the initial CAPS program were the Metal Spectacular and the Wooden Spectacular. Both of these pieces were identical in size (48″ across, 20″ deep, and 92″ high), but the retail objectives for these two pieces were considerably different. While both pieces were designed to be able to use 5 of the 18″ by 18″ image squares in the header of the piece, one was to be used as a permanent display (metal) and one was to be used as a temporary display (wooden). These pieces were to be used for big lobby display in grocery stores and in larger liquor stores and were designed for big holidays, like Bud Bowl, Bud Summer, July 4th, and Bud Holiday, where stacks of 75-100 12 packs of Bud Family products were the norm. The sheer weight and heavy structure of the metal spectacular lent itself to be a permanent item in the beer section of the grocery store where the much less overpowering wooden display was used for quick in and out lobby displays, like St. Pats, Halloween, and Mardi Gras.

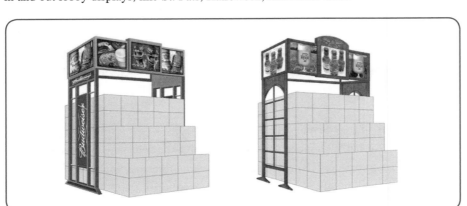

C.A.P.S. Elements,
left to right:
Metal Spectacular and
Wood Spectacular

C.A.P.S. Elements
Applications:
Image or Pricing Inserts
fit Frames

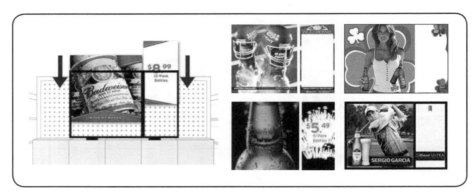

The benefits derived from this CAPS program for all the stakeholders are many. For example, benefits for the beer wholesaler who distribute the merchandising materials at retail and deliver the beer to the retailers are:

- Standardized approach simplified ordering, warehousing, and distribution of the marketing at-retail materials. Fewer and more standard sizes to all the materials made it easier to store and inventory.
- Provided simple turn-key display objectives for store merchandisers which saved time and created cost efficiencies for the wholesaler.
- Marketing material cost efficiencies were obtained as all our printed graphic pieces are the same size which made print bids more efficient and the end result was that the overall cost of the display was sometime as much as half the cost of the old Image POP displays
- Signmaking savings were obtained by the wholesaler as a result of not having to mount the vinyl pieces made in their warehouses to any type of foam-core material. They could easily use the framing system with their custom printed vinyl pieces.
- The universal frames and rack system provide maximum flexibility to merchandise and complete the showcasing of the entire Anheuser-Busch beer portfolio without having brand-specific frames/racks/bins.
- The simple weight and presence of the metal frames and heavy metal racks helps secure more semi-permanent space at retail.
- And most importantly from where we were with the Image POP, the CAPS system delivers both the image/theme and pricing inserts in the same retail merchandising vehicle. Bottom line, one piece gets the job done that used to be done by at least two.

From the retailer's perspective, the CAPS program:

- Provide clean, high-quality merchandising that can help upgrade the store image and supports the evolving retailer mantra of uniform and limited signage.
- In addition, the racks provide a moveable, flexible means of merchandising beer and related items.

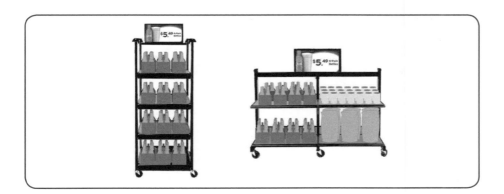

From an internal A-B sales department perspective, they benefited by:

- Short custom run promotional merchandising costs can be cut considerably by using the frames and racks and customizing them via use of the wholesaler sign-making machinery. Prior to CAPS, to do short run printing for a small wholesaler geographic program could be very costly.

- By having a full of line of everyday generic branded marketing at-retail materials and also using the themed programming materials, geographic marketing managers could reduce the cost of the creative used to develop a program.

- With reduced cost of individual programs and marketing materials came the opportunity to do more programs and provide heavier retail coverage for a program.

- Again, as with the wholesaler, geo marketing managers can apply custom creative to frames, rack, bins, etc., giving them more tools to support local programs and bring the brand to the grassroots marketing level.

And finally, from a brand perspective, they loved the clean, uncluttered look that their brands received as a result of implementing this program at retail. In addition, every brand, from the large Budweiser and Bud Light brands to the very small Michelob Amberbock and O'Doul's brands, benefited from the program by having all these non-logoed tools at their disposal in the retail marketplace. Any brand could be highlighted on any holiday by using the CAPS tools, and then the very same CAPS pieces could deliver a different brand and thematic the very next day.

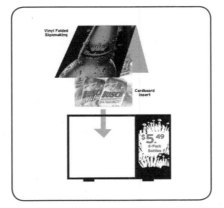

12

At-Retail Digital Media

Laura Davis-Taylor
Founder & Principal
Retail Media Consulting, Inc.

INTRODUCTION

For the past few years, the retail industry, like all other industries, has become increasingly impacted by technology. However, only recently has the notion of in-store digital media gone from interest to steady adoption, a trend partially driven by the increasing popularity of digital signage. For those of us who have been living, breathing, waiting, and watching this industry evolve, there's little doubt that the oh-so-talked about "tipping point" for this new genre of shopper communication is near. However, we are carefully balancing excitement, potential, and new paradigms with fear, uncertainty, conflicting strategies, and wobbly results for how this media is truly affecting our retail businesses and shoppers.

While digital signage is a key focus regarding in-store digital media, it is but one of many current and burgeoning tools that make up the toolkit of opportunities to engage with shoppers. We hope that this chapter gives you a solid foundation for not only what tools are available, but also how to think about applying them to your unique strategic challenges.

STORE MEDIA

We know you're not in the dark. Media is just not what it used to be. Did you know that the average person is exposed to 3,000-4,000 media messages a day? And, according to a recent industry forecast from Veronis Suhler Stevenson, Americans will spend 9.5 hours of each day immersed in it. Even NBC is seeing changes — their in-house team found that a startling 75% of GenX, GenY, and Baby Boomers are overwhelmed by the amount of media swirling around them. Given this deluge it should come as no surprise that it doesn't pack the punch that it used to.

Research coming out of Ball State University has cemented another communication challenge worth noting — very little media happens in a vacuum anymore. They conducted a study on "concurrent media exposure" and found that more than one-third of media exposures happen simultaneously with some other form. This is so common that most of us aren't even aware of it anymore. We refer to this phenomenon as "media A-D-D," but the experts call it "Multi-tasking Media." No matter what it's called, as video on demand, satellite radio, PDAs, MP3 players, and hand-held video game devices become more prolific, it's only going to get worse.

What does that mean for in-store digital media? The most important is the glaringly obvious — unless you're going to use in-store digital media to communicate something that matters to the viewer, don't do it. People aren't making room for yet more superfluous media, and we can only capture that treasured consumer attention if we earn it by saying something worth listening to. That said, here are the high-level reasons that in-store digital is becoming a new media darling:

1. Guaranteed "reach": Unlike many other forms of media, shoppers walking our stores are bankable bodies. Some industry veterans have erroneously coined the term "captive audiences" to define these people, implying that they can be trapped like netting fish and forced to watch our messages. (News flash: they aren't captive because they have feet.) Regardless, the logic is that their physical presence is ensured and this, in turn, has a tremendous amount of media value to a person chasing today's elusive consumer.

2. Recency: This is a fancy term that means people tend to recall — and respond to — the messages to which they were most recently exposed. Naturally, this makes hearing or seeing a message in-store very powerful, as recall is very important to media people.

3. Aperture: Quite simply, if you see a message in-store and the product is nearby, you've got aperture. Chances are good that you have a much better opportunity for people to actually respond to or buy a product that's within arm's reach.

So, we've established that inside of stores we can reach people, there's a good chance that they'll remember our messages and we can even stimulate on-the-spot response to the product. This said, there are still challenges.

It's human nature that when something new is introduced, we impose our status quo logic, experiences, and processes on it. In the case of store as media, it's no surprise that there are a lot of people viewing the store media opportunity from whatever media lens they see the world through. The most overlooked "aha"? The store is not a "new media channel." It's always been one. It's only become new to those that have never seen its value until now.

Most recently, the onslaught of "store as media" interest is coming from digital signage vendors and agencies. Though not always the case, many are unfamiliar with how the store operates and are driven by financial incentives selling technology or making a "traditional media" sale out of store real estate. Those who have lived in the store world for many years are not as apt to embrace pitch, as they're trying to make the store experience better, not turn it into a media zoo. They are, however, willing to take a look at powerful new digital tools for the store and try to figure out how to best activate them for the good of their shoppers.

So is the store a media channel or not? Yes, the store is a media channel. However, it is inappropriate to approach it strictly with a mindset rooted in an existing legacy media vehicle that may or may not be right for a store environment. More importantly, leave the note that its only value is about capitalizing on the number of people being reached as a "store audience" outside the store doors. This media channel exists in a busy, distracted environment where people are shopping and it's our challenge to use it to engage effectively, not simply disrupt the shopper gaze to make a GRP (media Gross Rating Point) dollar.

AT-RETAIL DIGITAL MEDIA: A 101

In its most simplistic definition, in-store digital media can be classified as any type of shopper communication that's powered by an electrical current in which messages can be controlled and changed on proactively. The most common — and popular — form of in-store digital media is retail digital signage (RDS). It's currently the new "redhead on the block" in this category and referred to by many different names. It is a true catalyst to the industry because of the doors that it opened within the shopper aisle. Here are the most important ones:

- Digital signage is most commonly powered by software that allows a brand to target specific content to the individual store, even at the individual screen level. This enables willing retailers the ability to practice targeted, direct marketing into the store without the cost and operational complexity of printing numerous versions of printed signs. Better targeting means better customer response. And what does that mean? If executed correctly, happier shoppers and more money for the store.
- Compliance — meaning the sign is actually up when it's supposed to be — is often guaranteed with a digital sign. This isn't a big deal to you if it's not your headache, but it's a huge industry challenge if you consider that as many as 50% of signs sent to the field aren't installed or taken down as directed. Not only is this expensive, it's doubly tragic due to missed opportunities to speak to customers effectively.

- RDS creates an open pipeline to distribute your message to the field at-will. This comes in handy not only for marketing and media promotions, but to train employees, respond to emergency situations, hold in-store live events, and even patch IT fixes.
- Measurement. As critically important as this is, we're still in our infancy stage and cannot track results as in-depth as we'd like. In the future, however, digital media in-store will be as accountable as online media and proving its value will not be such a challenge.

Retail Digital Signage is a very powerful form of in-store digital media, but there are new technologies, applications, cool devices, and tools popping up that have the potential to snap into the in-store media arsenal for building exciting customer experiences. Almost all of them share the powerful features above, and as technology continues to advance, we'll probably be looking at this chapter a few years from now and snickering at how fundamental this seems. For now, let's just say that in-store digital media has tremendous transformation potential and the key word is "flexibility."

THE DIGITAL TOOLBOX

Many powerful enabling technologies are rapidly appearing in the digital media toolbox. These technologies are being incubated by multi-national corporations, university laboratories, and small entrepreneurial ventures. There is a litany of definitions used to describe the participating products and services that are now available, the following being a quick categorized list of those most relevant to retail.

Digital signage
The high-level benefits duly noted, it's the potential of the next generation of this in-store digital signage that holds the most exciting potential. While it's true that digital signage provides very specific content scheduling so that we can target messages to exact times and locations, few are using this feature to its full capability. Many are testing the waters and targeting store messages on a high level, but the complexities of doing unique messages for each store are still being worked out. While we work through this, the next wave of digital signage is being cooked up inside of the labs. This "2.0" version will allow better interactivity, real-time results measurement, and the potential to "auto-populate" relevant content specifically for the person standing in front of the screen. These functionalities have been successfully implemented online and will translate powerfully into the store environment.

Next generation kiosks/interactive screens
Kiosks and interactive screens are rapidly becoming part of the same category, as kiosks are being redefined in how they look, the level of information they can provide, and how

shoppers can use them. Many have morphed beyond the typical permanently placed machine and are now mobile so that shoppers have one-to-one, helpful information while they shop. Others are showing up in surprising enclosures or surfaces and can be gesture or even voice controlled. There are many variations but here are a few compelling examples:

- Interactive store windows, the most common example being Ralph Lauren's SOHO store last year, tempt pedestrians to stop and interact with the window. This is done via motion activation on a screen-projected interface or by mounting an actual screen inside the window. Interactivity can be motion or touch activated and Ralph Lauren even had a slide card outside so that browsers on the street could purchase and send the items home.

- Interactive "foil" is an interactive adhesive film that you peel and paste to turn any shop window, display, or static surface into an interactive screen. It may sound far-fetched, but it's real and enabled via a proprietary touch sensor technology. Just think about the creative implementations for this one that have yet to be explored.

- A shopping cart "kiosk" is typically a small interactive screen that sits on the shopping cart and helps shoppers locate products, check prices, and/or scan products for purchase. Shopping lists can be scanned or emailed to the device and accessed while shopping. And, via location intelligence, relevant promotions and coupons can be served up based on where the cart is in the store.

- Interactive surfaces are being developed that combine an overhead projector, a rotating mirror, a video camera, and special software to turn walls, floors, tabletops, or any surface into a virtual, interactive touch screen display. Combined with complementary technologies like Radio Frequency IDentification (RFID), there are some fabulous possibilities in play.

- Handheld tablets are also worth calling attention to, as they allow shoppers or employees to pick up a lightweight, kiosk-like screen and walk around the store with it to use as desired. Some field tests have shown these devices to be quite promising when used for employees to better sell products (especially complex ones). Further developing these tablets as a shopper self-assist tool is also merited, especially if we can make it simple for shoppers to get deep product information with a touch.

Shelf edge systems

These are small digital screens that sit snuggly on or within a store shelf system. They offer tremendous short-term potential because of their cost, functionality, and ability to drive sales. They range from tiny 2-color OLED displays (the same technology used in mobile phones and PDA screens) that add juice to an otherwise stale and static POP display to slightly larger LED or LCDs that can become interactive. The beauty of these little gems is that they sit directly next to the product and, in most cases, no longer require a network connection; brands can update their content via cellular phone networks. Additionally, there are models in development that will operate for up to four years off of a single battery charge. The combination of no required network and power connection will be ideal for store environments, where anything that requires wired connectivity can be both disruptive and costly.

Immersive displays

These technologies allow users to play and engage with multi-media images projected on a floor or wall. They're unique in their capabilities, enabling brands to engage shoppers to do all kinds of things: play a game, ripple a logo, break open a floor virtually... the creative opportunities are boundless.

Other immersive displays are appearing with a unique twist, one being a thin curtain of "dry" fog that serves as a translucent projection screen and displays an image that literally floats in the air. It has to be in a somewhat dark setting, but it sure makes an impact.

A final genre to be aware of are the 3D product images that literally float above kiosks, shelves, and even outdoor signs. Although still being perfected, this virtual reality product is one to watch.

Electronic paper

Electronic paper holds an incredible amount of promise for retail. Xerox's Palo Alto Research Center created it in the 1970s as an alternative to printed price tags for the shelf. It's made of a thin sheet of plastic containing millions of black-and-white charged beads. When the paper is fed through an "electronic paper printer" (which can be done about 1,000 times), the beads take on a black or white state that create a digital image. It's fascinating but can be limiting in its creative presentation — kind of like how Atari game screens looked. There are 4-color designs in development and sources tell us that the lab prototypes look promising, recent news touting such a viable solution by 2009.

Other flavors of electronic paper have emerged, one that's more of a flashing electronic display perfect for POP. It uses no backlight or front light and is viewable from almost any angle or lighting condition, an important consideration with any digital screen. It's also extremely versatile in that it doesn't need AC power, with a small display capable of running off of 2 AA batteries for up to 6 months.

Digital store customer assistants

There are two new solutions for digital customer assistance: the first using real-time access to a live person and the second using 3D animation. With the "live" version, the shopper walks up to the screen, selects their inquiry, and, via a real-time connection, a highly trained customer support person is introduced to help them with their immediate needs. This implementation is very similar to a video teleconference. Alternatively, the 3D flavor is a customized, animated brand character that offers their support as directed by shopper. The character's responses are preprogrammed and driven by a menu or by complex and intelligent business rules. Once again, this has become commonplace online and is a natural fit for the store world when properly designed and implemented.

Mobile

The ubiquitous "3rd screen" holds massive potential in-store. Not only can mobile tools be used to quickly follow through on a promotional call-to-action, but groups can use them for virtual rain checks, instant coupons, social networking, purchase, and much, much more. One of the more exciting applications on the rise is a form of "local search," where a shopper can text in an SMS code to download promotional offers while in a mall or store. Even better, users can dig into the product promos to check price and store availability, sometimes targeted to the GPS location emanating from their cell phone signal. Of course establishing "permissions" for such marketing efforts are critical, but the potential for this kind of marketing is vast and priceless once it truly becomes one-to-one.

There are many resources on mobile marketing and we recommend that you get out there and learn about it. We're all watching how GPS and RFID will play further into mobile devices, and only time will tell if the phone one day becomes the "store cookie." Which gets us to the next category...

The brick-and-mortar "cookie"

Online, a cookie is the information morsel that gets embedded to track the user's online activities. It holds personal information and Internet usage data and does a good job of making Web visits more personalized and convenient. In-store digital media tools will become more relevant and beneficial when the equivalent of the computing cookie is implemented and integrated into the physical space. Provided this technology is deployed with tight consumer permission controls, the many benefits to the consumer, the store, and the brands will be extraordinary.

Many in the industry believe this will happen, but don't yet know what the technology will be or what it will take to garner acceptance. Radio Frequency IDentification (RFID), GPS, and/or some form of mobile phone tracking systems are the most likely candidates for this capability. Its acceptance will be driven by the perceived benefits to the shopper, the trusted relationship with the brand, and how much they are incented to allow each level of personal access.

Destination displays

More and more retailers are creating a specific zone within their stores designed as a specific destination for their shoppers. This zone can be built to provide information, customer support, entertainment, self-assist, training, product demonstration ... the list goes on. Regardless of how it's used, unique display screens and creative combinations of today's technologies are appearing to bring this store destination to life and keep shoppers coming back.

One of the more simplistic ways of "cutting" the various in-store digital media technologies is to think about them by: (a) how intimately they can connect with the shopper; (b) how mature the technology is; and (c) the complexity of deployment. Many retailers choose to start with one-way, less complex tools and build future efforts on them as a foundation.

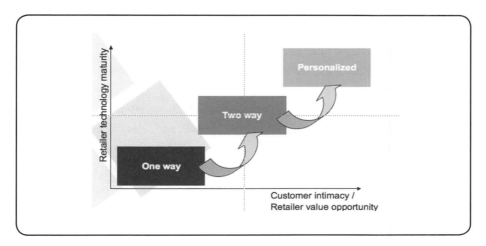

Very few people have the time to track and digest every emerging technology tool in the retail landscape, but it's important to stay informed about them on a high level and think about how they could and should be strategically deployed. After all, how we strategize, deploy, and snap these many in-store digital media tools together for store experience design will help pave the retail store future.

DEFINING THE ROLE OF AT-RETAIL DIGITAL

Like any other technology-based media, in-store digital can serve varying strategic roles. First, let's explore the true meaning of a few of them:

- Advertising: the business of drawing public attention to goods and services, performed through a variety of media.
- Retailing: the sale of goods/merchandise for personal or household consumption.
- Merchandising: promotion of merchandise sales by coordinating production and marketing, and developing advertising, display, and sales strategies to increase retail sales. This includes disciplines in pricing and discounting, physical presentation of products and displays, and the decisions about which products should be presented to which customers at which time.

Looking at these things, it's a natural assumption that in-store digital is a hybrid of many things and its role will depend on its intended use. Thus, our opinion is that the closest model for its potential place in the retail media industry is not television, but the Internet. Why? Due to the flexible nature of it, we can use it for many things;

- Entertainment (delight your shoppers)
- Awareness (show advertising impressions)
- Response (entice them to touch, download offer, pull a coupon, etc.)
- Engagement (motivate them to explore a product or sample)
- Purchase (stimulate a buy)
- Loyalty (engage them in dialogue)

So, when you think about this media, please don't classify it as simply a one-way "TV" proposition. Like the Net, its role is directly driven by what you aim to achieve with it.

OWNERSHIP CHOICES AND REVENUE MODELS

Determining the ownership and revenue model for your in-store digital media is directly correlated to:
(1) how much you want to control it;
(2) how much you want to spend; and
(3) your appetite for risk.

There are three ways to own your digital network or tool;

- You own it; therefore you invest the cash and take on the risk. You also get full control of how it's used as well as the content on display.
- You share it with a third-party network operator or funding partner, thus also sharing in the cost, risk, reward, and control.
- A network owner or funding group owns it and you share a percentage of the revenue generated by selling content for the advertising media value. You have limited control, but you also don't spend any money to have it in-store.

There are pros and cons to each of the above models and we can't stress enough how critical it is to determine which one is right for you up front. Not only will you save yourself and your company a great deal of time, you'll also save plenty of money and hassle.

Regarding revenue models, there are quite a few opportunities to recoup costs and generate an impact. Here are the primary categories:

- **Direct revenue:** This is measurable, bankable revenue generated from merchandising, advertising, or sponsorship dollars as well as increased sales that can be directly correlated to the content displayed on your digital screens.
- **Indirect revenue:** This is the more intangible category, where you know that you're creating inferred value, but it's not quite as measurable via actual dollars. This can include creating a better environmental brand experience for shoppers, increasing how long people stay in the store, securing more shopper loyalty, making stores more operationally productive, providing better employee training, and even helping to defray the expense and time involved in field communications.
- **Bartering credits:** This one is pretty easy. If you own a digital media tool or network, you can barter space on it to reduce the cost — or trade time for — your own promotional and marketing initiatives with a brand partner.

Just like with your ownership model, figuring out your potential revenue stream is critical to work out up front. If you remember nothing else, remember this: it doesn't matter how cool, innovative, and impactful the technology proposition is, every digital program will eventually come down to "show me the money" in the eyes of the financial decision makers.

THE MILLION DOLLAR QUESTION...DOES IT WORK?

Does it work? In relation to ISDM, the answer is very clear: it depends.

To determine if it works, you must first know what you want out of it. Then develop a rock solid strategic game plan as well as the appropriate measurement strategy. If these foundations are in place, you'll quickly see a pattern to the program's effectiveness out in the field and at least you'll know where you stand.

The good news? It's technology. The flexibility of digital messages means that you can respond very easily to what doesn't work without reinventing the wheel.

We don't want to completely dodge this question, so here's what we do know: 70% of decisions are made in the store; people tend to notice motion messages more than printed ones, and, no matter the media, people like stuff that makes a difference in their daily lives. We've been able to prove that digital media in-store can indeed work with the right foundational formula. But, like anything else, we feel compelled to quote Professor John Greening from Northwestern University here by saying, "it's the not the gun, it's the bullet." Be a sharpshooter.

BRANDING VERSUS SALES?

One of the hottest debates out there is in relation to if ISDM is best utilized for branding or sales. Most experts are in favor of using in-store digital media for generating sales lift, while the branding function is also supported but performing in the background. There are agencies and individuals with a vested interest in focusing on the branding element first, as it can support their services foray into this media. This is short sided, as using ISDM to "close the communications and purchase loop" and actively sell the product simply makes more sense. Supporting points:

- Marketers need to look at in-store for what it is rather than trying to transfer another medium's strength and weaknesses onto it. In the store, shoppers are trying to accomplish something — shopping or buying. We need to support this with the technology that they encounter during this process, not simply hit them with more brand advertising messages.
- Shoppers have very little need to hear about the brand in-store unless the brand message is tied to something useful. Valuable, helpful information at the point of purchase builds the brand in a direct way (like direct-response TV does) while still focusing on results generation. TV entertainment spots (AKA branding messages) are not the kind of messages that will do this.
- It's simply *easier* to push 'brand-building' instead of 'sales' because deep down many industry constituents simply don't know how to build sales more productively. So they go for the 'easier goal': gross rating points.
- In-store digital offers much more than just branding interactions. It offers measurable interactions such as engagement, behavior, purchase, and repeat purchase behavior. From the marketing perspective, this is worth its weight in gold. So, why would we focus simply on brand messaging? We miss a world of opportunity if doing so.

Whatever your perception of branding is, it is a means to an end — and that end is sales. Do we spend millions and millions of dollars on marketing to create positive brand perceptions just for fun? No. We do it to ultimately translate into business and dollars. Do stores want to expand on "store as media" just to give people cool places to go? No. They want them in stores, coming back often, and buying more with each basket. Branding is one of the many tactics to support this, but sales will always be the ultimate goal.

STRATEGICALLY SCREENING SOLUTIONS

If you find one or many of the in-store digital media technologies in this chapter mentioned intriguing and would like to take the next steps, the first thing that you need to ask yourself is pretty simple: why? As great as these technologies are, they are not doing their job if they are not "curing some kind of disease." There is a common C-level behavior emerging of "falling in love with a shiny new tech toy" that isn't legitimately adding value or solving a problem for the brand or shopper and this should be avoided.

To get a solid strategic intent clarified, start by determining your problems, then get into the appropriate conversations both internally and externally to figure out how you can combine technology, creativity, and a mindset of customer service to do something about them. After that, secure the experts to help you create, test, and evolve your programs. This sounds extraordinarily basic, but for some reason it's an often overlooked step of the process and the cause for many "failed" ISDM efforts.

The following are the most critical questions to ask of your project team to define your project intent and immediate next steps:

- What shopper problem are we solving?
- What business problem are we solving?
- What internal and external barriers exist?
- What "big ideas" do we have for utilizing new in-store media technologies?
- Are any of them "quick wins"?
- How will they strategically integrate with the shopper experience both in and out of our stores?

Once these items are flushed out, use the answers to focus your project team on the desired end results.

HOW TO THINK ABOUT COST

Inevitably, whenever someone contemplates an in-store media network, one of the first questions is "how much does it cost?" This is followed closely with some form of "is there an average cost per store that includes content creation, equipment, installation, etc.?"

Answering this question is like asking how much a Web site or new company brochure is going to cost; there are simply too many things to factor in to have a clean answer. There are no simple cost averages for the many things that make up the price tag for each digital project that you undertake. That said, there are some key cost drivers, the following being the main ones to think about:

- How many locations
- How many screens per store
- How many store channels
- Amount of content per channel
- How often the content is refreshed
- Selected hardware and software
- Screen types (can include quality and functionality)
- Installation
- Program management
- Measurement tools & support
- Desired field research
- Desired field support (monitoring, troubleshooting, etc.)

When thinking about cost, you can go about mapping yours out one of two ways: (1) make up your project wish list and work with the right people to cost it out accurately; or (2) create a budget per store and let the experts help you do the most with what you have. Just ensure that you think about this up front or there may be some unwelcome surprises down the road.

THE PROJECT ROADMAP

There are loads and loads of white papers and resources that scrutinize the foundations for an in-store digital media program. We're going to break it down in digestible, easy-to-grasp chunks of information.

From our view of the world, there are five key phases to this kind of project: Discovery, Business Planning, Activation, Measurement, and Evolution.

Discovery

As noted a few times, you need to start by figuring out why you want to do the project. To do so, you need to spend the time with each and every camp that has the potential to benefit from the technology, and then map out a very high-level business case for each. From there, all opportunities should be summarized into a project brief so that everyone is on the same page with the initiative's overarching intent.

Business Planning

This is the hardest part. But it's also the most important.

The business planning phase, if done correctly, takes 8 to 12 weeks and provides the initial strategy for the following items:

- What is the creative brand strategy of this new media?
- How does it fit with other outside- and inside-store creative?
- What will success look like and how will we measure it?
- How will it integrate with media and promotional calendars?
- Based on requirements, what will it cost?
- How will it make money and how will this be evaluated?
- How many channels and in which zones? Why?
- What is the content loop or screen creative made up of?
- What are competitors doing that we need to take into account?
- How will it be delivered to the store?
- What should content cost to purchase?
- Who will be purchasing it?
- What do shoppers ideally want to do with it? How will they get value out of it?
- Who and how will the operations of it be managed?
- How will we ensure that content is appropriately licensed?

Activation

This is most often referred to as a pilot phase, but some folks move right into roll-out if they feel passionately about the project. Regardless, activation typically includes:

- Project process design
- Technology specification (hardware and software)
- Workflow and budgeting
- Content creative and programming
- Vendor selection and management
- Site selection
- Installation

Measurement

This phase is all about monitoring the field to get a handle on program results. This is typically done via technology tools, customer and employee intercepts, corporate interviews, category sponsor interviews, and/or good old sales and category analysis.

Evolution

When it comes to innovation, you're never done, especially when technology is constantly evolving. Based on what's happening in-field as well as emerging, complementary technologies, the evolution phase is critical and ongoing. If you don't stay on top of this, trust us when we say that your competitor will.

BUILDING TEAMS

Building the correct team is absolutely crucial to the success of an ISDM project. Here's a team-building checklist for success:

- Learn from past challenges. We experienced significant challenges when the Internet emerged as a new media in relation to the team structures to support it. History is repeating itself now with in-store digital media projects and we should look to the past to avoid some of the pain we're experiencing in the present.

- You can't build your dream team if you don't know what you're seeking to accomplish. Determine your digital media project goals first; then look for the experts to make them real.

- Get critical team stakeholders involved early and add any others who may contribute specific value during key phases. Know the difference and understand that your effort is going to take a village of cross-functional experts.

- The ideal team is one led by a seasoned, savvy, impartial, open minded, can-do, and EMPOWERED leader. This person can be internal or external, just be sure they have the subject matter expertise necessary for your unique project.

- No one can be the best at every facet of this new media category; there are simply too many unique skill-sets involved, so weed out the commercial salesmen who are pitching the "best one-stop-shop" claims. If it were credible, we'd be surrounded by indisputable, successful case studies.

- Create clear rules of engagement for the team and hold everyone accountable.

- If a team member starts derailing the project out of a personal or departmental agenda, have the empowered leader deal with it or replace them. This is not always easy or possible, but these folks can cause major damage to the potential for a successful project.

- If anything creates a team "stalemate," remember that NOTHING MATTERS MORE THAN CREATING A BETTER SHOPPING EXPERIENCE FOR THE CUSTOMER and filter the decision accordingly. It's simple: if the customer likes what you created, we all win.

- There is no pretty little manual for innovation. It's messy and full of surprises. However, it's also fun, exciting and ripe with opportunity, so embrace the challenges and focus on the end game.

- Coming up with great ideas and making them happen are two very different things. If you commit to innovate, it's likely that you're going to end up ahead of the competition and become a retail leader. If you don't, there's going to be a lot of catch-up to do and it's going to be a long, hard road ahead.

A WORD ABOUT TECHNOLOGY DECISIONS

Many challenges can emerge when the strategic or more "right brained" teams engage with the each other for in-store digital media projects. All should remember that technology is simply an enabler to a holistic in-store digital media network, not the solution. It's very important to successfully answer the "why" and "what" questions for your initiative and then work with IT on the "how" (and necessary feature functions) to support your goals. When making the vendor choices, look beyond the simple features and functions of products — understand the design and business philosophies of the people and companies behind them.

When considering technology solutions, it's also important to think media-centricity as well as techno-centricity. You must design and integrate your in-store digital media initiative seamlessly into an overall experiential retail environment to maximize the full potential and benefits of this "4th-screen"™ world. To do so, think multi-sensory and don't overlook the importance of making the right decisions around audio, lighting, and usability as well.

Finally, let your rules of commerce and customer engagement rather than the technology define your in-store digital media initiative(s). With clarity of your business needs comes focus. With focus comes the right technology choice to help lead you to profitability.

CONTENT

There are many wonderful resources that dive into the subject of content for in-store digital media. To keep it simple, follow these rules for successful store content:

- Start with the intent and remember that few people are on couches in the store.
- Know your "who" and engage the shopper with information that is both relevant and helpful.
- Make your "how" holistic to channels.
- Create positive "Delta Moments" that break through the messaging clutter and adds value to the shopping experience.
- Engage the appropriate team members and skill sets to create your content.
- Gear content toward the typical behavior at the screen location; if shoppers are moving by quickly, it should be a "glance message." If the dwell time is longer, plan accordingly.
- Make sure this happens by writing a killer creative brief.
- Measure for results and, if the results are sub-par, try new content and "optimize" your content for success.
- Protect your creative IP carefully.
- Pay for rights usage for anything that's in rotation.

- Ensure that you have a pre-ordained workflow between any vendors and agencies that will be serving as a resource for content development.
- The same goes for asset management and storage. Know how you're going to do it and with whom.

MEASUREMENT

We are still creating opportunities for value with all out of home digital media in the minds of both brand advertisers and consumers. In-store, it's simply critical and measurement will be key to making this happen sooner than later. That said, it is universally accepted that any digital sign, kiosk, or store digital media tool has value in the fact that it's the last stop on the road of an integrated, multi-channel brand campaign focused on creating awareness and sales. What's holding us back? We don't have true market penetration with solid results, and much of the content on the screens is not seen as a premium value to shoppers.

In this industry, there are many things that create value. We have a long way to go to effectively establish and measure each "value factor," but there are some important things to keep in mind as you take on this challenge. The most important is how to think about measurement. Once again, the Internet comes to mind.

The new tools and techniques for measuring the impact of your programs get more exciting every month. The emergence — and ultimate adoption — of the Internet and its measurement tools can teach us a lot in the industry. We need to find inspiration from those past lessons learned and push for the same level of real-time results analysis. This would be easier if the many organizations in our landscape would band together in a unified effort, but until then, retailers and brands should exert as much influence as possible to motivate resources and suppliers to make "storestream analysis™" real.

What is storestream analysis? Just as we have "clickstream data" to measure user engagement online, we have the opportunity to create "storestream data" for our retail locations to determine who was present, who looked, at what, for how long, what the did behaviorally as a result, and the sales impact created. Creating legitimate models for storestream analysis has not happened yet, but it will, as it's critical to valuating and monitoring true in-store digital success. When this happens, the Value of Engagement (VoE) will range from pennies to dollars depending upon each customer's degree of interaction, resulting behavior, and the degree of validated historical data with a digital media touch point.

Many resources are building ISDM ROI forecasts on a handful of known variables. From our experience, there are more than 153, each with a potential "butterfly effect" on the 5-year P & L of a network. Accurately forecasting when, and if, a network will go "cash flow positive" is invaluable to secure the required funding. Ensure that you're working with resources that know how to do this for you.

What indicates value for your in-store digital media is linked to your goals ROI is everything, but a rewarding return on investment can be very different currencies depending upon the economic perspective of each stakeholder. Many tools and techniques exist to measure against these goals, some requiring human intervention and some technology-based. Both are critical, so spend some time educating yourself on your options and find the right resources to execute your measurement plan.

Therefore, to identify funding buckets, determine where the money to pay for a store media program originates, why it is being pulled for use, and for what it will be used. Knowledge is power, and people who stand behind the value of their offering aren't afraid to be accountable to their results. If your programs (or resources) aren't pro-accountability, we urge to you think hard about the long-term repercussions.

THE INNOVATOR'S MINDSET

Innovation has become a business and cultural imperative, as it is core to life as we now exist. No longer can we create strategies, technology tools and marketing plans against specific systems, processes and ideas and expect to be successful year-to-year. We now have to put forth the effort to understand current and emerging trends, change agents, and evolve our own status quo consistently. This happens by employing an innovator's mindset.

No matter which side of the brain you tend to utilize, we all have an ability to innovate. We do it all the time, just not always in our business life. This is likely due to the work processes that we are forced to operate within. Process is indeed critical, but why not create processes for innovating? There are a slew of wonderful books, magazines, and Web sites to inspire this within your firm, but here are a few principles to embrace:

- Employ your curiosity. What are you doing right now that can be improved in a fresh new way? What is one thing that you can do differently that will create a "quick win" for the company or your shoppers? What does your instinct say you're doing right or wrong? What did the competition do that you might be able to improve upon?
- Get out there. Read, watch, listen, and ponder. Carry a pocket notebook and scribble it down when a thought strikes — no matter what time of day or night. Do like we do and start an "inspiration" file to revisit when you're in the mood. In time, you'll train your subconscious mind to be on the lookout for new ideas.
- Understand what holds you back. Breakthrough thinking can be held back by habit, company personality or culture, mental blocks, or even a specific individual. If you can identify the deterrent, you'll be closer to finding a way around it. If you're not sure, ask others. They'll tell you, so keep your mind open in case it turns out to be you.

- Become a trend watcher. Many changes are rooted in emerging trends. They may be cultural, technology-oriented, or behavioral. A good ad agency planner is a trend watcher, as they have a constant eye peeled for what's happening in the world so that they can make predictions and stimulate ideas for responding. If you don't have an interest in being a trend guru, appoint someone to the job and make it a monthly habit to have them lead strategic discussions and brainstorm with your team.
- Test. As mentioned earlier, the only way to know if you're onto something is to test it and find out if you're right.
- Get support from the top down. The most innovative companies typically have open-minded leadership at the helm. Innovation carries successes and failures and both must be supported and awarded. After all, you only know what works when you also find out what doesn't.
- Bring in the young people. They are idea generators and grew up and thrive in the very culture in which we aim to create. Rather than keeping those college kids quietly in the corner with a limited job description, bring them into brainstorm meetings and see what they come up with. You'll be amazed, we promise.
- Get into the field. Salespeople have a pulse on what's happening and they are excellent idea sources. After all, no one spends more time with your shoppers. Tap into them.
- We've indicated the numerous moving parts and stakeholders that need to function cohesively for an in-store digital media initiative to meet your success objectives. However, when this many people, opinions, and agendas collide an "innovation project," there will inevitably be challenges and surprises. No matter how well you plan, design, conceive, organize, or model, your ability to adapt and react dynamically to change is a critical element to the success of your initiative. And in most cases, the challenges that arise have nothing to do with the technologies, but with the business aspects of the project. Keep this in mind and avoid it if possible.
- Reward big ideas. There are some retailers out there that keep a constant flow of innovative ideas cooking by offering rewards and accolades for those that are selected to test. Most will tell you that many of the winners came from the most unexpected people.
- Embrace the challenge. Why not change your attitude away from how much work and complexity your ideas may create to how exciting it's going to be to impact your shoppers and business for the good of all?

With a new mindset and a few "quick wins," we promise that you'll be on the road to evolutionary thinking with new in-store digital media enablers. Innovating and seeing "wow" results is fun. It's contagious and with it comes better team spirit, confidence, and optimism. People will start to behave spontaneously and work collectively to make the necessary changes to foster it. We've seen naysayers and obstructionists become leaders of creative thought once they experienced the success accompanied by trying new things.

It may not be a smooth road, but don't you want to be an organization known as inventive, creative, and inspired? Don't you want to cultivate people are buoyant, open-minded, confident, and can-do?

Embrace — and inspire — the innovator's mindset and use in-store digital media to light up your retail strategies.

13

Metro Group
Future Store Initiative:
A Platform for The Future
of Retailing

Susanne Sorg
POPAI Germany

METRO GROUP FUTURE STORE INITIATIVE: A PLATFORM FOR THE FUTURE OF RETAILING

Just a few years ago, the image of the retail sector was still characterized by attributes such as "down to earth"! and "pragmatic." This has fundamentally changed. Retailing is undergoing a fundamental process of innovation. The use of innovative technologies not only creates new opportunities for optimizing the business processes but also opens up new possibilities for individual customer marketing. Over the next five to ten years, the relationship between retailers, manufacturers and customers will change fundamentally.

Today, retailing is marked by the capacity of innovative and technological expertise: retail companies like the METRO Group are pioneers in the development and implementation of new, future-oriented technologies. The METRO Group Future Store Initiative has made a key contribution to facilitate this transformation.

The future of retailing is the core topic addressed by the METRO Group Future Store Initiative. The initiative pursues the goal of promoting innovation in the trade sector on a national and international scale. Consumer wishes and expectations have changed a great deal in recent years. These growing demands on the consumer goods sector call for customer-oriented retailing concepts. In the context of the initiative, the METRO Group, SAP, Intel, IBM and T-Systems, along with other partner companies from the consumer goods industry, information technology and the service sector all work together. They aim to evaluate and further develop forward-looking yet feasible technologies in practical tests, while also developing visions and prospects for the future of retailing. In the long term, they intend to establish uniform worldwide standards.

The objective of the METRO Group Future Store Initiative is to test and further develop new concepts and technical systems geared towards increasing efficiency in retailing. The focus is on the closest possible orientation towards the individual expectancies and needs of the consumer. Under this initiative, solutions to make shopping more comfortable and easy for the customer by using the latest technologies are demonstrated. This involves the further improvement of service and product quality, which have already reached a high standard in retailing, as well as the multiple forms of individual customer address.

The METRO Group

The METRO Group contributes its competence as one of the leading future-oriented retail groups to this strategic cooperation. It already demonstrated its significance as a motor for innovation and a driving force in trading in many sectors. The use of the latest technologies in all phases of the value added chain represents an important element in the consistent optimization of the METRO Group's sales concepts.

Intel is a world market leader in the production of microprocessors. It will contribute its solutions for system architecture and hardware components to the projects of the METRO Group Future Store Initiative.

SAP is the third largest software producer in the world with activities in more than 50 countries. The company supports the METRO Group Future Store Initiative with solutions relating to software and application technology.

The Initiative also integrates numerous partners from the consumer product industry and information technology as long-term sustained solutions in retailing are only possible with the cooperation of the largest possible number of participants. The objective is to develop uniform standards for retailing that can be widely implemented across the world.

The Future Store as the central component of the Initiative

The Future Store in Rheinberg, Germany is a key project in the Future Store Initiative. There, the application and interaction of various new technologies in retailing are tested under real-life conditions. The Rheinberg store is not a "lab store", but a very normal store, where customers do their ordinary shopping. The goal of the initiative is to develop benefit-oriented solutions, which offer advantages to the customers, to retailing and to the consumer goods industry. Until now, the retailing sector has implemented new technologies only in the form of individual applications or isolated systems, whereas in the Future Store, various modern technologies are linked together in complex ways for the first time ever. Radio Frequency Identification (RFID) is particularly important in this context, as it provides the basis for the efficient control of the supply chain. This technology makes it possible to identify objects without contact and to access data wireless – using RFID transponders, also called Smart Chips: special labels containing a computer chip and a miniature antenna. Smart Chips permit the instant identification of goods in process flow, ensuring traceability and optimum control along the entire supply chain. The METRO Group's pilot tests in the Future Store also include the use of Self Checkouts and convenient payment with Personal Shopping Assistants (PSA). Both cashier systems make the payment process more efficient and lead to shorter waiting times for customers. Additionally, customer communication in the store is being reorganized. Modern information media devices, such as information Terminals and Personal Shopping Assistants, provide additional information and help customers find products.

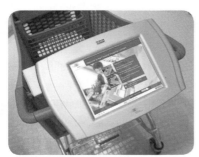

Source: METRO Group, Future Store Initiative

THE NEXT STEP TOWARDS THE FUTURE

The goal of the tests in the Future Store in Rheinberg is to ideally adapt new technologies to customer demands and to prepare the innovations for use in retailing. Only systems that enjoy acceptance by customers will be implemented on a broad basis. Existing concepts are being continually improved and developed further. This effort has been supported not only by the numerous technical tests which have been taken place, but also by the results of customer surveys from the Boston Consulting Group, a partner in the Future Store Initiative.

The Personal Shopping Assistant (PSA) received a new, more user-friendly interface at the start of 2004. Now, second-generation PSA software, which offers customers improved services such as adding or removing products or items is more convenient and the payment procedure has become even faster. Also the hardware of the PSA was changed. New scanners make it easier for customers to read barcodes. In the future, consumers can take advantage of yet another PSA function: using a PC at home or at work, they will be able to create an Electronic Shopping List and send it directly to the Future Store via Internet. The list can then be accessed with the Personal Shopping Assistant at the store.

Since the Future Store opened, over 25,000 interested visitors from businesses, politics, associations and other organizations, as well as schoolchildren and university students, have participated in tours of the store. About 44 percent of the visitors to the Future Store are from various countries including groups from North and South America, Asia, Australia and Russia who all traveled to Rheinberg to have a look at the future of shopping. Visitors also come from numerous retailing companies, consumer goods manufacturers and from IT sector companies.

Radio Frequency Identification (RFID): A key technology and its significance for the trade sector

The technologies and systems being explored and developed in the METRO Group Future Store Initiative are meant to achieve one goal in the particular: to make the processes involved in retailing more efficient. This applies specially to the RFID technology. With RFID, the route that merchandise takes from production along the transport chain and all the way to the store can be documented at all times. The inventory of goods can be checked automatically. Order processes, warehousing and transport can be simplified and accelerated, which in turn facilitates demand–oriented production. Out of stocks are easier to avoid.

RFID in practical testing: implementing the technology throughout the supply chain Since November 2004, the METRO Group has been introducing RFID technology throughout the supply chain and in merchandise management on a step–by–step basis. Starting with logistic units (pallets, packages and hanger–goods deliveries) and later adding retail units (cartons and subcartons); items all along the supply chain are equipped with Smart Chips in this process. Gradually, around 100 suppliers, 8 warehouses and 250 stores and outlets of the METRO Group's sales divisions Metro Cash & Carry, Real, and Kaufhof are going to participate in the introduction of the new technology. As soon as new–generation transponders are available in sufficient numbers, even more industry partners will equip their logistic units with transponders. The METRO Group actively supports its partners in the integration of the new technology. In July 2004, the company opened the RFID Innovation Center in Neuss, Germany. In 1,300 stores, the METRO Group offers its partners the opportunity to test reading devices and transponders for use with various product groups.

Benefits for the customers

Modern technologies support retailers in meeting the expectations of customers. Among other things, these technologies guarantee clear, accurate price labelling, quick payment procedures, smooth self–services processes and the permanent availability of goods. They also make it possible to provide individual offers geared to the customer's needs. In the future, customers will be able to take advantage of services that are tailored to them personally. Shopping will become quicker, more convenient and more individualized. At the same time processes at the back-bone systems can be standardized.

The METRO Group plays an active role in modernizing retailing

With its Future Store Initiative, the METRO Group is demonstrating its strength in innovation and performance. It generates momentum in the development of concepts and technologies for the retailing industry and for the customers of tomorrow. The METRO Group is thus underscoring its significance as a driving force in the trade and retailing sector.

Following five highly successful years in Rheinberg, Germany, the METRO Group Future Store Initiative is now moving on to test the future of retailing at a store operated by the sales division Real. The METRO Group will announce the opening of the new Future Store in due time.

The store in Rheinberg, Germany will be converted as one of the first locations in Germany – to the latest Extra concept, which, in the future, will offer customers a number of benefits. Better service, higher quality of the diverse assortment and an even more pleasant shopping atmosphere are guaranteed. Popular and frequently used technologies like the self-checkouts and the Smart Scales for fruits and vegetables will of course continue to make shopping more convenient.

Editorials

John C. Anderson

Peter Kornhaber and Brian McCormick

Merrill Howard

Robert Plante

TRENDS IN MARKETING AT-RETAIL FROM THE PERSPECTIVE OF A RETAILER

John C. Anderson
U.S. Manager of Marketing/Merchandising
BP Oil Corporation

In this busy world, retailers have less and less a share of the customer's attention as they try to entice the customer to purchase ever more goods and services. The question for the retailer becomes, "How can that be done?"

For many years, point-of-purchase materials have been increasingly used to better educate consumers. Retailers want consumers to better understand that the retailer has the product they want, that the price is "everyday" fair and low, and that the product is available for immediate purchase. Studies by BP have shown that in most cases our consumer is "on the run," coming into our convenience stores not always knowing what they want – but that they can and will make an impulse purchase decision if products are presented to them within the store.

We at BP also had to take into account the fact the average consumer is in our convenience stores for 90 seconds or less, so how do we draw attention to their needs and wants within that short a timeframe?

Seven years ago, we decided to make our point-of-purchase materials colorful and direct and to use specific product imaging. We reviewed what "best-of-class" retailers were doing around the country. We reviewed what POPAI research was finding about the effectiveness of different types of point-of-purchase displays. And we conducted internal studies with our consumers, matching that information to what POPAI had learned in previous studies.

Once we figured out how we wanted to target our messaging specifically to consumers, we created a new look and feel for our P-O-P materials.

We discovered that our point-of-purchase materials should be strategically placed in the consumer's pathway and that the P-O-P messages should be reinforced throughout the consumer's journey. Doing so has helped us get and keep consumers focused on whatever kind of purchase we want them to make. Such strategic and repeated messaging has given BP an edge in daily communications with the consumer, thereby increasing our effectiveness and in-store revenues.

Our next challenge was deciding how to combine point-of-purchase advertising with our different site graphics packages. This was not an easy task. We had to review all the different color options, along with placement options for the P-O-P display. We wanted to ensure that the display would stand out and give the consumer a message that would be carried throughout the store. Once we agreed on a strategy, we placed the P-O-P display in a test store and evaluated how well the color and font choices stood out from environmental factors including store design and other point-of-purchase signage. Then we conducted customer intercepts to ensure that we had hit our targets with the consumer. We now use this process in testing all of our new point-of-purchase advertising in-store.

In 2006 and 2007, BP participated in the MARI (Marketing at-Retail Initiative) project. BP understands that it is very important to be able to measure shopper engagement, while focusing on the changing needs of the customer. The MARI project has reinforced the strategic action plans that BP is using to target their customers daily with shopping incentives to purchase more during each visit.

As you know, the point-of-purchase advertising industry has changed dramatically over the past 10 years. As it continues to change, it will be essential that marketers use the innovative ideas and suggestions developed by POPAI and others. People are always looking for ways to get things done faster, cheaper, and more effectively. That is why one must always look for new ways to improve business—for both for the customer and the shareholder.

TRENDS, CONTINUING AND EMERGING, FOR PERMANENT MARKETING AT-RETAIL DISPLAYS

Peter Kornhaber and Brian McCormick
Rapid Displays

The retail environment is changing more quickly and dramatically than ever. Increased use of the Internet, faster product development cycles, and the growth in online and in-home shopping drive this changing environment. These developments, along with increased congestion on our roads, mean less free time for the average working American. In response to this new reality, trends have appeared in the marketplace relating to the design, development, production, and implementation of permanent display programs. Listed below are a few of these trends, with brief discussions of why they are taking place and what they mean.

Account-specific designs: No more "one size fits all" programs

As retailers increasingly understand the power of their own brand and their ability to deliver customers to the brand marketer, they demand more and more displays customized to tie in with their own brand identity and separate them from their competition. Brand marketers who sell in competitive retail environments must find a way to consistently communicate their own brand message and product benefits, while still allowing the retailer to customize the look to fit with the store's brand. Creative ways to do this will spell the difference between winning and losing in the placement game. Solutions that allow for common parts to be customized with simple graphic or logo changes are becoming increasingly attractive to brand marketers as they seek to meet retailer demands for customization without spending more money.

> *Multi-format retailers require multiple display versions for national rollouts:* Many national retailers have evolved their store designs over the years to the point where they have multiple formats in the field. As they try to provide a consistent look to their customers, brand marketers and designers must come up with display designs that can work on different fixtures, with differing shelf depths, heights, and color formats.
>
> This added level of complexity extends the developmental, prototyping, and testing phase of projects to accommodate these different environments. Often, established retailers do not have an accurate database of each store's specific details: Is it version one or version two? Single-level or multi-level? Newer retailers may be easier to deal with: they don't have as much variety in their store layouts and can thus be served more quickly and easily with a single solution working for the entire chain.

The need to accommodate these varying store formats makes development and production more expensive — added costs of packing a variety of kits, matching them with a correct database of store address, and shipping everything to arrive on time. The P-O-P producers who have the infrastructure and IT teams to handle complex distribution programs are best suited for these types of programs.

Creating a dialogue: Interactivity in retail displays

As more people become connected to the Internet, retailers and marketers are finding that consumers have become accustomed to having layers of information at their fingertips before they buy anything. While many consumers will seek out this information online, at home, or at work, others want to access that same depth of information in the retail environment.

Increased use of interactive elements due to reduced cost of hardware and memory products: This increased desire for information, reviews, and specifications has accelerated the trend toward interactive displays. In addition, recent reductions in the cost of memory and playback devices, as well as the advent of reasonably priced small flat screens, have made these types of displays accessible to both retailers and brand marketers. At the simplest levels, these interactive displays play media content to add excitement to the store environment. At their most complex levels, they include access to the Internet or Internet-like environments where consumers can scroll through options to gain the knowledge they need to make an informed and comfortable buying decision. These interactive devices also allow retailers to reduce the number of employees on the sales floor with specific product knowledge.

The trend toward increased use of interactivity in retail will likely accelerate as technology leads us into the world of Tom Cruise in *Minority Report*: billboards that read retinal scans and talk to you with directionally focused audio. These are real possibilities that many of us will see in our lifetime.

Displays on the go: Units that are easy to build and move

More and more permanent units are built with mobility in mind. Because retailers are continually working to reduce the labor costs of managing, stocking, and merchandising their stores, most of today's permanent displays ship fully assembled to retailers. The days of sending a KD permanent display with a four-page instruction sheet and an Allen key (type of wrench) are all but gone. As a result, many of the larger permanent displays produced today are built with locking casters or are designed to be easily lifted and moved by a fork lift. In addition to the reduced store labor that this mobility provides, it also allows the retailer to move these fixtures around the store to keep its layout fresh and to allow for floor cleaning and other maintenance work.

Permanent displays are increasingly used for higher-end, longer-lived projects. Increasingly, higher-end and pricier products find space on more permanent displays. The permanent display for the $300 shoe might incorporate an interactive screen, for example, and be regularly updated with changeable graphics and a new data chip to accommodate next year's version of the same style. One exception to this is that a "permanent display" can be used to help introduce new products for a few months, during which time the retailer can judge the popularity of the new product and decide whether to keep it in their planogram.

Move away from mass merchants and grocers into boutique and specialty. Grocers and mass merchants, while still using some permanent-branded fixtures, are increasing the number of in-line product presentations that utilize permanent displays while using temporary displays for promotional products. At the same time, boutique and specialty stores depend more and more on the marketer-provided branded fixture. A great example of this is in the flooring industry, where the small flooring store is completely outfitted with marketer-supplied fixtures. Small office-product outlets also fall into this category, especially compared with office-product superstores, which have their own fixtures and feature areas where they rotate the products they want to emphasize to prominent positions. These feature areas in superstore environments provide an added revenue stream to the retailer, who often makes brand marketers pay for placement and signage opportunities in these high-traffic, high-visibility areas of their stores.

TRENDS IN MANUFACTURING

Shorter lead times: Display producers become faster and more efficient

The lead time allotted to produce displays is shrinking across the board, and permanent displays are no exception. There are a few reasons for this.

Retailers are specifying some timelines: Retailers are taking longer to "pull the trigger" on key programs going into their stores. Many retailers will not allow any new displays moving into their stores after early November in preparation for "Black Friday."

Lead times shift to prevent error and allow changes: Many brand marketers are allowing more time for orders to flow in from the field, so they don't have to "guesstimate" quantities and risk producing too many or too few displays. Also, late-breaking changes to display programs are happening more and more. These changes from the brand marketer or retailer can take a normal timeline and compress it significantly, as additional engineering and development must happen while production of non-affected components continues. Obviously, these changes have to be made quickly in order to catch up to the original timeline of the project.

Going green: Sustainability impacts the marketing at-retail industry

Most of us try to be aware of the environmental impact of the choices we make in our daily lives — and that extends to our professional lives as well. Who doesn't want to make a positive impact? It may be as simple as taking mass transit or as complex as tracking our carbon emissions and trying to live carbon-neutral. The environmental movement has become a mainstream and important part of society and commerce.

Sustainability concerns are visible in board rooms at every major brand marketer and retailer. Many companies worldwide also are making an effort to be aware of the ecological impact of their products, as well as their manufacturing methods and materials. This effort has become an increasingly important part of their business plans, as it can increase brand value and profit margin and, ultimately, decrease production costs. These companies, many of which are ISO 1401 Certified (certification of an Environmental Management System) want to make sure that their environmental impact standards are upheld throughout the supply chain. This impacts how permanent displays are manufactured.

New concerns about materials for manufacturers: Display manufacturers and producers are making an effort to recycle and reduce waste that comes from display production. They're also looking to use materials high in recycled content, like steel, plastic, paper, and wood.

It takes slightly more effort to find environmentally friendly materials. It is easy today to get 100% recycled corrugated with as much as 90% post-consumer waste content. But you need to look for it -- not all producers provide it. Steel is the most recycled material on the planet. But again, steel comes in varying degrees of recycled content, from 0% to 95%, depending on the type of steel and its origin. U.S. steel producers have achieved a higher recycled content than all other countries and are 240% ahead of the Kyoto Accord goals.

Producers are also trying to reduce the amount of non-recyclable substances in packaging materials, like expanded polystyrene (EPS).

Thinking differently about shipping: Producers are also looking at the environmental impact of their shipping methods. Carbon dioxide emissions from the transportation sector are the largest source of energy-related carbon dioxide emissions. At 1,958.6 MMT, the transportation sector accounted for 33% of total U.S. energy-related carbon dioxide emissions in 2005.

Rail transportation can be a very carbon-friendly transportation method. Scientists calculate that as much as 4.5 times the energy is required to ship goods via truck vs. rail in high-density goods shipments. Rail shipments accounted for only 1% of the transportation sector's energy-related U.S. carbon dioxide emissions in 2005, which was disproportionate to its volume.

Carbon-neutral shippers have appeared on the scene. While they are relatively new to the market place, they are a fast-growing sector of the transportation industry and are sought out by firms that have interest in shipping their goods in a carbon-neutral fashion. Carbon-neutral shippers calculate their carbon footprint and then purchase equivalent investments in alternative energy projects.

Examples of these carbon-offsetting investments include:

- The Owl Feather War Bonnet Wind Farm, a 60 MW wind farm being developed near the town of St. Francis on the Rosebud Sioux Reservation in South Dakota.
- Farm methane projects on family farms, principally in the Mid-Atlantic region, which reduce on-farm methane emissions from fossil fuel use, and which produce electricity that displaces grid generation.
- A series of distributed 40 KW wind turbines on family farms in the Midwest, in partnership with Next Generation Power systems.
- A series of mid-size (65 kW to 250 kW) wind turbines in Alaskan native villages which will displace electricity generated by diesel generators in the villages.

Purchasers of transportation through a carbon-neutral shipping company (i.e., TransNeutral) are assured that their goods (including M.A.R. materials) arrive at their desired destination 100% carbon neutral. They also have the comfort in knowing their investment has increased the production capacity of green energy.

Going abroad: Production of displays and display components in low-cost countries

While the trend of producing permanent-display components and complete displays in low-cost countries such as China is not new, it is certainly continuing to grow. While there may not be statistics to empirically document this, there is plenty of anecdotal evidence. The number of display companies that have offices in China is at least 30 times what there was only five years ago. This trend is fueled mainly by the desire to reduce cost.

Drawbacks of cheaper production abroad: While the advantages to producing in low-cost countries such as China are obvious, the negatives sometimes are not. Some accompanying negatives to producing M.A.R. materials in China and other low-cost countries include increased lead times due to overseas shipments, less flexibility to make last-minute changes, increased carbon emissions from freight-

CHAPTER 14   EDITORIALS: PETER KORNHABER AND BRIAN McCORMICK   247

liners, lack of responsibly produced raw materials, and lack of respect for human rights in some countries and factories.

Increased creativity and quality in the display industry

Permanent-display professionals are getting more creative. There are a few different reasons for this.

Technology today can efficiently produce almost anything that can be designed: Lasers can cut shapes that were not possible before, without requiring anyone to spend tens of thousands of dollars on tooling. Robotic welders can weld with greater consistency and efficiency than ever. Similarly, computer-guided equipment (lasers, routers, turret presses, etc.) is very efficient at creating more complex shapes more easily than their older, non-computer-controlled counterparts.

C.A.D. (computer aided design) software — particularly those 3D packages that integrate design, engineering, and production engineering — speed the overall process by using the work done by the designer as the platform for engineering and the work done by engineering as the platform for equipment programming. 3D software presents a very accurate depiction of what the display will actually look like and allows for fast modifications prior to prototyping. 3D plastic printers allow a 3D-designed component to be prototyped quickly without the use of molds or labor-intensive fabricating methods.

Increased variations of displays required: All retailers are looking for the magic formula in retail formats. Some retailers, like Circuit City, have reduced square footage dramatically from 40,000 square feet to 15,000 square feet, while others are increasing the square feet of their new formats. Widths of aisles and end caps are changing, as are the heights and depths of fixtures. Retailers are adding islands to their stores where long runs of aisle existed before.

Also, retailers have done a good job of tailoring product offerings to their shoppers' demographics. Those changes in product mix and number of pieces per SKU can require adjustments to displays.

The retail environment continues to be an important aspect of modern social life. It is a place that people go not only to purchase products, but also for entertainment and human contact. As the electronic world and the physical world continue to intertwine, retailers and brand marketers face the challenge of keeping the shopping experience fun, relevant, informative, stimulating, and safe. They need to entice online shoppers to return to the physical world – to try on that outfit before they buy it, sample that fine wine before they sip it at home, touch that new faucet before they wash the dishes. These are some of the new challenges facing the brand marketer, retailer, and display producer.

TRENDS IN MARKETING AT-RETAIL TEMPORARY DISPLAYS

Merrill Howard
General Manager, Display Division
Artisan Complete

Temporary displays fill a large portion of the point-of-purchase market. They are often used to promote a newly introduced product or a product that the producer wants to have as a stand alone to separate it from the competition. They can be shipped flat for assembly at destination or as prepacked displays, which many retailers prefer, to save stocking costs at the store level.

A major benefit of producing temporary displays versus permanent ones is cost. Many displays are needed at the retail level for only a short period of time, to increase sales during a high-volume period (e.g., candy at Halloween).

Because of the low cost, companies with many brands to promote can afford to produce temporary displays separately for individual products. A promotional impact can be created with a unique design and vibrant colors, without the high costs of a permanent fixture.

In the past, many temporary displays were produced as cheaply as possible—and looked it. As if the appearances weren't bad enough, there was poor construction that often did not support the product, creating havoc on the retailer's floor.

This still happens today. However, the trend—directed especially by the larger retailers who are now more specific in what they will allow in the retail environment—is to produce an attractive display that will enhance their store's image. Retailers want a temporary display that will not fall apart and, most importantly, will attract the consumer to it and increase product sales.

Today, budget concerns are increasingly driving the development of temporary displays. Attractive displays, some including 3-D pop-offs, lights or motion, and stronger fillers to support the weight, will obviously cost more. Many brand marketers recognize the importance of point-of-purchase advertising and will opt for more durable, more attractive displays to increase product sales. Others do not see the value in the extra expenditures and need to be educated on how the improved display will improve the return on their investment.

Using research information from POPAI, the P-O-P producer can demonstrate that investing a bit more in the point-of-purchase display will result in a more powerful, more effective display that will show immediate results.

Some of the standard temporary displays long used in retailing—such as sidewinders/sidekicks, pallet displays, and base/tray/header—can easily be designed to create an image that will attract the consumer. Don't forget, whether selling hardware or candy, it is the consumer who makes the decision as to which brand to buy, and it is the display's job to attract the consumer's attention.

How are these added features achieved on a display? One of the most effective techniques is to integrate new or different materials into the manufacturing process such as the use of transparent, colorful plastic inserts that catch overhead light. Another effective technique is to add motion, either battery-driven or from in-store air currents; LED lights; or dimensional add-ons for a 3-D effect. There are many additional things that producers are asking for, to draw attention to their products.

What trends are expected in the future? There will be a lot more store identification added to the displays along with the product branding, especially by the larger retailers. This added retailer customization means additional costs, specifically in the printing process. However, these additional costs ensure that the brand marketer is gaining access and getting the retailer's cooperation for the most advantageous placement.

We can also expect to see an increase in prepacked displays to save labor costs at the retail level, again increasing producer costs. Many of these displays are for one-time use and are disposed of when the contents are sold out.

Yet, contrary to this trend toward disposability, many producers are asking to make a display that can be refilled with product to amortize the display cost and be more environmentally friendly. This usually adds only a slight cost, in order to increase the durability for longer usage in-store.

An added feature that now can enhance a temporary display is the ability to incorporate Digital Signage. This is a great way to add video/sound to a display, these all-in-one units are as easy as 'plug-and-play' and can be touch screen interactive or activated by motion sensors. Although LCD screen costs are coming down, there is still that initial investment, this can be overcome by simply supplying replacement temporary displays or shrouds and a Media Card with the new content. This becomes a cost-effective method to change over a promotion monthly, seasonally or for the introduction of a new product, this will help amortize the cost of the screen over time. The key to making this work is to ensure that the existing screens can easily be inserted into the replacement displays at the retail level.

Another trend will be point-of-purchase advertising's increasingly larger portion of the advertising budget. Brand marketers and retailers, bolstered by research conducted by POPAI and others, are proving that marketing at-retail is proving itself in return-on-investment analysis.

Where do we go from here? Although there will always be a need for the cheapest of displays to shelve product, display designers and manufacturers need to listen to producers, retailers, and consumers as to what is needed. More and more, we are being asked to stay away from the boring "square" display and create a display with innovative design and stunning color that will capture attention at the retail level.

Today, the display manufacturer is challenged with the opportunity to be uniquely creative and produce an attractive display by introducing new materials and complex shapes that will present the customer's product for a cost-effective, throwaway price.

TRENDS IN MARKETING AT-RETAIL
FROM THE PERSPECTIVE OF A BRAND

Robert Plante
Kiosk Programs Manager
BMW of North America LLC

The Iceberg Analogy: with kiosks you only see the tip

As I was thinking about what to write for this piece I was dialing in to the first of the two regular weekly conference calls we use to keep our dealer kiosk program running smoothly. When we started back in 2001 I had no idea how important these calls would turn out to be. Or that we would still be doing them several years later. It struck me that the relevant analogy for a kiosk program might be an iceberg. The bulk and complexity of most programs are largely unseen. Be advised however that running one is not unusually difficult. It's just that, like many other things in life, there's a lot more to it, and it helps if you are prepared to work through it all.

BMW's kiosk programs have won 21 industry awards over the last few years. Along the way we learned a few things. I will try in what follows to share some of that learning with the caveat that I can only describe the BMW experience. Hopefully others will find some useful nuggets in this tale.

For BMW the obvious underlying kiosk elements were fixture design, kiosk operating technology, hardware, high speed internet connectivity, and help desk support for these essentials. In today's marketplace these things are all readily available. But once you have these elements together it's very important to remember, they are all only there to support the content — which is all the customer sees. More about content in a moment.

The other key elements of a successful program are less tangible. It should go without saying that management support is essential – so communication on this front needs to be ongoing. Team building among your vendors and internal staff takes time but pays big dividends. Communication to key user groups is also essential. Communication to other stakeholder groups within your organization that could participate or benefit from the program will also help it to succeed. The other element often overlooked but very important is training. Teach your user groups how to benefit from the program

And then there is content, often referred to as the Graphic User Interface or GUI, (pronounced gooey) geek-speak for what the customer sees on the screen. Many deployers have a hard time getting this part right. It comes at the end of the whole kiosk build process when money and time are often limited so it gets rushed, cheapened, or is not well thought out. Yet, on screen content is the most important part of the program. It's all the customer sees. Equally important, ongoing content costs need to be estimated and communicated so decision makers are fully aware of what it will take to maintain that content over the life of the program.

For some applications a few simple screens may be all that's needed. However, even in these cases those screens should be designed by a graphic artist who understands the medium. Do not let your technology provider do it. Remember what's on the screen is what makes things happen. It pays to do it well.

For a brand marketer like BMW there is so much more too it. We think of our kiosks as a private, interactive video channel that must engage our customers' heads and hearts, with an occasional visceral response thrown in. That works out to be high-quality video, much of it produced specifically for the channel, or if it's re-purposed video, edited for the channel. Informative, entertaining, brief, updated often, are words we live by – all meat as Law & Order's Dick Wolfe would say. These kiosks have a voracious appetite that we feed constantly.

As we said at the beginning, a kiosk is like an iceberg. For most projects there's more to it than you might think at first. But if you do everything well, kiosks really work. So read, learn, and go for it. Below are some real-life concrete examples of what's involved -- the steps we went through for our most recent BMW dealer kiosk deployment. And I may have missed a few along the way:

- Fixture design competition
- Prototype technology partner selection
- Prototype content partner selection
- Hardware spec
- Prototype build
- Prototype technology build
- Prototype content build
- Internal review with management
- Internal review with BMW IT
- Preview with feedback survey at X5 launch dealer meeting
- RFP for dealer project to select fixture partner, technology partner, content partner
- Bid review and partner selection with Purchasing & internal management
- Team building and weekly conference calls with all partners begins
- Ongoing face-to-face meetings with Reality Pictures, the content partner team. Communication and meetings with this partner are frequent, ongoing, and will continue for the life of the project. While all the moving parts are important, content is really the only thing the customer sees. It must be entertaining, informative, and brief. Most important it must be frequently changed and always up to date.
- Two revised prototypes: fixture, technology & content builds
- Prototypes deployed in two BMW Centers within driving distance of BMW HQ
- Ongoing weekly review of prototype installations with Center personnel, team partners, BMW management, and BMW field staff (6 weeks)
- Ongoing communication about program with BMW field staff begins

- BMW's training group engaged. They review prototype installations and create a training video on kiosk use for dealer sales personnel
- Key learnings incorporated into revised fixture, technology, and content builds
- BMW IT reviews technology and participates in a major way in planning for connectivity and support for beta test
- Weekly support conference calls begin with BMW IT, BMW's connectivity vendors Reynolds & Reynolds, ADP and Reality Interactive, the program's technology partner
- Beta test deployment: 11 dealers nationwide selected from list of major problem sites from previous program
- Key learnings from beta test incorporated & rollout begins
- Two weekly conference calls continue – one with all build partners, the other with all support partners. Regular calls with all build partners will eventually discontinue
- Weekly calls with support partners will be ongoing for the life of the program
- Internal communication about the program, especially success stories, is ongoing
- Internal presentations for management about various aspects of the program, new content, etc., also ongoing
- Meetings with BMW field staff, dealer groups, and dealer sales personnel, ongoing

15

Retail Terms and Types of P-O-P Advertising Displays

Kat Chociej
Marketing Director
Weyerhaeuser

RETAIL TERMS AND TYPES OF P-O-P ADVERTISING DISPLAYS

This chapter will provide some short descriptions, terms, and illustrations of various displays to consider using for in-store marketing efforts.

RETAIL TERMS

Action alley

High traffic area in a main aisle of the store, usually where displays and 4-way fixtures are placed. Sometimes, there are specific guidelines that dictate these displays. Usually a term reserved for Wal-Mart.

CPG company

Producer of consumer product goods — i.e., Procter & Gamble (P&G), Unilever, Kimberly Clark, etc.

C-Store

Convenience Store

Channels

Various outlets for products and services that are distinctly different from each other. There are six primary channels in the U.S. — mass (Target), grocery (Kroger), club (Sam's), convenience (Circle K), dollar (Dollar General), and specialty (Toys R Us). In addition, hybrids of these channels have gained popularity in recent years — i.e., super-centers (combination of grocery and discount stores) such as Wal-Mart and Meijer.

Club Store

Warehouse membership stores — i.e., Sam's, Costco, BJ's

DSD logistics system

Direct to store delivery — vendor managed delivery of product direct to individual retail store locations. Popular logistics system for milk, bread, beer, soda, snacks, etc.

Gondola

Metal fixtures, shelving, walls, and bases used to create in-line or stand-alone merchandising areas in-store. A series of gondolas make up an aisle fixture.

In line

On shelf area where product is merchandised in pre-determined planograms.

In-run modular

Modify an in-line gondola section to highlight a category of products or a specific brand.

Knees to chest

Desirable shelf space/placement where product is easily accessible and highly visible.

Price points

Retail unit price groupings of common/competitive products — i.e., opening/low price (private label), mid-point (Gain), and high-point (Tide).

Redemption

Taking advantage of the terms and conditions of a promotional item, resulting in delivery of "payment" for special values (ex: $.50 off at checkout).

Register cap

Endcap fixture located at checkout.

Specialty stores / Category dominant

Store that is primarily focused on one, or very few categories (i.e., Toys R Us, Office Max, AutoZone, etc.)

Store perimeter

Outer "loop" of store floor plan; typically a high traffic pattern vs. aisle traffic.

Super Center

Large store format that offers both general merchandise and grocery categories. This store format has been around for quite some time (Meijer), but has become very popular with national retailers such as Wal-Mart and Kroger.

Third-Party Merchandiser

Independent vendors who set-up displays, assemble fixtures, and stock shelves in-store. Usually act as agents to consumer product companies to service their "space" on the shelf.

Valence

Overhead, horizontal signage panels often attached to tops of gondolas.

DISPLAY TERMS

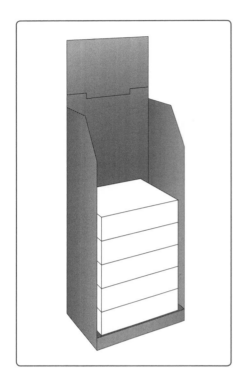

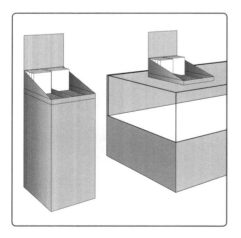

Case-stacker displays

A display component that serves as a three-sided wrap to encase product or other display components. Using a case stacker provides side panels for graphics and allows for header card placement. These displays are created by simply cutting product cases open to expose the product and stacking the cases side by side and on top of each other to create a mass display. Case-stackers are usually used in conjunction with a pole display, easel card, or a table tent. This is a very economical approach to getting a large quantity of product on display and is also an easy and effective way of merchandising. These displays can be built from very small to very large and are readily adapted to most market sizes.

Clip strip

Hanging display strip that displays small products that are hooked onto the strip. Clip strip material can be vinyl, metal, or fiber. Small size is conducive to multiple placements throughout a store to drive impulse purchases (i.e., batteries).

Combination counter/floor displays

The adaptability of this display approach is ideal based on where the display will be used by the retailer. If they have more floor space than counter space, the floor base can be used with the product tray. Otherwise, the product tray can be placed on a counter top and the base may be discarded. This display is highly likely to be utilized, as it gives the retailer the option of what is most appropriate for its market. The type of retailer these displays are most commonly seen in are:

Counter displays

Counter displays are typically small and compact in size, due to limited counter space in most markets. Like floor stands, they can be designed as a one-sided, three-sided sell or even as a revolving display. This option can be readily utilized from home improvement to convenience stores to all distribution types in between.

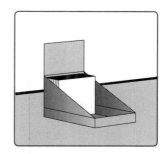

Coupon dispensers

These displays are generally battery operated and offer instant coupons to the consumer. Placed next to a product, they attract attention through the use of graphics and color and often use blinking lights. These are generally utilized in supermarkets and chain drug stores.

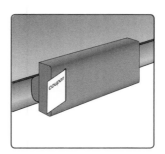

Dealer-loader displays

These displays are typically called "dealer incentives" and incorporate some type of take-home unit for the dealer, such as a table, cart, or grill. The display makes a premium offer to the consumer and a sample of the premium item I part of the display. Once the promotion has ended, the dealer is free to keep the premium item as thanks for the use of the retail space.

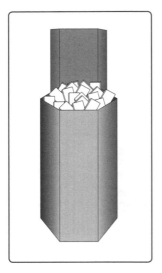

Dump bins

These displays are designed for bulk merchandise in a variety of materials, from corrugated, wire, sheet metal, and other materials. A dump bin is an open bin used to display merchandise that is "dumped" into the display body. This style often is placed on a base or directly on a shelf. It is intended to convey the idea to the consumer that this must be a special limited time offer. These displays are easy to assemble and are generally placed in multiple locations throughout the store, such as in the snack foods department, produce, or even at the checkout lanes.

Duplex displays

Duplex refers to a self-contained floor stand shipper display that holds both a base and the product. It typically will contain a planogram and will have a header attached. The display is received at retail, the shipping tape is cut, and the unit is literally turned inside out, creating a display out of what had originally been a shipping carton. These are relatively inexpensive displays and easy to assemble.

Easel cards

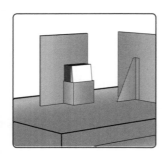

These displays are usually flat, two-dimensional displays that have a simple chipboard easel attached to the back. The retailer opens the easel and sets the display on a counter, shelf, or case stacker of a product. Easel cards are often included in a complete P-O-P advertising kit, along with items such as mobiles and table tents.

End-cap display

Metal fixture and shelving at the end of an aisle (sizes vary per store — typically 36″ or 48″ for grocery and mass; home improvement ranges from 48″ to 84″+)

False bottom

"Dummy" area at the bottom of a display where product sits raised off the pallet base. Internal components are used to support the weight of the product on the display.

Four-way

Permanent store fixture that holds PDQ trays in a pin-wheeled presentation.

Floor displays

Displays not placed on a pallet, store fixture, or shelf (i.e., display designed for direct floor placement). Like all displays, these are intended to educate the consumer about the product's attributes, qualities, and sometimes price.

Header/Riser

Primary graphic billboard that attaches to the base of a display.

KD displays

"Knocked-down" displays are shipped partially assembled in an effort to reduce shipping, storage, or actual production costs. The retailer is expected to unpack the display components, carefully assemble the display as per the instructions provided, place the display in the desired location within the store, and then fully load the display with product from the cases. The degree of assembly required varies.

Kiosk

Free-standing display that often offers consumer education as well as product. Usually constructed of more permanent materials and often has interactive features.

Inside/outside shipper

Floor display that has cosmetic graphics printed on the interior of the shipper carton. Once shipper is opened, flaps are folded back to create display tray and riser. Display tray is then placed upon base (included in shipper).

Lug-on

An "add-on" piece of material (cardstock, plastic, etc.) attached to the main display body. Often used to add high-end graphics to a display panel in a cost-effective manner or to customize a header (i.e., retailer logo, etc.).

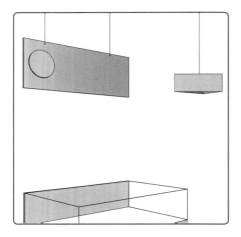

Mobiles

Mobiles are displays consisting of several counter-balanced pieces suspended in such a way that each piece moves independently in a light current of air, but can also be motorized so as to always be moving and attracting attention. They tend to be used as image-building displays, not to merchandise product. Mobiles do not take up floor space or counter space. They hang above retail spaces, can be seen from a distance, and are sometimes used to identify specific departments and centers. They are normally sturdy and lightweight and can be developed into more than just a flat, two-dimensional hanger.

Modular display

Display consisting of common, interchangeable/stacking pieces.

One-way sell displays

These are the most common type of floor stands. They can be backed up against a wall, placed on an end cap, or placed back-to-back. The product is only merchandised at the front.

PDQ tray

A tray that can be pre-loaded with product, placed inside an HSC carton, banded, and shipped. This allows for easy shelf placement at retail. PDQ — "Pretty Darn Quick."

Near-Pack/Pack-out displays

"Near-pack" displays are received at retail either knocked down or assembled. Both the display and the product are received at retail at the same time. Display design that requires the retailer to place pre-loaded trays of product into the display base as part of the display set-up.

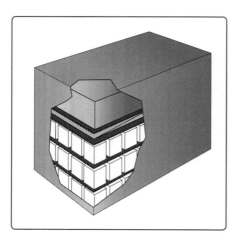

Pallet displays

This type of display is created by a mass display of product built on a pallet and contained in corrugated or other structural components on the retail floor ready for display merely by removing the protective shrouding and, in some cases, by also adding a riser.

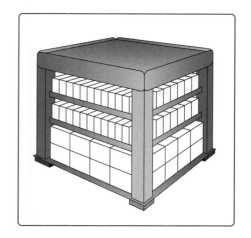

Master Pallet

Serves as a carrier pallet for several pallet displays that have a smaller footprint. Wrapping four quarter pallets atop a 48×40 master pallet is an example.

1/4 pallet

Quarter pallets are typically a 20″×24″ footprint. Size can vary slightly depending on the retailer and product. Pallets materials can be wood or plastic. Components that make up a pallet display are a base, trays, a stacker, and a header/riser. All pallet displays have height restrictions based on retailer specifications.

1/3 pallet

Midsize footprint that falls between a 1/4 pallet and 1/2 pallet.

1/2 pallet

Half pallets typically have a 20″×48″, 24″×40″, or 24″×48″ footprint.

Full pallet

Full pallets typically have a 40″×48″ or 48″×48″ footprint.

Split pallet

When two 1/2 pallets are banded together for shipment to a store. Sometimes one side goes straight to the retail floor, and the other side remains in the back store room.

Pin-wheel

Presentation/layout of product on a fixture or display that accommodates four-sided shopping by the consumer.

Pole-topper displays

These displays can be part of a floor display, functioning as the sign or header for the display. A quantity of product is generally stacked around the pole at the floor level. They carry the advertising message, mounted on top of poles, which are usually paper tubes, in either a two-dimensional or three-dimensional form, often with lights and motion to attract the attention of the shopper. They are usually supported at the floor by a simple corrugated pedestal or a set of wire feet.

Power panel

Flat panel display that holds pegged product; length and width dimensions are similar to a power wing — just not the same "tray" style.

Premium displays

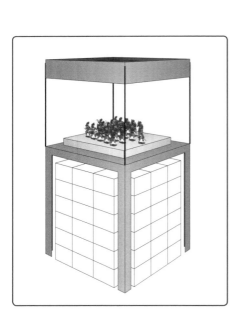

These displays include some sort of item used to attract attention to the display or product in a secondary manner. A gimmick is used to create interest in itself, and then transfer interest to the product. The customer may purchase a product, send in a proof-of-purchase along with the price of the premium, and then receives the premium item in the mail a few weeks later. This type of promotion is used to encourage a consumer to trial a brand he or she has not used in the past.

Pre-packed displays

The P-O-P producer packs the merchandise within the display and ships to the retailer as one single unit, ready to be placed onto the store floor. Retail management appreciates pre-packed displays because store labor tends to be scarce and this option cuts down on in-store labor for assembling and stocking the display. This type of display may be more likely to be used for this very reason.

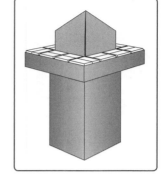

Rolling rack / lane blocker

Floor display that has castors built into the base to allow movement throughout the store. These displays are often used to "block" a closed checkout lane, while offering shoppers a chance to purchase another item.

Revolving-floor displays

The consumer can manually spin these displays, ideal for corners where the product on a regular walk-around display would be hidden from view and tend to be inaccessible.

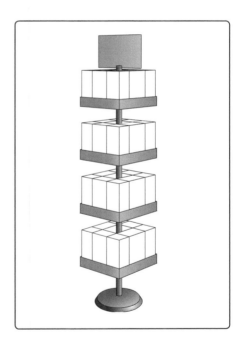

Shelf talkers

These are small signs affixed to the display shelf edge to call attention to the product.

Shipping shroud

HSC cover, or similar design, that is placed over a display for shipping purposes.

Sidekick/Power wing

These types of displays are most commonly used in supermarkets, chain drug stores, hardware stores, and convenience stores. They are designed to attach to the ends of endcap shelves and are intended to create display spaces to encourage incremental sales of products not normally sold in that location of the store. Sidekicks can be designed in temporary or permanent materials, but are generally considered to be promotional and designed as temporary displays sent to the stores already assembled and pre-packed with product. Sidekicks can be used in multiple units, creating a large floor display or even larger full-sized pallet displays. They can be added to a base to create a floor stand or can also function as a counter display. This design offers the retailer many options, based on individual store needs. It fits inside a metal rack usually on the side of an endcap. The product in power wing displays can be pegged, trayed, or dispensed product. The metal racks usually have an ID of 14″ - 14.5″ wide and the height is typically 48″ (22″ - 24″ for WM).

Mini-sidekick

Display similar to power wing that fits on the side of a power wing rack. The width is usually 5″ or less.

Standee

Large signage piece for floor placement, usually requires easel for support/set-up. Often does not contain product, may feature tear pads and/or small ballot boxes.

Store spectacular

Large eye-catching display placed in a high-traffic area. This may consist of multiple displays and signage components as well as multiple brands.

Table tents

Single-fold cards, set like a tent, are used on counters, bars, or tables, carrying an advertising message, typically on both front and back sides of the card.

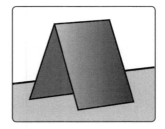

Three-way sell displays

This display is ideal for location at endcaps or back-to-back with other three-way sell displays. It allows the display to be accessed from the front, left, and right sides.

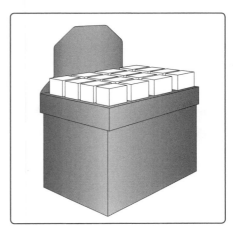

Walk-around displays

Offers product on all sides and allows the consumer to shop all sides of the display. It is not always accepted by retailers due to the amount of floor space required for the consumer to comfortably walk around the entire display.

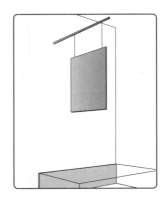

Wall displays

Designed to be hung on a wall of a retail outlet or the back of a store fixture, this option creates retail space on both sides for copy or product.

Weekender

A one-piece, die-cut, corrugated tower display that folds into a shelf unit to hold lightweight products (i.e., potato chip displays).

NOTES

NOTES

NOTES

NOTES

NOTES

NOTES

NOTES